DAVID LIVINGSTONE

David Livingstone

David Livingstone

The Truth Behind the Legend

ROB MACKENZIE

Rob Mackenzie

KINGSWAY PUBLICATIONS

EASTBOURNE

Unless otherwise indicated, biblical quotations are from the
New American Standard Bible © The Lockman Foundation
1960, 1962, 1963, 1968, 1971, 1972, 1973

ISBN 0 85476 387 2

*Cover design based on original concept
by Mark Cerfonteyn*

Produced by Bookprint Creative Services
P.O. Box 827, BN23 6NX, England for
KINGSWAY PUBLICATIONS LTD
Lottbridge Drove, Eastbourne, E Sussex BN23 6NT
Printed in Great Britain

This book is dedicated to my mother,
whose gentle love for Christ
purposed me to draw close to him

Contents

DAVID LIVINGSTONE

Foreword

In this book Rob Mackenzie has brought together all his many talents to have another look at the life of the legendary David Livingstone.

Rob is a man who is undaunted by the size of the task. He is a stickler for detail, and yet has an imagination that graphically sees the larger picture. He looks past the mundane and captures the heart of the matter.

Rob has lived most of his life in Africa, and this adds an extra dimension to the book. Here are minute details, and yet a balanced insight into the real character, nature and emotions of Livingstone, exposing both his strengths and his weaknesses.

I feel sure that those who read this book will be enriched and inspired by the story of a man whose courage, determination and faith proved more than a match for life's great challenges.

Bob Edmiston
Chairman and Chief Executive,
International Motors Group Ltd.
Director, Christian Vision.

Acknowledgements

To compile a book of this nature requires a dedicated team and I am truly indebted to those who gave this project so many undivided hours of attention.

Those who deserve particular credit are Linda Christenson for patiently wading through my writing and typing out the original manuscript, Jillian McCracken for spending countless hours diligently editing the initial drafts and Hilda Olivier for painstakingly checking the references.

I would like to thank Rev George Canty for assessing the work and whose words of encouragement helped to inspire me. I would also like to thank Harold Westwood, Dr Martin White and Afric Hamilton for reading the draft manuscript. I value their advice. Thanks to Bob Edmiston for his personal input and for the Foreword; to Mark Cerfonteyn for the cover; Suprine Murove for the maps; Lou Seng Joo and Bok Ai; Richard Greenwood and my wife, Hilary, for their support.

I would also like to acknowledge the services of the staff of the National Archives of Zimbabwe and the host of previous researchers of Livingstone for their contribution; as well as thank Pastor Reinhard and Anni Bonnke, Pete and Evangeline Vanderberg and the Christ for All Nations team.

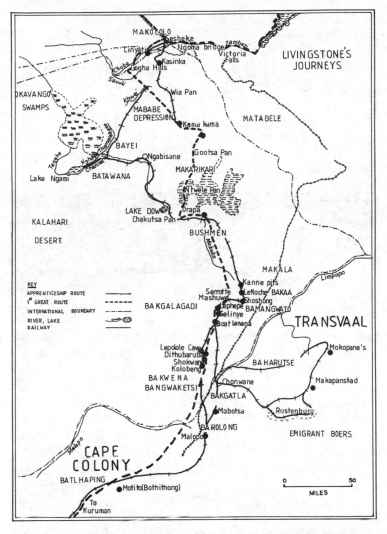

It will be noted that the maps show some present-day names of countries and man-made lakes, eg Zimbabwe, Lake Kariba.

To show the spread of Christianity several mission stations, established shortly after Livingstone opened the interior, have been inserted.

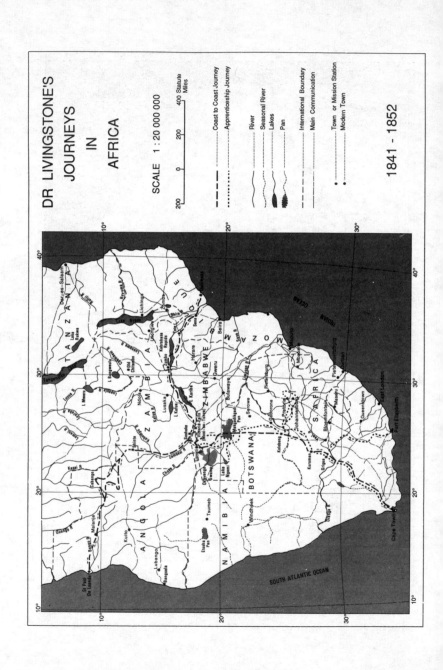

DR LIVINGSTONE'S JOURNEYS IN AFRICA

SCALE 1 : 20 000 000

200   0   200   400 Statute Miles

Coast to Coast Journey
Apprenticeship Journey

River
Seasonal River
Lakes
Pan

International Boundary
Main Communication

Town or Mission Station
Modern Town

1841 - 1852

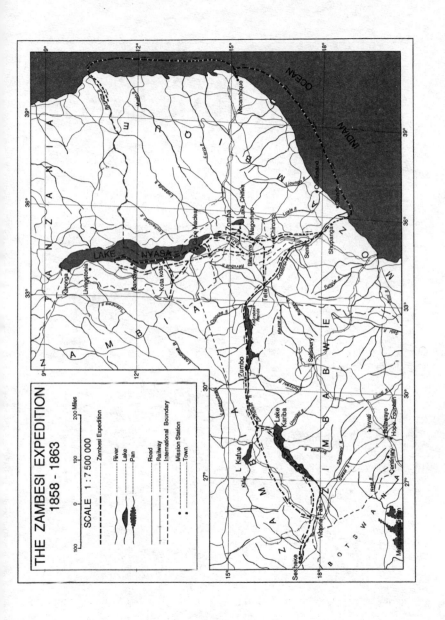

THE ZAMBESI EXPEDITION
1858 - 1863

SCALE   1 : 7 500 000

River
Lake
Pan
Zambesi Expedition
Road
Railway
International Boundary
Mission Station
Town

100   0   100   200 Miles

INDIAN OCEAN

TANZANIA

ZAMBIA

MOZAMBIQUE

ZIMBABWE

BOTSWANA

LAKE NYASA

Karonga
Livingstonia
Bandawe
Kota Kota
Lake Chilwa
Zomba
Magomero
Blantyre
Chironde
Mazaro
Sena
Shupanga
Tete
Zumbo
Kebrabasa Rapids
Salisbury
Lake Kariba
L Katue
Victoria Falls
Sesheke
Inyati
Bulawayo
Hope Colbeath
Centenary
Matopos

9°   12°   15°   18°
39°   36°   33°   30°   27°   15°   18°

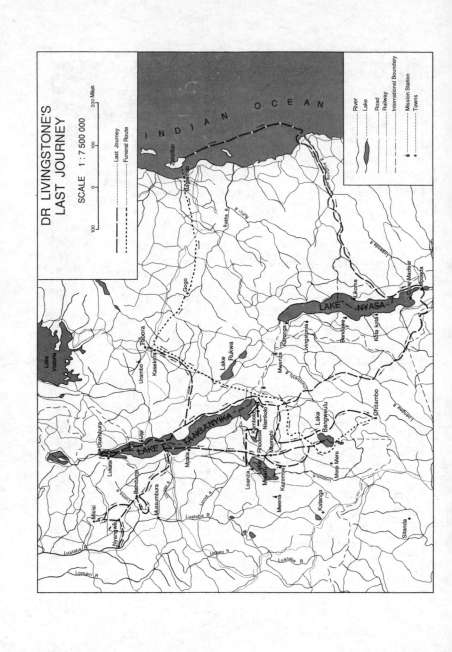

DR LIVINGSTONE'S
LAST JOURNEY

SCALE 1:7 500 000

— — — Last Journey
.... Funeral Route

100   0   100   200 Miles

River
Lake
Road
Railway
International Boundary
Mission Station
Towns

INDIAN OCEAN

Zanzibar

Bagamoyo

Ruaha R.

Rufiji R.

Ruvuma R.

LAKE NYASA

Likoma

Cape Maclear
Mponda

Kota kota

Bandawe

Livingstonia

Matonga

Mwenzo

Chitambo

Lake
Bangweulu

Loangwa R.

Lake
Rukwa

Tabora

Kasekera

Urambo

Gogo

Lake
Victoria

Ujiji

Usambura

Lukata

LAKE TANGANYIKA

Moliro

Kasumba

Rhodes

Niamkolo

Meereshi

Loanza

Muinda

Kazembe

Mwena

Katanga

Merb Mere

Chindani R.

Sitanda

Lualaba R.

Lugani R.

Lualaba R.

Lomani R.

Lomani R.

Nyangwe

Misisi

Mussumbura

Belmbarga

Luela R.

Lueula R.

Lualaba R.

List of Illustrations

Preface

In writing a biography one is invariably asked to justify the addition of yet another publication. My purpose in compiling this book is fourfold.

First, to correct several popular misconceptions I had formulated concerning Livingstone. To me he was a nebulous colonial explorer who pottered around the countryside with little or no purpose in life.

This fallacy was corrected when I noticed the high regard the African people have for David Livingstone. In many countries where independence from colonisation has occurred, the names previously given to streets, buildings and even towns bearing the names of early pioneers have been withdrawn and replaced.

This has not been the case with Livingstone. In Zambia, a town near the Victoria Falls bears his name, and Blantyre, the capital of Malawi, was named after Livingstone's home town in Scotland. Countless streets and buildings throughout Africa still bear his name.

On the edge of the Zambezi River I questioned an African on Livingstone. I was told, 'Ah, Livingstone, he has a good name.'

Livingstone, contrary to many western beliefs, is greatly respected and admired by a large number of Africans—a sure testimony to the man who spent the majority of his life among them.

Secondly, in recent years there has been a tendency by diverse writers to produce works that condemn or at best criticise many great pathfinders. Though this was done to correct several of the hagiographies which were the fashion in Victorian times, many, for the sake of readership, have swung the pendulum too far. This publication will, hopefully, redress Livingstone, the man, and bring a much needed balance to the popular beliefs surrounding him.

Thirdly, the most accurate and comprehensive biography written to date on Livingstone was by Tim Jeal, published in 1973. This book, as with many others on Livingstone, is out of print. A new publication may help fill the gap and fuel the revived interest in early explorers and missionaries.

Lastly, as other biographies tend to lean on a particular aspect of Livingstone's life, be it his personal character, his work as a Doctor of Medicine, his 'colonial vision' or even his style of writing, this publication assesses both his motives and his life as a Christian. Thus extensive quotations from his personal notes and letters are included. In giving an overall assessment of Livingstone this conspectus covers his failings as well as his accomplishments.

Indeed, many regard him a failure. As a missionary he brought only a couple of people to know Christ. Here it should be noted that Livingstone was a man of very high standards: he only considered a man to be a Christian when the believer produced the relevant fruits of righteousness and maintained them after several years.

Furthermore, to assess the impact of this man on civilisation one needs not only to examine his life but also his legacy. Livingstone was a man who, according to the biblical truth, sowed in tears. It was only after his death that his greatest desires were granted—the cessation of the slave-trade and the opening up of Africa to Christianity and lawful commerce.

He had the grace to see that his vision was part of a divine plan to set many souls free from slavery, both physical and spiritual. Although he was considered a failure for not locating the source of the Nile, his motives in searching for it were to gain a platform from which to denounce the slave-trade.

Livingstone was not the first to hate slavery, but few when

he was a child had done anything about it prior to the philanthropists of Britain. It was endemic, or simply not one's business. Then political considerations produced a Levite reaction—at least in Africa—when one complex eccentric's extraordinary career finally snapped the threads of self-interest and apathy.

Thus Livingstone's ultimate goal to bring to the world's attention the plight of the African slave-trade was achieved, and this largely due to the work of Henry Morton Stanley.

The Epilogue is an observation of the Christian work in Africa and in keeping with the biographical theme, I have chosen Reinhard Bonnke, an evangelist who is witnessing multitudes of Africans express a desire to serve Christ. He is reaping with joy the harvest of souls that Livingstone and fellow missionaries sowed in tears.

The house where Livingstone was born

1

Boyhood in Blantyre

The little manufacturing town of Blantyre, in Scotland, has grown up on the edge of the River Clyde. In places the green banks are sheltered by oak, ash, birch and hawthorn trees. Elsewhere, the broad calm mirror of the stream is marred by weirs and rapids which break up the glassy reflection of houses, trees and banks with foam and angry whirls of water.

Below Blantyre and on the further side of the Clyde stands the Old Mill and above it a weir. Opposite on the green grassy bank lies a young, rather thin lad who is totally engrossed in a book.

The Mill house is home to two children, a girl and a boy who have rather a naive enthusiasm for adventure. The little girl puts her younger brother aboard a boat and, without anyone noticing, ventures into the mainstream. All is well until an oar slips and slowly drifts away. The relentless current is bearing the boat towards the weir. The girl, realising the danger, shrieks for help. The youngster on the bank hears the cry, assesses the situation and at some risk to himself, dives into the icy cold water, swims out and rescues the oar and the trembling children.[1]

This lad, David, was the son of Neil Livingstone, a humble tea merchant. Little was said of this mishap, and the harsh life in Blantyre continued. David enjoyed a life which thus far

---

[1] Macnair p 38.

had not been easy for him, but neither was it for other poor children of those times.

His entry into the world took place on 19th March 1813, a special moment for his parents who had seen death take two other babies, both boys, in their infancy. David had one elder surviving brother, John. They enjoyed each other's company and their relationship was not diminished by the arrival of yet another brother, Charles, and later two sisters, Janet and Agnes.

The Livingstone family was close in every way, for they cooked, ate, sewed, spoke and slept in a tiny room fourteen feet by ten. A solid wooden table stood in the centre of the room and upright chairs were placed around it. The black brick fireplace was well used, providing not only much needed warmth against the cruel, cold winters, but heat for cooking and for boiling water. There was neither hot nor cold running water, and David and his brothers lost count of the times they had walked down the tightly curved cold brick staircase to fetch water from a pump in the yard, and heaved it back up the stairs and along the corridor of the third floor to their room.

The Livingstones shared a tenement with twenty-four other families who generally took an optimistic view of life as conditions there were not as severe as those in Glasgow. Nonetheless, the poor continued to fight a never-ending battle against the vicissitudes of life. Bed-time was an exacting affair. Truckle beds were pulled out from under the two main beds which were set into recesses in the wall. Privacy was non-existent and as the family grew, space seemed to shrink. David and John were eventually boarded with their grandparents in a neighbouring cottage.

David's father, Neil Livingstone, was a committed Christian and his whole life was consecrated to serving and revering God. In his youth he had seen the ravaging effects of alcoholism, and as a result he abstained totally.

As a child, like his son, he was put to work in the mills,

but when old enough he was apprenticed to a local tailor. Neil disliked tailoring from the outset, but he persevered long enough to convince the tailor's daughter, Agnes, of his worth.

Having won her heart they married in 1810 and moved to Glasgow where their first child died. Before David's birth they returned to Blantyre where Neil became a travelling tea-salesman; a job which paid little but gave his main interest— that of preaching the gospel—greater dimension, as it enabled him to distribute tracts to his customers.

He also taught children at Sunday school and was a zealous member of a missionary society, persistently promoting meetings for prayer and fellowship.

He was far 'too conscientious ever to become rich as a small tea-dealer, by his kindliness of manner and winning ways he made the heartstrings of his children twine around him as firmly as if he had possessed, and could have bestowed upon them, every worldly advantage'.[2]

David respected his father and years later said: 'He deserved my lasting gratitude and homage for presenting me from infancy with a continuously consistent pious example.' Yes, his father was a godly man who took great pains to bring his children up as God-fearing Christians. They realised this, for they often felt the smarting sting as he disciplined them in order to enforce his principles.

Young David had a mind of his own and strength of character to match. Once his daily duties were done, he would scramble off in search of new discoveries concealed in the Scottish countryside.

At other times he would swiftly become absorbed in a book borrowed from the local library, particularly books on travel and science. Neil Livingstone would far rather have seen his offspring pore over the pages of Wilberforce's *Practical Christianity*. but this did not appeal to David. He stubbornly

---

[2] M T, p 3.

refused and his father unhooked the rod from the black fireplace and discipline was dealt out.

David's hidden distaste of religious writings remained until later he experienced a change within his heart. Nonetheless, as a young lad he enjoyed studying and was not against reading the Scriptures. At the age of nine he took up the challenge of learning the 119th Psalm, and undaunted he repeated the 176 verses on two successive evenings with only five errors. For his labours he received a copy of the New Testament.

David's Mother, Agnes, was a gentle woman whose loving kindly nature served as a valuable counter-balance to her husband's strict and austere rule. She managed to keep alive in the hearts of her children a love and respect for all things sacred. She did not have an easy life, and David grew very conscious of her difficulties—'that of the anxious housewife striving to make both ends meet'.[3] Despite the difficulties 'Nannie Hunter', as David's mother was called by her friends, maintained her sweet gentle nature. Small and delicate, her chief characteristic was markedly bright eyes, a feature which her middle son inherited. She was always active and orderly, and possessed a keen eye for cleanliness. She trained her family in the same virtues, and the training proved valuable much later when, during his roughest times in Africa, David never slackened his scrupulous care for his personal appearance.

Despite their frugal lifestyle, the family budget was deficient, as times were very difficult in the aftermath of the Napoleonic wars. David, at the tender age of ten, was called upon to share in the upkeep of the home.

Accepted for employment, he entered the Monteith & Company cotton spinning factory where his work was spelled out for him. He was to be a 'piecer', which meant that he had to piece together threads in the spinning frames if they

---

[3] *Ibid.*

threatened to break. The noisy dimly-lit humid atmosphere was to become his environment for the next decade.

In summer, and throughout the bitterly cold dark winters, he was awakened at five-thirty in the morning by the mill bell, which hung on the outside corner of the building. He, like the other children who worked at the mill, would tumble into scanty clothing, gulp down a plate of scalding porridge or, if late, seize 'a piece' that his meticulous mother had ready and rush downstairs round the corner, past the bell and down the short path to the gate of the grim building.

There they would work from six in the morning till eight at night in tremendous heat and humidity, for steamed temperatures of 80–90°F were considered ideal for the production of thread. They only had half an hour's halt for breakfast and an hour free for lunch; a working day of twelve-and-a-half hours, six days a week.

'The management claimed that times were too hard to shorten working hours, and constantly referred to cotton shortages to back up their case; but James Monteith, the owner of the mills, in five bad years made a personal fortune of eighty thousand pounds.'[4]

Piecers needed sharp eyes and the power of constant attention if they were to avoid frequent beatings. They also had to be unusually agile since their work often involved climbing under the machinery or balancing over it. Piecers walked anything up to twenty miles a day in the mills, and much of this distance was covered in crawling or stooping positions. Long hours on their feet often led to the development of bow legs and varicose veins.

Each adult spinner had three piecers attending to his machine and, since he was paid in proportion to what he produced, it was in his interest to force the children on. Often

---

[4] G Hewart, *Curiosities of Glasgow Citizenship* (Glasgow, 1881), pp 112–13, in Jeale, p 8.

towards evening they started to fall asleep on their feet, but a beating with a leather strap or a dousing with a bucket of water generally renewed their energies. Many of the children ended up with 'limbs deformed and growth stunted'.[5]

By the end of the working day most piecers were too tired to play and certainly in no frame of mind to learn. David Livingstone and a handful of studious children were more ambitious. They defied aching limbs and tired minds, and wearily made their way to the company school to work from 8–10pm. David would then return home to study, often until midnight, his mother frequently having to take his book away before he would go to sleep.

With part of his first week's wages he purchased Ruddiman's *Rudiments of Latin*, the language he studied for many years. The remainder of his wage went towards his upkeep.

David managed to read in the factory by placing his book on a portion of the spinning jenny so that he could catch sentence after sentence as he passed at his work. Thus he maintained fairly constant study, undisturbed by the roar of the machinery.

The other workers often pitched bobbins, aiming to knock his book off its perch, and they used to try to turn him from the path he had chosen with words such as: 'I think you ought . . .', until young Livingstone snapped back with: 'You think! I can think and act for myself; don't need anybody to think for me.'[6]

As a fervent reader, he did not gain admiration but rather earned the reputation of being unsociable and remote. His superiors in the spinning mill were not sympathetic towards

[5] Parliamentary Papers. Report of the Minutes of Evidence on the State of Children Employed in Manufactures of the United Kingdom 1816 (397), Vol 3, in Jeal, p 9.
[6] J P R Wallis (ed), *The Matabele Mission 1858–1878* (London, 1945) in Jeal, p 10.

his steadfastness in studying as it tended to slow him down and distract him from his work.

From the age of thirteen he attended an extra Latin class given by the village schoolmaster. When the others gave up, he remained. The master, not seeing much response for his labours other than that of an over-zealous son of a tea merchant, decided to abandon the lessons. This did not deter young David who, fixing his own goals, pressed on studying by himself.

Not merely content with his reading, he often scoured the countryside with his books in search of stones, rocks or botanical and zoological specimens. On one such exploration David and his brother entered a limestone quarry. David began to collect the shells in the limestone, and turning to a quarryman asked, 'However did these shells come into these rocks?' The man looked at him with the pitying eye which the benevolent assume when viewing the insane. 'When God made the rocks, He made the shells in them,' was the dampening reply.[7]

However, his interest in science was not limited to procuring plants and inedible specimens. If a salmon came his way while he was fishing for trout, he landed it as an added bonus. Once, to ensure safe delivery of the dinner, he deposited a salmon in the trouser leg of his younger brother Charles. He, for his part as a porter, gained immense sympathy from the villagers for his swollen leg.

David's enquiring mind probed many things from the use of herbs to the 'still more perplexing profundities of astrology.'[8] However, he retraced his steps as 'it seemed perilous ground to tread on farther, for the dark hint appeared to my youthful mind to loom towards "selling soul and body to the devil"'.[9]

---

[7] M T, p 5.
[8] *Ibid.*
[9] *Ibid.*

His cautious sentiments were synonymous with Scripture, as the prophet Isaiah warned of the weakness in studying the signs of the stars when he stated: 'Let now the astrologers, those who prophesy by the stars, those who predict by the new moons, stand up and save you from what will come upon you. Behold, they have become like stubble, fire burns them; they cannot deliver themselves from the power of the flame.'[10]

Furthermore, from the age of twelve another battle had been raging in the Scottish lad's heart and mind as he worried about 'his state as a sinner'.

Great pains had been taken by his parents to instil the doctrines of Christianity into his mind, and he had no difficulty in understanding the theory of free salvation by the atonement of our Saviour, but it was about this time that he began to feel the necessity for a personal application of the doctrine to his own case.[11]

He was deterred, however, from embracing the free offer of mercy promised in the gospel by a sense of his unworthiness to receive so great a blessing. Conceiving it to be his duty to wait for this, he continued expectantly. Finally, his convictions were addressed and he saw himself as forgiven in the eyes of his Saviour. He likened the change to that of colour blindness being healed. 'The perfect freeness with which the pardon of all our guilt is offered in God's book drew forth feelings of affectionate love to Him who bought us with His blood.'[12]

He had found the peace he sought, and he used a phrase which was to become the constant undertone of his life: 'In the glow of love that Christianity inspired I resolved to devote my life to the alleviation of human misery.'

Young Livingstone faced the future with more confidence and care. Acts of self-denial, very hard to practise under the

---

[10] Isaiah 47:13–14.
[11] M T, p 4.
[12] *Ibid.*

iron law of conscience, became a willing service under the glow of divine love.

A major contribution to his breakthrough was the understanding that the Holy Spirit was available to all and willing to abide in those who asked. Until then he was led to believe that the Holy Spirit only anointed a select few who were appointed by God.

Another factor which helped him to receive the peace he much sought was the reading of works by the rather eccentric yet likeable old scientist, Dr Thomas Dick, who enforced David's own conviction 'that religion and science were friendly to each other'.[13]

Livingstone seldom revealed his inner feelings in public, but it is plain from his letters and lifestyle that from this point onwards to his death, his life was influenced by a calm but mighty inward power.

Many influential men are motivated by their desire for gold. For others it may be glory and the fame and fortune that follow dramatic discoveries which they covet. But for a few, their main object in life is to glorify God. One servant was that unsophisticated Scotsman, David Livingstone, who little realised he would have a profound effect on the world as he continued to labour for Christ. Three themes were to dominate his life: evangelisation, exploration and emancipation. But for a time, little change was recorded in the quaint village of Blantyre.

At first he had no thought of becoming a missionary. However, feeling 'that the salvation of men ought to be the chief desire and aim of every Christian', he made a resolution 'that he would give to the cause of missions all that he might earn beyond what was required for his subsistence'.[14] Later this came to mean his life.

---

[13] *Ibid* (Jeal dates the year of breakthrough as 1832).
[14] Blaikie, p 15.

David took a greater interest in his church and warmed to several characters who gave him sound religious instruction. One such person was Thomas Burke, an old soldier who incessantly urged the people of Blantyre to yield themselves to God. By ringing his bell and shattering the peace and quiet of Blantyre village at the crack of dawn every Sunday morning, he would attempt to rouse people to attend his early morning prayer meeting. Despite Burke's brusque temperament, the Livingstones appreciated his genuine worth, and they faithfully supported him.

Another teacher was David Hogg, who addressed David from his death bed with the words: 'Now, lad! Make religion the every-day business of your life, and not a thing of fits and starts; for if you do not, temptation and other things will get the better of you.'[15]

Much earlier David's grandfather had also left him a challenge. He related that one of their forefathers, a poor islander renowned for his wisdom, gathered his children around him on his death bed and said,

> I have searched most carefully through all the traditions of our family, and I never could discover that there was a dishonest man among our forefathers. If therefore any of you or any of your children should take to dishonest ways, it will not be because it runs in our blood . . . I leave this precept with you: be honest.[16]

The dying grandfather probably overlooked a little bit of sheep stealing, for that did not come out in his closing speech. As far as we know, the Livingstones remained upright, steadfast and above reproach.

David laboured at the mill six days a week, year in year out. He saw this irksome mill as part of his education and bore it with patience. Promotion came in his ninth year, to

---

[15] M T, p 6.
[16] *Ibid*, p 2.

the rank of a spinner. This labour was still 'excessively severe on a slim loose-jointed lad, but it was well paid' and enabled him to save for university, where his greatest goal to date would be realised.

The year 1832 was special in the Livingstone home: David had the dramatic breakthrough with regard to his reasoning that science and Christianity were compatible, and his father had a further change of heart.

During this time there was a stirring in Scotland and many Christians became dissatisfied with the strict austere conduct of the State church. Several believers in Blantyre, including Neil Livingstone, changed their fellowship to that of the Free Church. Every Sunday the Livingstone family would as usual don their best dress and walk, regardless of the weather, to Hamilton, a small village near their home. They were not a family to live off the goodwill of others and they refused the generous hospitality of the congregation to dine with them. Accepting only a kettle of boiling water, they made do with the few provisions they had brought. It was not that they were a proud family; they knew only too well the restrictions placed on everyone who was poor, and feeding an extra family would severely tax the finely balanced budget.

After lunch, the family treated themselves to their weekly luxury—a barley sweet each—and Mrs Livingstone would indulge herself by enjoying a pipe, another rarity.

Moving to the new church in Hamilton had an additional impact upon David's life for it brought him into contact with a far wider social circle. Several members of the congregation were wealthy, well-read men who corresponded with theologians in America, where a simultaneous religious revival was taking place. The new American theology was far more liberal than that evident in the Scottish churches. Livingstone read much of this literature and was greatly influenced by an American Pentecostal believer, Charles Finney.

The impact on the rest of his family was just as great. Charles, his younger brother, sponsored by Henry Drummond, a member of the congregation, was shortly to leave Scotland to attend Oberlin College where Finney taught.[17]

David completely accepted Finney's proposition that 'the Holy Spirit is promised to all who ask'. In a letter sent much later to his friend Rev George Drummond, David urged him to read the works of Finney, stating that ministers of the gospel must be able to adapt to whatever circumstances in order to save souls, and if sinners are not saved the blame is theirs; the sinners' blood will be required at their hand.[18]

With this same solemnness of spirit, and with a message of eternal salvation, he strove to reach out to a lost and dying world.

The new congregation in Hamilton also had more dynamic views with regard to missions, and they were to win the hearts of father and son alike. Neil Livingstone's change of heart brought him closer to David; old rifts were completely healed as the love which had been frustrated for so long flourished and fed an even deeper relationship.

The year 1832 was also significant in Britain's history as the Reform Bill was passed through Parliament, stipulating demands for social and educational reform. The secular and humanitarian reformers joined with the Temperance, Bible and Tract Societies in demanding better conditions for the poor. It was not enough merely to stamp out drunkenness and vice by preaching. The conditions that bred them would also have to be destroyed.

This revival of evangelicalism was closely linked with the anti-slavery movement which in 1833 recorded its greatest triumph. After a long battle, slavery was abolished throughout the British Empire by an act of Parliament. This victory against massive vested interests had been achieved by the concerted

---

[17] Jeal p 13.
[18] D L to Rev George Drummond 10/03/1841 in Chamberlin, p 20 (posted on his arrival in Cape Town).

action of many Christians. Success also spurred members of the missionary societies who considered the freeing of slaves to be the first step towards spiritual freedom; the heathen had to be given the gospel. This was the optimism that stirred young Livingstone.

As he returned to face the daily drudgery of the spinning mill, his heavenly Father kept his hand on David's life, holding, teaching and gently moulding. Another year elapsed and he stood firm to his hopes and convictions.

His father returned home one evening with a pamphlet which had been issued at the church. It had been released the previous year from Canton by Karl Gutzlaff of the Netherlands Missionary Society and was an appeal for medical missionaries to be sent to China. Gutzlaff maintained that medical missionary training, a new concept in Christianity, made the missionary far more effective in converting the lost souls to Christ, for gratitude often followed the relief of physical suffering. David rejoiced that his father, duly convinced, finally supported his desire to become a doctor and to preach the gospel. The path ahead, though, was not easy. It was plagued with problems.

For the vast majority of folk at the mills the idea would have been unthinkable. However, David had learned enough Latin to be able to understand most medical terms, and considering his background he was remarkably well read. University entrance requirements at this time were hardly stringent—lack of finance was the main obstacle. David had to find an enormous sum but, with his parents' encouragement and his own dogged determination, he saved most of his money during the next eighteen months, and with a little help from his older brother, John, the goal appeared attainable.

In the autumn of 1836, Livingstone faced his next formidable hurdle; he had already achieved something that statistically was immensely improbable. Less than ten per cent of all the children put to work in the mills during the first three decades of the nineteenth century learned to read or write with any proficiency. For one to manage to do this and devote time to Latin, botany, theology and simple mathematics was exceptional. At the age of twenty-three David Livingstone had already shown himself to be the exception.

2

Medicine and Missions

Early one morning David and his father set out to trudge the eight miles to Glasgow in search of accommodation. The pressed snow crunched beneath their feet. They had a list of likely lodgings, but it was not until evening that they found an affordable room at two shillings a week. After settling David in, Mr Livingstone, cold and tired, returned home.

It was not long before David discovered his landlady's taking ways regarding his tea and sugar, and refusing to accept this state of affairs he found more expensive lodgings in the High Street, but at least his supplies were safe. Although he came home at weekends David confessed to his sister Janet how lonely he was during his early days in Glasgow.

During the first two academic sessions, young Livingstone studied Greek at the university, theology under the Revd Dr Wardlaw and medicine at Anderson's College. He had great admiration for Dr Wardlaw and generally accepted his theological views, though Livingstone was not much of a scientific theologian.

His chief work in Glasgow was medical study, although the training he received from 1836–1838 was by today's standards primitive. Surgical operations were performed at hazardous speeds because of the lack of anaesthetics. Chloroform and ether were not introduced until seven years later and the discovery of antiseptics lay twenty-five years ahead. The study of chemistry was growing, but that of physics had hardly started, and biochemistry and bacteriology were unknown.[1] Furthermore, nothing at all was known about the tropical diseases he was to encounter, such as malaria and black-water fever.

The sale of bodies for dissection had only been legalised four years prior to his initial training, so knowledge of anatomy was not extensive. Before the legalisation, body-snatchers raided graves in order to provide the medical profession with corpses to dissect.

His training, despite many inadequacies, equalled that of the finest in the world at that time and proved invaluable.

He later kept himself abreast of new information, and whenever possible had medical manuals sent to him. These he studied intently and so learned about chloroform, with which he later helped his wife through several birth processes. This wide reading also drew his attention to the benefits of quinine in the treatment and prevention of malaria, without which his life might have been shortened.

At university he also broadened his knowledge of surgical instruments which would assist him in later years as he needed to be a Jack-of-all-trades in Africa.

David enjoyed his visits home to Blantyre each weekend, and although Fergus Ferguson—the kind, wealthy draper from the church—would offer him a lift in his gig to Glasgow each Monday morning, Livingstone would refuse, preferring a long walk in the snow to missing part of the morning's lectures. This refusal of the offer also meant that he had to be up before five in order to reach Glasgow by eight.[2]

New acquaintances were made and Livingstone became a great friend of Mr Young of Kelly, the founder of a great paraffin industry in Midlothian. Their friendship was firm and Mr Young remained Livingstone's best friend. With his

---

[1] Gelfand, p 1.
[2] Neil Livingstone to London Missionary Society 26/04/1838, LMS Archives in Jeal, p 16.

wealth, Young later generously supported the explorer's expeditions.

During his second year at Anderson's College, David began to think seriously about applying to a missionary society, and after thorough discussion with his father contacted the London Missionary Society. This Society had worldwide operations, taking the gospel to the remotest parts of the earth and accepted candidates from all Protestant denominations.

In January 1838, after a delay of three months, Livingstone was sent a small booklet by the directors of the Society. He was to write in it his answers to seventeen questions regarding his background and reasons for wishing to be a missionary.

The young bachelor answered the marriage question:

> Unmarried; under no engagement relating to marriage, never made proposals of marriage, nor conducted myself so to any woman as to cause her to suspect that I intended anything relating to marriage; and so far as my present wishes are concerned, I should prefer going out unmarried, that I might be without that care which the concerns of a family necessarily induce, and give myself wholly to the work.[3]

The booklet was posted and the Livingstone family waited what seemed like an age for a reply. Neil Livingstone became anxious. What if the form had not been answered in the way the directors expected? He felt compelled to write to them, telling them a few facts which his son in his modesty might not have divulged. He informed them of his son's diligence in attending lectures, even at the cost of declining a lift to town; his refusal to be tempted by a secure teaching job and his early quest for Latin proficiency.

Neil concluded by assuring the directors that he had not told his son he had written to them and would rather David never knew, for he would most certainly disapprove. This

[3] Chamberlin, p 1–2.

touching, heartfelt letter must have taken him some time
to compose and write, for Neil was a man of minimal formal
education.

Eventually, David was invited to appear in London on
13th August 1838 for an interview. Fergus Ferguson gave
him money for his fare and David made his way to London.
He was interviewed, but was given no decision and told
nothing except that a further interview would take place.

After the second scrutiny in September, the directors
decided to accept Livingstone on probation. The young man
was sent to pursue his Christian education under the Revd
Richard Cecil at Chipping Ongar in Essex. His medical
studies would for the moment have to take second place.
He lodged with six other students in a long, low building
where they lived by themselves, doing their own cooking,
washing, ironing and so on. His room was over a central
arch that led to the Congregational chapel where they
worshipped.

The keen students assembled for teaching in Richard
Cecil's house which was close by. The set curriculum of
Greek, Hebrew and Latin was hardly inspiring, as the
peoples whom they would eventually teach would have at
most a limited knowledge of English and none of the dead
languages.

Richard Cecil was an elderly, pedantic man who took his
work seriously and judged his students by exacting
standards. By January 1839 he had the following view of
Livingstone, and stated that 'his heaviness of manner, united
as it is with a rusticity, not likely to be removed, still strikes
me as having importance, but he has sense and quiet vigour;
his temper is good and his character substantial, so that I
do not like the thought of his being rejected.'[4]

However, rejection was still a distinct possibility. In spite

---

[4] R Cecil to LMS 26/01/1839, LMS Archives, in Jeal p 19.

of his strong character and vigour, his academic progress was slow. In February, the Revd Richard Cecil wrote again to the directors and regretfully told them that Livingstone was 'hardly ready in point of knowledge to go to a theological college, whatever plans had been entertained for him'.

This judgement was very hard on him, for he was almost entirely self-taught and had fought a long, weary battle for his education. The other students, while not exactly from privileged homes, had had several years of continuous formal education in the past. The reticent Reverend considered Livingstone 'worthy but remote from brilliant' and described his progress as 'steady but not rapid'. He ended his report with the hope that his stolid Scottish student 'might kindle a little'.[5]

Livingstone was not noted for great oratory in his preaching. As part of their training, students had to prepare sermons which were submitted to the Revd Cecil and, when corrected, were committed to memory and then repeated to their village congregations. On one occasion a minister fell sick after the morning service and David was called to preach that evening. He chose his text and read it out very deliberately. Suddenly his sermon wavered as his memory failed him. In a staunch Scottish accent he abruptly said, 'Friends, I have forgotten all I have to say,' and hurrying out of the pulpit, left the chapel. This did not impress the directors and the report sent to the Board after three months was unfavourable. His lack of confidence was evident in his public praying and preaching and in his hesitant manner when conducting family worship. When the report was read and a decision was about to be taken against him, a wise man pleaded hard that his probation should be extended. He was granted several extra months and so the course continued.[6] He undertook many preaching commitments

[5] R Cecil to LMS 23/02/1839, *ibid*.
[6] R Cecil to LMS in Blaikie, p 29.

in the villages surrounding Ongar, submitting himself to the
authority of those over him.

The compassion of Christ continued to move him as he
strove to fulfil this, his latest challenge, preaching. He was
not a man given to tears, but as he continued to walk with
Christ his heart ached. He allowed the things that were
troubling God's heart to trouble his.

On one occasion in Ongar it was David's turn to conduct
the family worship. He was so completely overcome while
reading an Old Testament passage on slavery that he broke
down, and for some time was unable to say another word.[7]
A fellow student, Mr Moore, was impressed that Livingstone
never prayed without the petition that 'we might imitate
Christ in all His inimitable perfections'.[8]

Apropos this prayer it is interesting to note, twenty years
later, the impression made by David Livingstone on a lady,
Mrs Sime. She only saw him twice, yet she wrote, 'I never
knew anyone who gave me more the idea of power over
other men, such power as our Saviour showed while on
earth, the power of love and purity combined.'[9]

Twenty years, however, is a long period of time and it
was one in which Livingstone's faith would be sorely tested.
As gold is put through the fire, so would his life be refined,
that his faith, being more precious than gold which is
perishable, 'may be found to result in praise and glory and
honor at the revelation of Jesus Christ'.[10]

Certainly in his Christian walk David Livingstone had high
aspirations for himself, and alluding to the remark of a friend
urged his sisters to seek to be 'uncommon Christians, that is,
eminently holy and devoted servants of the Most High'.

---

[7] Recollection of the Revd Thomas Fison, BA of Hendon in Ritchie, p 28.
[8] Blaikie, p 28.
[9] *Ibid.*
[10] 1 Peter 1:7.

Let us seek—and with the conviction that we cannot do without it—that all selfishness be extirpated, pride banished, unbelief driven from the mind, every idol dethroned, and everything hostile to holiness and opposed to the divine will crucified; that 'holiness to the Lord' may be engraven on the heart, and evermore characterise our whole conduct. This is what we ought to strive after; this is the way to be happy; this is what our Saviour loves— entire surrender of the heart. May He enable us by His Spirit to persevere till we attain it! All comes from Him, the disposition to ask as well as the blessing itself.[11]

Some may argue that the sincere Scot was not a saint. After all, his younger brother was later to nickname him the 'cursing Consul of Quillimane'. Nonetheless, it is plain to see that his heart was in the right place. He did seek first 'the kingdom of God and his righteousness' before any of his own desires. He steadfastly sought the Lord's will for his life as he persevered through the problems that ensued.

Walter Inglis, one of Livingstone's contemporaries, noted that David's 'face wore at all times the strongly marked lines of potent will'. It was not in his character to relax into the abandon of youthful frolic or play. He only really remembered seeing him play one practical joke. 'A man came with a ripe boil that only required to be lanced. He gave the boil an honest skelp with a book. He had a grin for dry Scottish humour . . .'[12]

Despite this cutting humour, he still won some fine friends, Joseph Moore being one of them. The aspiring missionaries met when they both came to London to be interviewed by the society, and touring London they enjoyed each other's company as they anxiously awaited the outcome of their examinations. Their friendship grew as they jointly suffered and studied under Richard Cecil.

---

[11] D L to his sister 5/05/1839, in Blaikie pp 29–30.
[12] G Seaver *David Livingstone: His Life and Letters* (1957), p 27 in Jeal, p 20.

Joseph admitted that 'there was truly an indescribable charm about him which, with all his rather ungainly ways, and by no means winning face, attracted almost everyone, and which helped him so much in his after-wanderings in Africa'.[13]

One person Livingstone warmed to was Miss Catherine Ridley, the first middle-class girl he had ever met. Sadly his poor background made him feel rather inept in her company and in a letter to her he confessed that he was 'not very well acquainted with the feelings of those who have been ladies all their lives'.[14]

Though they met often and exchanged little gifts, romance did not blossom. She preferred another student, Thomas Prentice, a fine friend of David's. David was to tell his son later that he 'broke off' with Catherine as she was too much of a lady to make a good missionary's wife.

However, he did write to George Drummond, a friend in Papaoa, Tahiti, and spoke warmly of the couple, saying that

> both he and Catherine seem possessed of the true missionary spirit, for when I told him I thought she was too much of the lady for a missionary's wife he said that ever since she thought of becoming a missionary she wrought just like a servant and did a great part of the household work, baking the bread etc . . .'[15]

Of Catherine's zeal he felt that 'she will require it all . . . as the difference between the elegant little carriage which they used to drive and the bullock wagon of South Africa is very great'.[16]

Livingstone was an idealist. He took his task and calling most seriously, and whatever he did he performed thoroughly. His character was uncompromising.

---

[13] Blaikie, p 26.
[14] D L to Miss Catherine Ridley 24/02/1841 in Chamberlin, p 16.
[15] D L to the Revd George Drummond 25/07/1840 in Chamberlin, p 8.
[16] D L to the Revd Henry Dickson 8/05/1840, *ibid*, p 6.

Very early one foggy November morning he set out from Ongar to walk twenty-seven miles to London to carry out some business for his elder brother, John, who had begun to deal in lace. In the morning darkness Livingstone tripped and fell into a ditch, muddying his clothes, which did not improve his appearance. Undeterred, he continued into London visiting various shops, including that of a relative of his father.

After a long day, rather than look for accommodation in expensive London, he started walking back to Ongar. Just beyond London, near Edmonton, Livingstone came across a lady who had been thrown out of a gig. She lay stunned on the side of the road. Livingstone went over to her and after lifting her up carried her into a house nearby. There he examined her and firmly recommended that a doctor be called. He bade them farewell and resumed his weary tramp, footsore and so tired that he mistook his turning and slogged miles in the wrong direction.

When he realised his error he felt exhausted. All he wanted to do was lie down and sleep, but finding a sign-post he climbed it and by dim starlight deciphered enough to learn his whereabouts. Lead-legged, he headed for home. About midnight, after a round trip of roughly sixty miles, he reached Ongar, white as a sheet, and so tired he could hardly utter a word. Joseph gave him a basin of bread and milk, and put him to bed. The intrepid traveller slept until after noon the next day.[17]

Thus Livingstone with each passing day prepared himself for the mission field. His commitment to his high calling in Christ took an ever stronger hold upon him.

At that time total abstinence began to be spoken of and the young man, together with Joseph Moore and Joseph Taylor, another trainee missionary, took a pledge to abstain.[18]

---

[17] Blaikie, p 27.
[18] *Ibid.*

In 1839, world events affected Livingstone's career in a greater manner than his encounter with Catherine Ridley. He had set his sights on China, but the British and Chinese were involved in the inglorious Opium War. The leaders of the London Missionary Society were not prepared to risk the lives of their missionaries unnecessarily. China was closed.

In July, the Society proposed that David go to the West Indies. These islands did not appeal to him, as they were partly developed and 'appeared so much like the Ministry at home'.[19] He felt that his medical skills would be wasted, as there were already doctors in that field, and urged the Selection Committee of the Society to grant him a further year in Britain, so that he might obtain more medical knowledge and then be put to labour in lands further afield.

On 22nd July 1839 the Examination Committee agreed that David Livingstone 'should continue with the Revd R Cecil until Christmas and then attend the British and Foreign School of Medicine to fit himself for some station in South Africa or the South Seas'.[20]

A happy year followed while he was studying medicine. The young man made many friends, one of whom was J Risdon Bennett, Physician to the Aldersgate Street Dispensary, who later became the President of the Royal College of Physicians. He was to become one of Livingstone's most trusted friends.

Dr Bennett had 'the highest admiration of his endowments, both of mind and heart, and of his pure and noble devotion of all his powers to the highest purposes of life. One could not fail to be impressed with his simple, loving, Christian spirit, and the combined modest, unassuming, and self-reliant character of the man.'[21]

---

[19] D L to LMS 2/07/1839 in Campbell, p 62.
[20] Minutes of 22/07/1839 of the Examination Committee (L M S) in Gelfand, p 21.
[21] Blaikie, p 31.

Regarding his medical studies, David placed himself under the guidance of Dr Bennett who

> was struck with the amount of knowledge that Livingstone had already acquired of those subjects which constitute the foundation of medical science. He had, however, little or no acquaintance with the practical departments of medicine ... Of these deficiencies he was quite aware, and felt the importance of acquiring as much practical knowledge as possible during his stay in London.

Dr Bennett was at that time also lecturing at Charing Cross Hospital on the practice of medicine and was able to obtain for Livingstone free admission there and to the ophthalmic hospital in Moorfields. 'With these sources of information open to him, he obtained a considerable acquaintance with the more ordinary forms of disease, both surgical and medical and a valuable amount of scientific and practical knowledge.'[22]

Another distinguished man with whom Livingstone became acquainted in London was Professor Owen, who was in charge of the Hunterian Museum where David achieved an excellent knowledge of comparative anatomy.

Many years later, on one of Livingstone's expeditions to Africa, he remembered that he had promised to bear his instructor in mind should a rare specimen come his way. After a long while and hearing nothing, the promise was considered forgotten by Professor Owen yet, true to his word, on his first return to Britain, Livingstone presented him with an elephant tusk which had a spiral curve. This was found in the heart of Africa, and despite the difficulties Livingstone was determined to deliver it.

This diligent fulfilment of a moral obligation illustrates Livingstone's inflexible adherence to his word. This kindness of character made a deep impression on all his fellow students

---

[22] *Ibid* pp 31–32.

and acquaintances. He had a certain brusque, bluntness of manner, but it was softened by his humble approach to life.

Alexander Macmillan, an eminent publisher who enjoyed Livingstone's company, did not notice any greatness of character, yet he did recognise that he was a man of 'resolute courage, singular purity and loftiness of moral aim, and an exquisite modesty of mind . . . I have heard it said of him, "Fire, water, stone-wall would not stop Livingstone in the fulfilment of any recognised duty."'

Little did they realise just how severely these aspects of his character would be tested.

While studying in London, David had little time to make friends, male or female, outside his sphere of work. However, during a stay in a boarding-house for young missionaries in Aldersgate, he met the remarkable South African missionary, Robert Moffat, whose journeys and friendship with the African Chief, Mosilikatse,[23] were legendary.

Six months earlier, Livingstone had set his heart upon going to Africa, and his meeting with the bearded gentleman from the back of beyond further strengthened his intentions. He asked Moffat many questions pertaining to the latter's work and by and by asked Moffat if he thought he would be suitable for Africa.

Moffat replied that he believed Livingstone should travel to new territory in Africa, specifying the vast plain to the north of the mission station, where sometimes was seen by the light of the morning sun 'the smoke of a thousand villages, where no missionary had ever been'.

This was the challenge that the young man was seeking. He focused his sights on Southern Africa.

However, there was something about Livingstone which bothered Mr and Mrs Moffat. He was single. They had tried

---

[23] Today his name is often spelt 'Mzilikazi'.

to suggest a Miss Collier who was ten years his senior as a suitable wife,[24] but to no avail.

Frustrated and rather forlorn, the would-be medical missionary wrote to his friend the Revd George Drummond in Tahiti and posed the exact question to him:

> I dare say you wonder if I am going to be married myself . . . I really don't know. If people would just let me alone I am quite easy but there are so many giving me advice, and all gratis, that I don't know what to think. I think if I know my own heart that I want to do what will render me most useful but whether my usefulness will be augmented by getting a wife I really don't know. So here I am in a pretty mess you will allow as deep in the mud as any man was; can't see three inches before me and am free as to any engagements. What may turn up you shall hereafter hear.
>
> I look forward with greater interest than ever to my mission. I can't say I have the least regret in leaving my native shores for ever. I rejoice that so great honour is to be bestowed upon me. How much reason have we to say, 'I thank Jesus Christ our Lord who hath enabled me for that he counted me faithful, putting me into the ministry.'[25]

A month prior to penning this letter, on 1st June 1840, Livingstone attended a meeting in Exeter Hall in the Strand, mounted by the Society for the Extinction of the Slave-Trade and for the Civilization of Africa.

There it was proposed that Africans would only be saved from the slave-trade if they were woken up to the possibilities of selling their own produce; otherwise, chiefs would continue to barbarically sell their own kind to pay for the beads, cloth, guns and trinkets they coveted. Commerce and Christianity could achieve the miracle, not Christianity alone.

These ideas proposed by Thomas Fowell Buxton,

[24] Mrs Moffat to Robert Moffat 27/06/1840, NAZ.
[25] Chamberlin, p 8.

Wilberforce's successor, had a major impact on David Livingstone.

So did the sick rooms of the London hospitals. In July he developed what he believed to be 'congestion of the liver and infection of the lungs' from inhaling 'too much of the effluvia of sick chambers, dissecting rooms, etc'.[26] This illness might have proved fatal, and he was sent by ship to Scotland to recuperate.

By the end of the summer he had recovered, and returning to London he completed the curriculum of medical studies. Sadly, however, he did not have the funds to sit the examinations in London. If he wanted a diploma, he would have to go up to Glasgow to write and be interviewed.

This he did, and unwittingly underwent an examination more severe than usual, as he considered the stethoscope to be of considerable value, whereas the Board was not convinced of its usefulness. A robust argument ensued.

He later admitted: 'The wiser plan would have been to have had no opinion of my own.'[27] But such a thought did not occur to him at the time. Anxiously he waited for his results which arrived in November 1840. To his unfeigned delight he had qualified as a Licentiate of the Royal Faculty of Physicians and Surgeons.

Now the young man lost no time in commencing his life's work.

A single night was all he could spend with his family, and they had so much to discuss that David proposed they should sit up all night. This, however, his mother would not permit.

'I remember my father and him,' wrote his sister, 'talking over the prospects of Christian missions. They agreed that the time would come when rich men and great men would think

---

[26] *Ibid*, p 7.
[27] M T, p 7.

it an honour to support whole stations of missionaries, instead of spending their money on hounds and horses.'[28]

It was still dark when the family rose at five that bleak November morning. Mrs Livingstone made the coffee, Mr Livingstone prepared to walk with his son to Glasgow, and David then led the household to the throne of grace in prayer. The thought embedded in his text was uppermost in his mind. He was leaving those who were dearer to him than life itself, yet there was One upon whom he could always rely. One whose words, 'Lo I am with you always, even unto the end of the world,' would still a raging storm in his heart when in his darkest hour he would fear for his very life.

In the dim, cosy glow of the lamplight, the twenty-seven-year-old selected Psalm 121. With a heavy heart he read:

I will lift up mine eyes unto the hills,
from whence cometh my help.
My help cometh from the Lord,
which made heaven and earth.
He will not suffer thy foot to be moved:
he that keepeth thee will not slumber.
Behold, he that keepeth Israel
Shall neither slumber nor sleep.
The Lord is thy keeper:
The Lord is thy shade upon thy right hand.
The sun shall not smite thee by day,
nor the moon by night.
The Lord shall preserve thee from all evil:
he shall preserve thy soul.
The Lord shall preserve thy going out
and thy coming in
from this time forth, and even for evermore.[29]

Turning to Psalm 135 he read of the glory, majesty and sovereignty of God, who alone is to be praised.

---

[28] Blaikie, p 36.
[29] Psalm 121, King James Version.

The humble family then bowed in prayer. Though their hearts ached, their distress was softened by the readings. The time came for the anguish of farewell.

In the grey light of that wintry early November morning, father and son set out on their long and cheerless tramp to the Glasgow Docks. On the Broomielaw pier they looked for the last time on earth at each other's faces. The ageing old man walked back slowly to Blantyre, no doubt with a lonely heart, yet praising God.

Decisive, David set out towards the far continent.

3

Running Risks in Rio

Young Livingstone arrived in London on 20th November 1840, and he was ordained as a missionary in the Albion Street Chapel, London. On 8th December of the same year, he joined the sailing barque 'George' for Cape Town, South Africa.

He was very conscious of what he had accomplished and the cost of doing so. He'd had no real childhood or adolescence, little or no play or recreation. To achieve what he had, against so many odds, demanded qualities that left little room for any but serious sentiments.

His heart had been tempered by his love for Christ, yet the obstacles he had overcome and the suffering he had endured had lasting effects. He could only judge others by the standards he had set for himself, and as time passed, these ideals would become less flexible, with little or no time for views that differed from his own. As he sailed, he knew that many humanitarians disapproved of missionary work abroad, believing like Charles Dickens that 'the work at home must be completed thoroughly or there is no hope abroad'.[1]

Livingstone would have brushed aside such arguments with scorn. 'All men had the right to hear God's word. No nation ought to hoard the Gospel like a miser . . .'[2] Christianity is

---

[1] 'The Niger Expedition' Charles Dickens, *Household Words* 19/08/1848 in Jeal, p 24.

[2] Jeal, p 24.

for all men at all times in all places. The labourers were few
and the harvest great.

Besides, Britain had a debt to Africa it could never repay.
For too long it had bought slaves from Africa. Africans had
a right to hear the gospel.

The three-month journey in the cramped ship was tiresome.
There were many storms near the Bay of Biscay, during one
of which Livingstone wrote to his friend Tom Prentice, who
at that stage had aspirations of visiting Africa, that the

> little vessel went reeling and staggering over the waves as if she
> had been drunk, our trunks perpetually breaking from their
> lashings, were tossed from one side of the cabin to the other,
> everything both pleasant and unpleasant huddled together in
> glorious confusion . . . Imagine if you can a ship in a fit of epilepsy.[3]

Livingstone's advice on the journey was simple: 'Expect to be
sick and take nothing from your trunks until that is over
except your Bibles. If you escape sea sickness it will be an
agreeable disappointment.'[4]

Captain Donaldson became the young doctor's closest
friend on the voyage. He was very obliging and taught
Livingstone 'all the information respecting the use of the
quadrant in his power, frequently sitting up till twelve o'clock
at night for the purpose of taking lunar observations'.[5] Thus
the young missionary gained another skill which was to serve
him successfully in the trying years ahead.

While the ship rocked and reeled over the perilous seas, the
Scotsman tried to help several folk who succumbed to sea-
sickness, including Mr and Mrs Ross, who were also from
the London Missionary Society. Unfortunately, the bachelor
from Blantyre brought on a jealous husband's fury and
accusations that the young man had designs on Mrs Ross.

---

[3] Chamberlin p 11.
[4] *Ibid.*
[5] Blaikie, p 38.

This offended Livingstone, and he wrote to the Revd Cecil, indignantly expressing that he would rather have flirted with his grandmother than with Ross' 'blooming bride of thirty-four or five'. From then on Ross was written off by Livingstone as a man with 'an exceedingly contracted mind', whose opinions should receive 'no more attention than an illiterate Hottentot child'.[6]

They were to remain rivals, Livingstone years later refusing to have Ross accompany him on research work.

In between staff and sea storms, Livingstone spent a lot of time studying theology, but wrote honestly to the London Missionary Society, saying that he 'knew of no spiritual good having been done in the case of any one on board the ship'[6] for though the captain rigged out the church on Sundays, Livingstone held out little hope for souls and said, 'I being a poor preacher, and the chaplain addressing them as Christians already, no moral influence was exerted.'[7]

More problems occurred. During a raging storm the foremast of the ship was split. This was a major problem and as a result they had to put into Rio de Janeiro to have it repaired.

Livingstone enjoyed his stay in Rio de Janeiro and, being true to his nature, took off alone to roam the luxuriant hills and 'valleys lovely beyond description. Their sides covered with plantations of coffee, sugar cane, Indian corn, etc. and the little shed-like cottages of the natives scattered here and there and peeping out from beneath orange trees or the spreading leaves of the banana.'[8]

Wanting to obtain some fruit, he wrote later:

I descended one of these valleys intending to seek a supply at the first cottage I came to, but no sooner had I emerged from the

---

[6] *Ibid.*
[7] *Ibid.*
[8] Chamberlin pp 13–14.

wood to an open space in front of one, than I was surrounded
by three half starved looking dogs who seemed inclined to
make an end of me but having a good stick in my hand I
soon convinced them that I was not a member of the Peace
Society.[9]

The noise, however, alerted the inhabitants who in turn
showed him exemplary kindness. Ushered inside, a prodigious
meal was laid before him and Livingstone battled profusely
to refuse bottles of liquor which were pulled out one after the
other in the hope he would have something to drink. For all
his knowledge of languages he was at a loss to convey to the
Brazilians the fact that he did not drink and was a Christian.
How he wished he had some Portuguese tracts with him,[10]
and he later prayed that heaven would direct the steps of some
missionary with the bread of life to their little cottage.

The husband seemed surprised that an Englishman
should refuse alcohol, for the American and English seamen
continually disgraced themselves in the streets of Rio by
getting intoxicated. Other nationalities generally controlled
themselves, yet the English and Americans would get into
scuffles and be stabbed and robbed. Livingstone bade the
family farewell.

Later another evening he took his life in his hands when
he went to a notorious waterfront bar and started handing
out gospel tracts. At one time, surrounded by twenty drunk
and angry sailors, he narrowly escaped with his life.[11]

He also visited the local hospital and saw a fellow
countryman, a young man of about twenty-two, who was
lying in a fit of raging drunken delirium, and secured by a
strait-jacket with blood still flowing from a wound.

Livingstone sat on the edge of his bed and vainly

[9] *Ibid.*
[10] *Ibid.* p 15.
[11] D L to T Prentice 5/03/1841, LMS Archives in Jeal p 25.

endeavoured to lead the intoxicated mind into a logical train of thought. However, if two sentences were sensible, the third was sure to be about blue devils or gin and the like. Livingstone turned away with a heavy heart for he knew by the nature and position of the wound and his system saturated with alcohol the man could not survive another night. 'O how much need have the Christians of Britain to exert themselves on behalf of seamen'.[12]

The zealous missionary also spent time with a Frenchman who had learned English while a prisoner during the Napoleonic War. The dying sailor said he thought that if he were sorry for his past sins and did as well as he could, God would forgive him. Livingstone explained his mistake to him. Only Christ could forgive sins; it was not enough to be merely sorry. He gave the Frenchman some tracts and 'left him never to see him more until we appear before that Bar where it shall be made apparent whether we have cast all our dependence on Christ or have trusted to a refuge of lies'.[13]

Before leaving Rio de Janeiro Livingstone wanted to have a good wash, after enduring seven weeks of almost no proper bath. Many times he had longed to dive into the sea, but the occasional appearance of enormous sharks prevented any of the passengers from enjoying that luxury.[14]

Thus he put his skills of exploration into practice and scoured the countryside for a natural waterfall. Finding one, he washed himself and without realising it, ran the risk of getting all his 'clothes stolen while in the state in which Adam was when he pruned the trees'.[15] Later he was to find out that a man and his wife had gone to the same place a few days before and were stripped of everything they had.

---

[12] D L to Catherine Ridley 24/02/1841 in Chamberlin p 15.
[13] Ibid.
[14] D L to T Prentice 5/03/1841 *ibid.* p 17.
[15] *Ibid.*

At last repairs were completed and the journey continued. Shortly he was to see the shores of Southern Africa.

He penned a letter to his friend Tom Prentice saying:

> This is really a fine world we live in after all. Were it not for that hateful rebellion against God, it would be quite a Paradise. I see more clearly now than ever the necessity of casting our whole being into the hand of Jesus. Our interests, cares and sorrows upon Him who careth for us. Why should we burden our hearts with these and go moping and melancholy beneath a cloud of our own vapours when He offers to look out for us?[16]

Little did he realise how his words would be tried and tested. The small ship 'George' edged its way into Simon's Bay on 17th March 1841, 'a warm but not roasting' day.

With the majestic Table Mountain silhouetted against the South African sky, Livingstone started off from the ship and within a few hours was staying with the superintendent of the London Missionary Society's African Mission, Dr Philip.

He had come into a continent that was plagued with problems.

---

[16] *Ibid*, p 19

4

Cape Town, The Karoo, Kuruman and Kalahari

As David walked through the picturesque avenues of oak trees which led to whitewashed Cape Dutch buildings with their green shutters, little did he comprehend the cancer of the barbaric slave-trade which continued to spread in the Dark Continent.

The interior of Africa was still a place of mystery to Europeans, despite the huge traffic in slaves. The Arabs, south of the Sahara, never ventured inland from the coast. They relied on native tribes to procure for them ivory, gold and slaves from the interior.

Early exploration of the interior had proved unprofitable. Rivers were riddled with rapids and sand bars. The deadly disease, malaria, was widespread and inhibited travel. The latter was a major problem, for it was known to decimate entire expeditions of three or four hundred men with such effectiveness and speed that the early explorers (mainly Portuguese) believed they had been poisoned by the Arabs or the Africans.

The African terrain was also difficult to negotiate. Floods would render traversable tracks into swamplands. Thick tropical forests also thwarted wheeled transport.

These hindrances dampened the dreams of the most enthusiastic explorer, and besides—what was there to search for? When one looked at the natives they were poor and their country offered nothing that was not easily obtainable elsewhere, except for one commodity: the African himself.

Robert Moffat

Livingstone was well aware of the new laws which had been passed to stop the sale of humans, but they had effect only in Britain and to some extent in the British Colonies. The colossal transatlantic slave-trade had been going on ever since European discoveries of the New World had required labour to work on sugar plantations, cotton fields and in mines. Livingstone soon learned that it was not going to cease suddenly.

In Cape Town, however, the citizens did not rely on the slave-trade to support their endeavours. It was a colony that had been established by the Dutch East India Company to provide fresh food for the spice ships sailing to and from the East. In fact, shortly after the Dutch settlers arrived in 1652, slaves were imported as was the custom from West Africa and Malaya to make up for the Hottentot labour which was scarce in the area.

When the Cape Colony was ceded to the British from the Dutch, many early Dutch settlers moved north, and continued until they clashed with the Bantu migration moving south. The British, whose rule was acceptable to those remaining in the Cape, met with opposition from the Frontier Dutch farmers who begrudged their interference.

Missionaries were seen as untrustworthy vassals of the British crown—particularly David's host, John Philip, who had reported to the Government in Britain that natives were being used as forced labour on the farms. Crown commissioners were appointed within months 'to inquire into the state not only of the civil government and legal administration of the Cape but into the general condition of the slave and Hottentot populations'.

This was seen as a slap in the face for the Cape Government, particularly when in 1828 Westminster, acting on the recommendations of the Crown Commissioners, decreed that all natives of South Africa be given 'the same freedom and protection as enjoyed by other free persons residing at the Cape, whether they be English or Dutch'!

The settlers did not disagree with the emancipation of the slaves. What did worry many of them was the dictatorial British influence, as well as the policy that the black 'heathen' be regarded as equal to white 'Christians'.

This feeling was not representative of the Boers alone. The colonists who were later to settle throughout Africa generally adopted this attitude. Thus the missionaries, whose desire was to see slaves saved for Christ, were hindered from the outset.

That was not the only challenge facing young Livingstone: the missionaries themselves did not get along well together. When Livingstone met Robert Moffat in London, the founder of Kuruman Mission Station had launched into a scathing attack against John Philip saying he had become senile, autocratic and more interested in politics than in converting the heathen.

Livingstone found his new host to be unlike the reports and rather shamefacedly acknowledged that he had expected to find a monster and had instead discovered 'an amiable man . . . who claims no superiority over us'.

Philip heard of Moffat's attack and replied in like manner. Livingstone learned from Philip that Mr Moffat is 'not on speaking terms with the Griqua Town missionaries and takes another route when visiting the colony to avoid seeing them. They in turn hate the brethren in the colony and amongst the whole there exists a pretty respectable amount of floating scandal one against the other.'[1]

In addition, he also learned that though the outposts did not talk to each other they were united in their attack against ministers in little towns who called themselves missionaries. This deplorable state of affairs worried the young Scot. From previous experience on the journey out, he had disliked Ross and was apprehensive of the strife that a local missionary

---

[1] D L to D G Watt 07/07/1841, LMS Archives.

committee, being planned to run the mission north of the Orange River, might cause.

In a letter to his friend George Drummond he poured out his heart, but also said:

> I am determined to live in peace and goodwill. I won't quarrel on any account and may God give me wisdom to conduct myself aright. I see it of great importance that missionaries should be united and not spend time grinning at each other while the Devil is leading sinners around and down the sides of the bottomless pit . . .'[2]

Livingstone held to his opinions dogmatically and expressed them with bluntness. His outlook was puritan and he would not deviate from the high standards he set both morally and within his Christian walk. Of the settler farmers he told Drummond they were 'exceedingly vexed with the British Government for emancipating the slaves here. O when shall the time come in which every man that feels the heat of this sun shall be freed from all other fetters but bonds of love to our Saviour?'[3]

His views regarding the exploitation of the Africans made him very unpopular, particularly as he was rather tactless. Few were sad to see him leave Cape Town on 16th April 1841 when he embarked the 'George' with his travelling 'companions', Mr and Mrs Ross, beginning a 450-mile journey to Algoa Bay, where they would disembark and buy provisions before setting off by ox-wagon to Kuruman.

Near Algoa Bay was a mission station called Hankey which Livingstone managed to visit. Some of the scenery was strange to the Scottish eye as it gazed upon 'a foreign-looking tree from which the bitter aloes is extracted, popping up its head among the mimosa bushes and stunted acacias'.[4]

[2] D L to George Drummond 10/03/1841 in Chamberlin, p 21.
[3] *Ibid.*
[4] D L to his parents 19/05/1841 in Blaikie, p 40.

The Hottentots of Hankey impressed Livingstone, who saw them as being in a 'state similar to that of our forefathers in the days immediately preceding the times of the Covenanters. They have a prayer meeting every morning at four o'clock and well attended. They began it during a visitation of measles among them and liked it so much, that they still continue.'[5]

As little time as possible was lost after their arrival in the small picturesque port of Algoa Bay. Provisions were bought and gathered together. These ranged from an ox-wagon and a span of oxen, to sugar, soap and candles. Many other necessities were purchased to help ease the discomfort of living in the interior.

The acquisitions were expensive. (An ox-wagon could cost between £40 and £75—approximately Livingstone's salary for the year.) But finally the purchases were completed and Mr and Mrs Ross and Livingstone set off on the 530-mile trek to Kuruman.

Travel was slow, even though the rough tracks were for a time flat and relatively easy going. The wagons themselves were miniature houses with large chests at the front and back holding daily supplies of tea, coffee, sugar and other commodities. Smaller lockers at the sides held the cutlery and china. Packing crates were stacked in the centre of the wagon, and on top of them the bedding was placed, With the odd sackful of meal dangling from the curved ceiling of sailcloth, little room was left below.

Two or three labourers would drive the procession of wagons, leading the oxen in the front or driving them from the back, cracking long whips made of giraffe or rhinoceros hide.

After the cramped conditions of his home in Blantyre, and the strict routine in Ongar and London, the freedom of Africa captured Livingstone's heart. He enjoyed learning to shoot

---

[5] *Ibid*, pp 40–41.

for the pot and exploring the continent which teemed with animals, reptiles, birds and insects. The nightly outspan was a memorable experience. After the oxen had been unhitched and led to the water, fires would be lit as the mighty orange sun in its final moments of glory bade goodnight to the weary travellers.

As the blaze leapt up from the crackling wood, flames licked the sides of the big black kettle which hung precariously over the fire, and the food was prepared. Pieces of one of the animals which had been shot that day were cut and cooked.

Tales were told as later coffee was sipped and the red embers of the fire glowed in retreat from the night air. As the travellers spoke and later slept, their weary bodies were lulled by Africa's choruses. Crickets quietly chirped continuously to one another, while an owl would let out a cosy 'coo oo' in call to a mate. Occasionally large animals such as the hyena and jackal would call out defiantly into the night as the thousands of twinkling stars awaited the moonrise.

Livingstone called this 'a protracted system of picnickings, excellent for health and agreeable to those who are not fastidious about trifles and who delight in fresh air'.[6]

The route took the missionaries through Graff Reinet, which Livingstone told Thomas Prentice was 'the prettiest town in all Africa', and he met there 'two Christians worth going a hundred miles to make the acquaintance of'. They were none other than Mr and Mrs Andrew Murray, a godly couple who were instrumental in establishing the Dutch Reformed Church. 'He is a Scotsman and a Dutch minister of the town.'[7]

From there the lumbering wagons creaked and rolled across the dry savanna scrub on to Colesberg, crossed the Orange

[6] Birkinshaw, p 30.
[7] D L to T Prentice 3/08/1841 in Chamberlin, p 24.

River and travelled along its north bank to the Vaal River near Douglas and over the veld to Kuruman.

At times the going was so bad that the young doctor feared the wagon might tip over and crush them all, and at other steep places he feared the oxen would stumble and the wagon would run forward out of control. Lumbering across the endless sun-baked terrain posed further problems, as the dry river beds were filled with boulders. Pulling the wagon wheels over them proved heavy work.

Where water appeared acacia abounded, as well as the low scrub and villainous *wag 'n bietjie* (wait-a-bit) thorns, which caused one to do exactly that. Their sharp needles pierced the toughest of clothes and urged the ardent explorer to wait a bit and cautiously untangle himself, only to be ensnared by another unsuspected bush.

When the wagons were safe, David scoured the countryside in search of specimens for Dr Owen and compiled detailed notes on the creatures and ecology. Herds of antelope, wildebeest, giraffe and zebra roamed undisturbed beneath the hot African sun.

Livingstone was delighted to see the Christian deportment in the local folk he met. On one occasion Livingstone and his fellow travellers had to travel on the Sunday morning in order to reach water, and they were reproved by a bushman for travelling on the Sabbath. Despite Livingstone's explanation, the bushman was not satisfied.

Near the water stood a Bechuana village, comprising about 100 houses.

It had a native teacher connected with the Griqua Town Mission, had seldom even been visited by a missionary, but they hold service regularly. ... after morning service the Chief, with the native teacher and principal people of the village, came and requested an explanation of our conduct. That being given it was next demanded why we had not come to Church since we had come early enough for that ... Next morning they purchased many

Sitchuana Testaments from us. I never saw such thirst for the Word of God before.[8]

On 31st July 1841 the weary oxen pulled the wagons into the mission village of Kuruman. Although an arid under-populated village, Kuruman still had a little vegetation which stood out like a small oasis against the dry, brown, parched countryside, riddled with sharp thorn bushes. The white-washed stone buildings were shaded by planted Syringa trees with green orchards and vegetable gardens enhancing the beauty. The missionaries, Hamilton and Edwards, gave them a warm welcome, but within a short while Livingstone was yearning to reach out to the lost souls of the north.

He was disappointed with the missionary work at the station, as out of a congregation of 350, only forty received Holy Communion. The vast majority of people had not even been baptised.

The zealous missionary wrote to the directors telling them that Kuruman's population would not increase and would probably even reduce in the future, since the Bechuanas were cattle-farmers and would inevitably choose better watered and more fertile places to graze their oxen and sheep. Livingstone was telling the truth, but the directors were not prepared to let some zealous young man tell them that their most publicised African mission station was an arid, under-peopled village that might soon be deserted.

It upset Livingstone to see so many missionaries living in safe and comfortable localities in the south—treading on one another's heels, and sometimes corns—while innumerable villages in the north remained unvisited.

He also strongly believed that use should be made of the African Christians, who would have a greater impact on the tribal people of their own culture than the white man would

---

[8] D L to Henry Drummond 3/08/1841, *ibid*, p 26.

have. Moffat did not support this principle as he wanted the local converts to receive the further training he was giving. Livingstone felt the urgency of the hour, and in theory he was right, but African teachers were then very hard to find.

As the frustrations gripped him, Livingstone wrestled within himself: should he leave and go to Abyssinia? There was a need for a missionary there. In writing to his friend Watt, he used words which were almost prophetic: 'Whatever way my life may be spent so as but to promote the glory of our gracious God, I feel anxious to do it ... My life may be spent as profitably as a pioneer as in any other way.'[9]

Moffat had worked hard at Kuruman, though the results appeared far from promising. He had had to build a station with little help and with no knowledge of the native language. Then he had written down and finally worked out its grammar. Once mastered, the Moffats then had to teach their own as well as other children the language.

Journeys to Cape Town for supplies took six months, and when the resident missionaries were at the mission station the wagons were repaired and maintained. Making cheese, butter, clothes, soap and candles were also other laborious tasks.

Moffat persisted for eight years before winning his first soul for Christ, whereas zealous Livingstone naively thought conversion would be quick and gave no thought to converts backsliding. Moffat could have told the doctor that it was almost impossible to tell whether a conversion was genuine or not. The locals might simply display gracious behaviour as gratitude for agricultural improvements or as a desire to please the 'gun mender'—a name many missionaries were given. Furthermore, low rainfall, disease and shifting pastures did not help. None the less, Moffat had persevered and this noble quality was also to be found in Livingstone. This same

---

[9] D L to D G Watt in Blaikie, pp 41–42.

quality is in fact part of the very fibre which constitutes any great man or woman of God.

The medical missionary continued to care for the sick, while taking every opportunity to investigate further areas to the north which might be used as future mission stations.

On 18th October 1841,[10] Livingstone and Rogers Edwards left Kuruman on their first journey northwards to tribes at the edge of the Kalahari desert. (Rogers Edwards had planned this fact-finding mission for some time, and with Livingstone's motivation they soon set off.) Conditions on the journey were harsh, and soaring temperatures plagued the men and cattle. Livingstone described the heat as so great that 'the very flies sought the shade and the enormous centipedes coming out by mistake from their holes were roasted to death on the burning sand'.[11]

They travelled 'over hundreds of miles of dreary wilderness, not a soul appearing in sight'.[12] This type of scene was hardly inspiring, yet Livingstone and Edwards continued to enjoy the sights of elephant and other game as their wagons took them into the unknown interior. A place which was largely untouched, hostile, yet enticing.

After many miles of travel they came to a large village. The chief had sore eyes which Livingstone relieved, and in gratitude he generously presented him with milk, beans and a buck.

When they were a few miles away a little girl of about eleven or twelve years of age came up and sat down under the doctor's wagon. She wanted to travel with them. Her sister, with whom she had lived, had recently died and another family had taken possession of her in order to sell her as soon as she was old enough to become a wife. Afraid, she determined to run away from them and stay with friends near Kuruman. David was

---

[10] Ransford p 26 (T Jeal, p 43 has this date as September 1841).

[11] D L to B Pyne 22/12/1841 in Jeal, p 44.

[12] D L to Janet L 8/12/1841, *ibid*.

impressed with the determination of the little girl who was prepared to walk over 150 miles behind the wagon. He gave her food, but was alarmed to hear 'her sobbing violently as if her heart would break' and on looking round he saw a man with a gun who had been sent to take her back. Pomare, one of Livingstone's guides, intervened and being the son of a chief, Pomare had sufficient power to persuade the man to take the beads she wore and depart. Livingstone 'took measures for hiding her, and though fifty men had come for her, they would not have got her'.[13]

On returning to Kuruman in December 1841, there was still no news for Livingstone. Moffat was in England and no one knew what year he would return.

Livingstone pursued his medicine and in a letter to Sir Risdon Bennett told him of an immense practice. 'I have patients now under treatment who have walked 130 miles for my advice.'[14] He was horrified that the poor Bechuanas had more disease than he had expected, but was not surprised when he saw that they had little clothing to protect them against the scorching heat of the day and the biting chill of the night. The young doctor, on being beseiged by the 'blind and halt and lame', wondered 'what a mighty effect would be produced if one of the seventy disciples were amongst them to heal them all by a word'.[15]

He was also astonished by their tolerance of pain.

In cutting out a tumour an inch in diameter they sit and talk as if they felt nothing. They say: 'A man like me never cries, they are children who cry,' and it is a fact that the men never cry. But when the Spirit of God works on their minds they cry most piteously. Sometimes in Church they endeavour to hide themselves from the eye of the preacher by creeping under the forms or hiding

[13] D L to Janet L 8/12/1841, in Blaikie, pp 44–45.
[14] D L to Sir J Risdon Bennett 18/12/1841 in Chamberlin, p 30.
[15] *Ibid*, p 31.

their heads with their Karosses as a remedy against their
convictions. And when they find that won't do they rush out of
the church and run with all their might crying as if the hand of
death were behind them. One would think when they had got
away there they would remain but no, there they are in their places
at the very next meeting.[16]

Though *Nyaka* (doctor) was one of his best-known native
names, he was always more the preacher than the doctor.
Livingstone never built a hospital, though his medical training
was never wasted. It taught him the importance of judging
objectively and of expressing an opinion based on his own
observations. Although he realised he was dealing with a
primitive people he did not summarily dismiss their customs,
practices and beliefs as being ridiculous or nonsensical. He
was tolerant as well as observant. Nor did Livingstone scoff
at the witch-doctors, but constantly requested them to reveal
their remedies. He experimented on himself with the different
herbs which they claimed would have an effect on malaria.
He appreciated the role the witch-doctors played in their
society, and realised that by gaining their friendship he would
be a step closer to converting them to Christ.

On 10th February 1842, after waiting three dreary months,
Livingstone left Kuruman on his second missionary journey
with two other guides, the purpose being to spend time alone
with the people so as to learn the Setswana language and
customs; as well as train the guides to be 'Native Agents in
spreading the Gospel'. They travelled through the dry savanna
bush for twelve days, following the narrow paths made by
animals and people, to the Bakhatla tribe. And then a further
100 miles to return to visit Chief Bubi, head of the Bakwain,
whose honesty greatly impressed the missionary. Livingstone
never put a guard on his wagon and was to learn later that
thieving was rarely practised except in the trail of the slaver.

---

[16] *Ibid.*

Seeing the need for water, Livingstone told the tribesmen that he, like the rain-doctor, could make rain too; not by enchantments like they did, but by channelling out their river for irrigation. The idea pleased mightily, and 'to work they went instanter. Even the chief's own doctor is at it, and works like a good fellow, laughing heartily at the cunning of the 'foreigner' who can make rain so.'[17]

Unfortunately, the chief came to an untimely end. He had quarrelled with his Paramount Chief Sechele, who later sent him a gift of gunpowder. Suspiciously, he examined it by burning it near a 'powerful magic' to see if it had any hidden evil. The ensuing explosion justified his suspicions.[18]

Livingstone moved on, visiting other tribes en route to the Bamangwato. The sand across which they had to travel tired the oxen, and Livingstone opted to walk the remaining fifty miles.

The chief, Sekomi (who was the great-great-grandfather of Sir Seretse Khama, the late President of Botswana), gave the weary walker a distinguished welcome. Presenting Livingstone with many gifts, the chief opened his heart to the missionary.

On one occasion Chief Sekomi entered the doctor's hut and having sat by him for some time said, 'I wish you would change my heart. Give me medicine to change it, for it is proud, proud and angry, angry always.' Livingstone lifted up the Testament and was about to tell him the only way in which the heart can be changed, but was interrupted by him saying, 'Nay, I wish to have it changed by medicine, to drink and have it changed at once, for it is always very proud and very uneasy, and continually angry with someone.' He then rose and went away.[19]

How close that chief had come to knowing the truth.

---

[17] Blaikie, p 46.
[18] Macnair, p 75.
[19] Blaikie, pp 47–48.

Another incident occurred which greatly moved Livingstone. A widow had been killed by a lion, and during the whole day after her death the surrounding rocks and valleys echoed the bitter cries of the orphaned children. As he listened to the loud sobs painfully indicative of the sorrows of those who have no hope, Livingstone thought that if some of the churches could have heard the sad wailings it would have 'awakened the firm resolution to do more for the heathen than they have done'.[20]

After two weeks Livingstone and his guides left Chief Sekomi. He sent thirty of his people to guard them and carry the presents. Four of these were to escort the doctor to Kuruman.[21]

Most of the second journey was on foot as the oxen were sick due to the drought. Some of Livingstone's African companions, who had recently joined the travellers, did not know that he understood their language, and he overheard them discussing his appearance. 'He is not strong, he is quite slim, and only appears stout because he puts himself into those bags (trousers); he will soon knock up.'

As Livingstone put it: 'This caused my Highland blood to rise, and made me despise the fatigue of keeping them all at the top of their speed for days together, until I heard them expressing proper opinions of my pedestrian powers.'[22]

The missionary then walked to the Baka tribe who were infamous for the murder of four white traders whom they had mercilessly poisoned and strangled. To walk unarmed into their presence was an amazing feat which demanded fearless faith. The steadfast servant of Christ, counting his life not his own, believed that they also needed to hear the good news of Christ's redemptive work.

---

[20] *Ibid*, p 47.
[21] D L to the Revd J J Freeman 3/07/1842 in Chamberlin, p 35.
[22] M T, p 10.

The sweltering heat and dry thorny scrub offered no comfort as the lonely man strode forward. He was the first European since the massacre to have visited the Bakas, and he believed that after that deed of darkness, their conscience loudly accused them.[23]

Fearlessly, while all eyes were upon him, Livingstone walked into the village, and all the people, except the chief and two attendants, fled his presence. 'In their faces they had evidence of perturbation such as I never saw in black countenances before.' He calmly squatted next to the terrified chief who only relaxed once Livingstone, showing trust, had eaten some food and lay down to sleep in front of them. As he slept, the people soon came around him in considerable numbers. To Livingstone 'there seemed to be something horrid in the appearance of these people but perhaps the impression on my mind', he said, 'may be accounted for by the fact that I saw as ornaments round their necks pieces of gun-locks etc. and one had a piece of sail cloth round his head' which Livingstone felt sure must have been taken from the wagon of the unfortunate Gibson, one of those murdered.

'I had more than ordinary pleasure in telling these murderers of the precious 'blood which cleanseth from all sin' and I blessed God that He has conferred on one so worthless the distinguished privilege and honour of being the first messenger of mercy that ever trod these regions.'[24] He preached the sermon in their own language, which he had managed to master.

Livingstone found himself within ten days of Lake Ngami and he could have been the first known white to explore it— but that was not his motive. His desire was to preach the gospel of Jesus Christ. He quickly retraced his route to Kuruman, for he was eager to hear if any news regarding his

---

[23] D L to the Revd J J Freeman 3/07/1842 in Chamberlin, p 36.
[24] *Ibid*, pp 36–37.

future had arrived. He completed his journey by June 1842
and had covered more than a thousand miles.

As no news had come, Livingstone continued work at the
mission. On 13th July 1842 he wrote to his father saying:

> The work of God goes on here notwithstanding all our infirmities.
> Souls are gathered in continually, and sometimes from among
> those you would never have expected to see turning to the Lord.
> Twenty-four were added to the church last month, and there are
> several inquiries. At Motito, a French station about thirty-three
> miles north-east of this, there has been an awakening, and I hope
> much good will result. I have good news too from Rio de Janeiro.
> The Bibles that have been distributed are beginning to cause a
> stir.[25]

Livingstone had a greater appreciation for Moffat's work now
that he had seen the 'facsimiles of what the converts were'.
He wrote that he was able to 'see in all their greatness the
wonderful works of the Lord. The contrast between what they
were, and have now become is most striking, and it forces on
my mind with greater power than ever the conviction that the
gospel has lost none of its pristine efficacy.'[26]

The foreign secretary for the London Missionary Society
wrote to him expressing gratitude for his 'vigour, perseverance
and fidelity', but the Society remained hesitant on the matter
of Christians being sent out as 'native agents', and with typical
British tact urged him to get involved with the District
Committee, which Livingstone dreaded. But, as he wrote to
George Drummond, 'If it will advance the cause I won't spend
time quarrelling ... O that none of my life may be spent in
vain jangling after I have had such an opportunity of devoting
it to Him who died to save me.'[27]

Waiting in Kuruman for instructions to come, or for the

---

[25] D L to Neil L 13/07/1842 in Blaikie, p 52.
[26] D L to the Revd J J Freeman 18/07/1842 in Chamberlin, p 38.
[27] D L to George Drummond 20/06/1843 *ibid*, pp 40–41.

return of Moffat, was not easy. Livingstone wanted to move north again to see Chief Sebehwe as he had promised him a visit. Sadly, in the interim, disaster had overtaken this tribe, for when moving out of the Kalahari region many were slaughtered by Chief Mahura. The native Christians from Kuruman who had been staying with the tribe were blamed.

However, Livingstone was confined to Kuruman for a total of eight months, as he was unable to get a guide to accompany him—the mission Africans having been terrified by the Matabele raids. To travel alone along the many meandering paths meant certain disaster. It was not until February 1843 that a guide volunteered to escort him. Livingstone ventured forth on this his third missionary journey; an unclerical moustache prevented sunburn of the upper lip and a common midshipman's cap covered his head.

He travelled to the Bakhatla and then continued for a further five days to the village of Sechele, chief of the Bakwains. Chief Sechele gave Livingstone a chilly reception, for he had been upset with the missionary for having paid more attention to Chief Bubi. However, it was not long before he became amicable again and Livingstone awoke on the Sunday morning to hear orders being given that the tribe should do nothing but pray to God and listen to the words of the foreigner.

The first time Livingstone attempted to hold a public service Sechele remarked that it was their custom to ask questions when any new subject was brought before them. The chief then enquired whether the missionary's forefathers knew of a future judgement. Livingstone replied 'yes' and began to describe a scene of the 'great white throne, and Him who shall sit on it, from Whose face the heaven and earth shall flee away'.

'You startle me,' Sechele replied. 'These words make all my bones to shake; I have no more strength in me: but my forefathers were living at the same time yours were, and how is it that they did not send them word about these terrible things sooner? They all passed away into darkness without knowing whither they were going.'[28]

Livingstone explained the geographical barriers and added his belief, as Christ had declared, that the whole world would be enlightened by the gospel.

Pointing to the great Kalahari desert, Sechele replied, 'You never can cross that country to the tribes beyond; it is utterly impossible even for us black men, except in certain seasons, when more than the usual supply of rain falls, and an extraordinary growth of water-melons follows.'[29] The challenge of crossing this obstacle fascinated Livingstone.

By March 1843 Livingstone had managed to translate several hymns into Sichuana, as well as compose a basic dictionary for himself, all the while knowing only one direction—forward.

He was determined to advance in the direction of the Matabele country, but the dread of their Chief Mosilikatse prevented him from getting the Bakwains to accompany him. Being unable to rig out a wagon, Livingstone was obliged to travel on oxback and wrote and told Sir Risdon Bennett:

> It is rough travelling, as you can conceive. The skin is so loose there is no getting one's great-coat, which has to serve for both saddle and blanket, to stick on. And then the long horns in front with which he can give one a punch in the abdomen if he likes, make us sit as 'bolt upright' as dragoons.[30]

In this manner he trekked over 400 miles. Unfortunately, the Baka tribe were out of humour with Livingstone, accusing him of having given poison on his last visit to a man who had been seized with fever. They therefore refused to feed him, and he had to dine on the 'sumptuous feasts of his imagination'.[31]

[28] M T, p 16.
[29] *Ibid.*
[30] D L to Sir Risdon Bennett in Chamberlin, p 52.
[31] Blaikie, p 55.

Worse was to befall him. Coming down a steep pass, he lost his footing and put out the hand in which he was carrying his Bible, to save himself. In so doing he wedged a finger between a rock and the Book and suffered a painful compound fracture.

The doctor had to tend to the open wound himself, pushing the shattered bone back into place and splinting it with a reed. There were no antibiotics or painkillers to relieve infection or suffering.

The painful wound was healing favourably when a visit by a lion in the darkness of the night caused great consternation. Without thinking, Livingstone fired his revolver and the recoil broke his finger again. The second fracture was worse than the first. His Bakwain guides tried to comfort him when they saw the blood by saying: 'You have hurt yourself, but you have redeemed us: henceforth we will only swear by you.'

This troubled the doctor who wrote: 'I wished they had felt gratitude for the blood that was shed for their precious souls.'

In writing to the secretary of the Missionary Society, Livingstone expressed his appreciation of his heavenly Father by saying, 'The Lord has been exceedingly kind to me, He has shielded me in many such dangers. May my heart be stirred up to love Him more ardently, and may His name be blessed for ever and ever.'[32]

His third missionary visit complete, Livingstone returned to Kuruman.

He was content, for he had been offered ground by the Bakhatla on which to build a mission station. All he needed was permission from the Society, which on his return in June was granted, though it was suggested he await the arrival of Moffat before venturing forth.

Edwards was to move with Livingstone. The young doctor was not keen to wait for Moffat, in case he changed his mind.

---

[32] D L to A Tidman 24/06/1843 in Mssny. Corr., p 40.

That, combined with the thought of the impending hot season, made Livingstone and Edwards opt to move in August.

Little did Livingstone realise that his life would soon be in jeopardy.

Chief Sechele and his wife

5

The Missionary is Mauled, Marries and Moves on

In early August 1843, Mr and Mrs Edwards and Dr Livingstone rolled their wagons out of Kuruman and headed for the beautiful valley of Mabotsa, about 200 miles to the north east.

Three other gentlemen, two from India and the other the son of a planter from the West Indies, accompanied them. They had come to the 'country in order to have their health restored by the exercises of hunting and travelling'.

Livingstone had little time for the man from the West Indies as he was living off profits from slave labour. Nor did he develop a long friendship with the Scotsman, Mr Pringle, although he was a keen collector of specimens of interest to the doctor. However, the third member, Captain Steele of the Coldstream Guards and Aide-de-camp to the Governor of Madras, struck a chord with him. He had come to Africa to recover from cholera and Livingstone found him to be 'polite, well versed in the classics and possessed of much general knowledge'.

David wrote to his sister Janet in Scotland: 'All are men of the world and would travel on Sundays if we were not with them. When will the time come when men will spend thousands in the cause of Missions? It will come. The silver and gold are the Lord's and He will yet bring it to pass that men will acknowledge whose right it is'.[1]

---

[1] D L to Janet L 21/08/1843 in Fam. Lett. I, p 80.

The hunters had many horses, labourers and a huge collection of paraphernalia, but were very disorganised. Despite months of travelling, even lighting a fire would take them several hours.

The missionaries and their close crew would offer the hunters cups of hot coffee before they had even heated the water. David could see that they were certainly 'enthusiastic hunters', yet he told Janet: 'We have a nobler subject on which to be enthusiastic'.[2]

Edwards and Livingstone traded ground from Chief Mosealele for a musket, gunpowder, lead and beads worth about £4, and commenced work immediately, carving a home and school out of the arid African land. They received little assistance from the tribesmen although one man, Mebalwe, who had come with Livingstone and Edwards from Kuruman to help them evangelise the local folk, proved invaluable. He was to risk his life to save the doctor.

Livingstone counted his life's calling a challenge and committed himself to it. He loved the people and was grieved to hear that Sehamy, a servant, had died. Sehamy became ill after leaving a certain tribe and some locals believed him to have been poisoned.

In a flurry of anxious thoughts Livingstone penned,

'Poor Sehamy, where art thou now? Where lodges thy soul tonight? Didst thou think of what I told thee as thou turnest from side to side in distress? I could now do anything for thee. I could weep for thy soul. But now nothing can be done. Thy fate is fixed. Oh, am I guilty of the blood of thy soul, my poor dear Sehamy? If so, how shall I look upon thee in the judgement? But I told thee of a Saviour; didst thou think of Him, and did He lead thee through the dark valley? Did He comfort as He only can? Help me, O Lord Jesus, to be faithful to everyone. Remember me, and let me not be guilty of the blood of souls.[3]

[2] *Ibid*, p 81.
[3] D L to Janet L in Blaikie, p 63.

He told Janet that Sehamy

> governed the others, and most attentive he was to me. He anticipated my every want. He kept the water calabash at his head at night, and if I awoke, he was ready to give me a draught immediately. When the meat was boiled he secured the best portion for me, the best place for sleeping, the best of everything. Oh, where is he now?[4]

Mabotsa Mission slowly began to develop in the 'most delightful valley' situated in an 'amphitheatre of mountains'. The range of hills to the rear were the Mabotsa Mountains. Translated it meant 'marriage feast'—a fitting name. As the missionary wrote: 'May the Lord lift upon us the light of His countenance, so that by our feeble instrumentality many may thence be admitted to the marriage feast of the Lamb'.[5]

Despite the excitement of the new Station, Livingstone battled with loneliness. While Rogers Edwards was married, he was not. He wrote to all his friends and implored them to write as often as they could. A letter would take between four and six months to reach England and the same time for a reply. One year was a long time to wait, even for the most patient of people.

Livingstone longed for letters. He wrote to his sister Agnes, saying: 'Next month I expect to receive letters from home. 'What are you all doing?' is a question that I sometimes ask myself, but no answer but the still deathlike quietness which you can almost hear in this wide wide wilderness land'.[6]

The two men and their team returned to Kuruman on 27th September 1843. There was still no news of Moffat's return and Livingstone occupied his time composing an account of the establishment of the Mabotsa Mission. In it he gave little credit to Edwards. Unfortunately, the Society published an

---

[4] *Ibid.*
[5] D L to D G Watt 27/09/1843 in Blaikie, p 65.
[6] D L to Agnes L 4/04/1842 in Fam. Lett. I, pp 56–57.

extract of his report which gushed over 'our intrepid Missionary, Mr Livingstone', but mentioned not a word of his colleague. This did not go unnoticed by Rogers Edwards.

Livingstone was anxious for Moffat's return. What would the missionary say? And the committee—would it crush his hopes to accomplish much for Christ?

The young man prepared himself for the worst and wrote to Arthur Tidman: 'I shall try to hold myself in readiness to go anywhere, provided it be forward'.[7] He recognised the need for one to get on with even the strangest tempers and in seeing his weakness wrote: 'May the Lord clothe me with humility and make me more like Himself'.[8]

At the end of November information was received that the Moffats were approaching. Gladdened by the news, Livingstone rode 150 miles to meet them near the Vaal river.

The dot in the distance soon became an ox-wagon as the lonely rider galloped up to greet them. This warm greeting in the wilderness was to the Moffats 'a most refreshing circumstance. Few can conceive of the hallowed feeling his presence produced'.[9]

It was here, the young missionary met Mary Moffat for the first time. The single, neatly dressed lady impressed David, and according to her father he was at once 'smitten with Mary's charms'.[10]

Much news was exchanged as the folk travelled on to Kuruman. Many of the Bechuanas met Mr and Mrs Moffat with tears of joy. One poor bushman who had been brought up by him wept aloud when he approached him; 'and as I had gone to meet him,' Livingstone wrote, 'I received many

---

[7] D Livingstone to A Tidman 30/10/1843 in Mssny. Corr., p 48.
[8] *Ibid.*
[9] Ransford, p 34.
[10] *Ibid.*

thanks for bringing him. They had believed he should never return'.[11]

Livingstone remained in Kuruman over Christmas and developed a firm friendship with Mary. His relationship with Robert Moffat strengthened, particularly when the Scot learned that the mature missionary was not opposed, as he had believed, to the idea of equipping and sending forth 'native agents'.

Livingstone and Edwards left for Mabotsa on 6th January 1844, immediately after the dreaded committee meeting. The ox-wagons loaded to capacity with stores for Mabotsa creaked and groaned beneath the cracking of the whip and cry of the wagon driver.

It was a rare response to a challenge which has been echoed for centuries. Livingstone, for all his many human failings, sought to take the gospel to every man. He never looked down upon the natives; he saw each person in relation to their standing with God. His manner was steadfast and the folk knew where they stood with him. He was intent on making friends of the folk he tried to reach with the gospel. From the time he arrived in Africa, Livingstone sagaciously studied tribal customs and treated Africans with patience and tact, seeming to have an instinctive understanding of them. This, along with his calm courage and persevering heart, meant that practically all Africans responded to him. However, with Europeans he was often tactless and, on occasions, even overbearing.

The doctor decided, after much thought, that missionaries had failed in the past to win the tribal folk by too readily condemning what they, as missionaries, did not understand. Here were a people who resisted the gospel, for they took it as a threat to their culture and customs. Livingstone went to great pains to try to convince the Africans that this was

---

[11] D L to Janet L 21/08/1843 in Fam. Lett. I, p 88.

not so. The presence of Christ would ultimately enrich any culture.

His heart was full of the missionary spirit, yet Livingstone could never quite shrug off the fear that personal ambition, rather than Christian service, was the driving force which carried him so far beyond the normally accepted bounds of missionary activity. He realised that some of the brethren did not hesitate to tell the natives that his object was 'to obtain the applause of men'. 'This bothers me, for I sometimes suspect my own motives,' he told his directors. 'I am conscious that, though there is much impurity in my motives, they are in the main for the glory of Him to whom I have dedicated my all'.[12]

Some may say today that missionaries exploited the natives. This is inaccurate; Livingstone certainly did not. It was his love for the people that won their hearts. He even stated:

> In our relations with this people we exercised no authority whatever. Our control depended entirely upon persuasion; and, having taught them by kind conversation as well as by public instruction, I expected them to do what their own sense of right and wrong dictated. Five instances are known to me in which by our influence on public opinion war was prevented.[13]

On 16th February 1844 Livingstone was working in the ditches of the water course when some folk timidly told him that a troublesome pride of lions had been located. The lions were notorious for destroying livestock, even in daylight, an occurrence so unusual that the people believed themselves bewitched.

Livingstone knew, however, that the death of one lion would send the others away. On hearing the news of the lion being sighted he seized his gun, threw on his tartan coat and calling Mebalwe to follow, hurried out to join the hunt. As

---

[12] Ransford, pp 35–36.
[13] M T p 19.

he put it later: 'I very imprudently ventured across the valley in order to encourage them to destroy him'.[14]

One beast had been located on a small bush-covered hill. The men slowly encircled the lion and gradually closed up as they cautiously advanced. Livingstone and Mebalwe were below on the plain and they could see one of the lions sitting on a rock within the ring. Mebalwe fired over the hunters' heads and the ball hit the rock on which the lion sat. He snarled and bit at the spot struck, as a dog does at a stick or stone thrown at him, and then leaping away broke through the circle unhurt; the hunters being too afraid to spear it.

The circle was reformed, trapping two lions, but Livingstone dared not fire lest he shoot someone. The beasts burst through the line and 'as it was evident the men could not be prevailed upon to face their foes' they bent their footsteps towards the village.

In going round the end of the hill, Livingstone saw a lion sitting on a rock, about thirty yards off, with a little bush in front of him. He took a good aim at him through the bush and fired both barrels into it. The men called out, 'He is shot, he is shot!' Others cried, 'He has been shot by another man too; let us go to him!'[15]

Livingstone saw the lion's tail standing up in anger, and turning to the people said, 'Stop a little while till I load again.' While ramming down the bullets he heard a shout, and half looking round he saw the big raging animal leaping towards him. His powerful, vengeful jaws connected with Livingstone's left shoulder, crushing the bone as they fell to the ground; locked in an embrace.

Growling in a paroxysm of dying rage, he shook Livingstone as a 'terrier dog does a rat. The shock produced a stupor similar to that which seems to be felt by a mouse after the

---

[14] D L to R Moffat 15/02/1844 in Fam. Lett. I, p 90.
[15] M T p 12.

first shake of the cat. It caused a sort of dreaminess, in which there was no sense of pain nor feeling of terror', though he was 'quite conscious of all that was happening'.[16]

With the animal's paw on the back of his head, Livingstone edged round to lighten himself of the weight and saw that the lion's eyes were focused on Mebalwe. Mebalwe was aiming from a distance of ten to fifteen yards, but his gun, a flint one, misfired in both barrels. With that, the angry beast left Livingstone and lunged at Mebalwe, tearing his thigh with one bite. Another man, whom Livingstone had previously rescued from certain death when he was tossed by a buffalo, attempted to spear the lion. The animal then turned from Mebalwe, seizing the other man by the shoulder, when at that moment the inflicted wounds took effect and the injured lion dropped dead.

Livingstone's injuries were the most severe. The bite resembled a gun-shot wound, the crushed bone having pierced through the skin, and the shaft of the left humerus was also broken. Not only was it extremely painful, but it took a long time to heal, for a secondary infection caused a copious purulent discharge through the eleven gashes.

Livingstone lay for weeks battling against the maggots in the suppurating sore. In his little dark hut, strength ebbed from him and he could not even move his limbs. He deliriously experienced dreams, seeing Dr Risdon Bennett, his friend and an able doctor, coming to his aid. He said later:

> I shall not soon forget the lively disappointment I as often experienced on finding that all surgical aid was still on the other side of the Atlantic. When only partially recovered I had to begin the erection of my house and a jerk received in lifting a stone has led to a false joint in my left humerus: I often think of putting a

---

[16] *Ibid.* Livingstone thought, 'This placidity is probably produced in all animals killed by the carnivores and if so is a merciful provision of the Creator for lessening the pain of death.'

seton through it but never have been able to plan a six weeks leisure.[17]

He remained curiously diffident, possibly because critics may suggest a missionary's duty does not include engaging in a lion hunt. He advised his parents: 'I don't think you ought to make any talk of this to any one. I don't like to be talked about',[18] and he tried to play down his dramatic encounter with death. Livingstone had won the respect of the people; indeed two had risked their lives for him, and a firm bond developed.

Edwards and the doctor built a school, and Livingstone began to instruct the children, though attendances were poor.

Livingstone told his parents that 'the nearer we come to Egypt we get more into the region of flies, fleas, puleys (lice), moths, vermin of all sorts, which eat everything except iron and glass etc'. On complaining to a native about the superabundance, the earnest reply was, 'O we have always plenty of these, but you have more than ordinary just now because they come to greet strangers.'[19]

He urged his family to spread the gospel and wrote:

Private Christians are not exempted from the duty of bringing sinners to the Saviour. Their lives are to be consecrated to the glory of God as well as those of ministers and missionaries. You hear fine sermons no doubt, but do they enter into your heads and come out again for the good of those who are not so favoured? Try what you can do, and don't content yourselves by listening and admiring and doing nothing. Some content themselves by the excuse of humility on account of inability, but should any one tell them they were not able to connect two ideas together so as to tell a plain story their humility would have some bristles standing straight up on its back.[20]

---

[17] D L to Sir Risdon Bennett 26/12/1845 in Chamberlin p 83.
[18] D L to his parents 27/04/1844 in Fam. Lett. I, p 93.
[19] *Ibid.* p 97.
[20] D L to Janet L. 21/05/1844 in Fam. Lett. I, p 99.

The Christian appreciated the need for the gospel to be understood by the simple, tribal people.

> If you look at the sermons of the Apostles in the Acts, you will see that to different people their address was different in order to make the truth profitable. The Jew was addressed differently from the Gentile, and though the object and the truths were the same, Gentiles of different localities were addressed differently.[21]

The arm took time to heal and it was decided that he recuperate fully at Kuruman, where Mary afforded him both attention and affection. The Moffats did little to bolster the bachelor's belief in celibacy, and under the shade of the orchard trees in May 1844 he asked Mary to become his bride.

She graciously accepted his proposal, though it was not her first, and their relationship, like the orchard in which they courted, was to bear much fruit.

The contented young man concealed his emotions in a letter to the Society, conscientiously informing them as only he could that 'various considerations connected with this new sphere of labour, and which to you need not be specified in detail, having led me to the conclusion that it was my duty to enter into the marriage relation . . .'.[22]

Mary was twenty-three. She was born at Griqua Town in the Cape Colony and had completed her education in London. They were ideally suited. Livingstone was not one for the love nest and described his fiancée to Watt as similarly 'not a romantic. Mine is a matter of fact lady, a little thick black haired girl, sturdy and all I want'.[23]

He returned to Mabotsa for five months and set to work in building his wife a house. He wrote and told her: 'It is pretty hard work, and almost enough to drive love out of my

[21] *Ibid*, p 101.
[22] D L to LMS 2/12/1844 in Mssny. Corr., p 59.
[23] D L to D G Watt 2/04/1845 LMS Archives in Jeal, p 60.

Mary Livingstone

head. But it is not situated there; it is in my heart and won't come out unless you behave so as to quench it'.[24]

In comparison to African housing, Livingstone built a large home as he considered it would be cooler. He said to Mary: '. . . we have nothing to put into it is no matter, for I shall think it furnished when you are here'.[25]

A few weeks later he wrote another long letter to Mary, the latter portion reading:

> To mother, too, give my kindest salutation. I suppose I shall get a lecture from her too about the largeness of the house. If there are too many windows she can just let me know. I could build them all up in two days, and let the light come down the chimney, if that would please. I'll do anything for peace, except fighting for it. And now I must again, my dear, dear Mary, bid you good-bye. Accept my expressions as literally true when I say, I am your most affectionate and still confiding lover.[26]

Labouring to win the lost to Christ was not easy. The resolute young man confided in Dr Tidman his disappointment that 'conversion among Bechuanas is in general by no means a quick process', and of the Bakhatla tribe 'their mind is darkness itself . . . O may the Holy Spirit aid our efforts, for without His mighty power all human efforts will be but labour in vain'.[27]

The labour of the missionaries and Mebalwe was not without hope, for the time would come when the light of God's glory and grace would shine from Africa and astound the rest of the world. However, they were not then to see the fruit; they were but planting the seeds.

Already Livingstone was eager to traverse new ground and

[24] D L to Mary Moffat 12/09/1844 in Fam. Lett. I, p 105.
[25] *Ibid*, p 106.
[26] *Ibid*, pp 107–8.
[27] D L to A Tidman 9/06/1844 in Chamberlin p 71.

he wrote to Mary in September saying, 'I don't expect to remain at Mabotsa long'.[28]

For all his talk about Prentice and his other friends being 'noosed' as they allowed the marriage bells to ring within their ears, Livingstone had coyly to admit to his friend of long standing, the Revd George Drummond, that he was: 'In love!! words yea thoughts fail so I leave it to your imagination and recollection—I am it seems after all to be hooked to Miss Moffat!'[29]

The bachelor returned to Kuruman, and on 2nd January 1845 was married to Mary Moffat. They shared ideals and partook of the cup of their calling in Christ with equal commitment. Mary in her marriage to David was to prove herself to be a sensible, submissive spouse as worthy as her husband of the reward to be received on the day of judgement.

Their marriage was not to be one of idyllic domestic felicity, but affected by the stern demands of a vocation unique in the annals of modern Christendom.

In Mabotsa they went vigorously to work, Mrs Livingstone with her infants' school and her husband with all the varied agencies, medical, educational and pastoral, which his active spirit could bring to bear upon the people. Their relationship deepened although always to take second place to their calling, and they suffered many hardships in order to bring the gospel to the local population.

Livingstone cherished the thought of a seminary which would facilitate the spreading of 'the Word of God'. He presented the matter to the missionaries, but without success. Some saw the scheme as being premature and opposed it. Others did likewise as they insinuated that his object was to impress the directors of the Missionary Society and so be promoted to Professor. Annoyed and hurt he withdrew the

---

[28] D L to M Moffat 12/09/1844 in Fam. Lett. I, pp 105–106.
[29] D L to George Drummond 21/11/1844 in Chamberlin p 74.

proposal and the burden for the school was to be put aside owing to the harsh words of a few stern men.

Despite this blow God was in control. Had Livingstone's wishes been carried out he might have spent his life training native agents, and while undoubtably doing a noble work he would not have traversed Africa, dealt the death blow to African slavery by closing the open sore of the world, nor rolled away the great obstacle to the evangelism of the continent.

Livingstone struggled with African superstitions and was amazed that they had 'no curiosity about God and eternity'. Their basic thought of God appeared as 'broken planks floating down on the stream of ages from a primitive faith'.

On top of the heat, harsh conditions and hardness of hearts, there was another problem with which to contend. Edwards, eighteen years the senior, was not content with playing second fiddle to a domineering young man who chose to take all the credit for himself. Edwards showed Livingstone a letter he had written to the directors, complaining that the young man was acting unfairly and assuming more than his due.

This spurred the Scot to write screeds to the Society, and self-justification was the order of the day as he poured out his heart, bringing to their attention even the most petty differences. The root of the problem was that neither man would be a mere appendix to the other.

Thus suspicion and half-truths were flung at each other in the midst of the hurt and confusion, no party being without fault. It appeared later that Edwards never sent the letter he showed Livingstone. However, Livingstone saw it as a brilliant excuse to push on to form another station.

Sechele, the lean energetic chief, wanted the young man and his wife to settle alongside him in Chonuane so, forsaking the house and garden they had built, the Livingstones moved north. Edwards was not aware of Livingstone's desire to move, and had he known he probably would not have caused the fuss. None the less, the wagon wheels turned as the young couple bade farewell.

For Mabotsa it was a sad loss—the people did not want to see Livingstone go. While his oxen were 'inspanned' and he was on the point of moving they offered to build a new house in some other place without expense to him if he would stay with them.

The Foreign Secretary of the London Missionary Society, Arthur Tidman, wrote to David on 29th October 1846. He said:

> The whole affair shews the extreme importance of mutual forbearance, generosity and meekness on the part of the brethren labouring together at the same station; and we trust the lesson it has supplied will not be forgotten either by yourself or Mr Edwards ... Let your ardour be sustained by incessant communion with Christ and your consolation drawn from the conviction of His power and sympathy, and then you will neither be faint nor wearied in your mind, whatever obstacles may exist or trials arise.[30]

This wise letter was a lesson to the young Scot. Replying, he said it brought him much solace and comfort as it 'soothed the bitterness of spirit under which I laboured'.[31]

On leaving Mabotsa Livingstone resettled some forty miles further north with Chief Sechele who showed a keen, intelligent interest in his preaching.

Financially they could not afford to move and rebuild. The Society did not give a grant and they 'endured for a long while, using a wretched infusion of native corn for coffee, but when our corn was done,' wrote Livingstone,

> We were fairly obliged to go to Kuruman for supplies. I can bear what other Europeans would consider hunger and thirst without

---

[30] A Tidman to D L 29/10/1846 in Mssny. Corr., pp 93–94.
[31] D L to A Tidman 30/12/1847 *ibid*, p 111.

any inconvenience, but when we arrived, to hear the old women who had seen my wife depart about two years before, exclaiming before the door, 'Bless me! how lean she is! Has he starved her? Is there no food in the country to which she has been?' was more than I could well bear.[32]

Sechele became a great reader, especially of the Bible, and had a high regard for Isaiah. Livingstone never went into the village without being pressed into hearing Sechele read some chapters of the Bible. The chief was wont to exclaim, 'He was a fine man, that Isaiah; he knew how to speak.'[33]

He shared the missionary's anxiety that his subjects should become converts to Christianity and said to him, 'Do you imagine these people will ever believe by your merely talking to them? I can make them do nothing except by thrashing them; and if you like, I shall call my head-men and with our litupa (whips of rhinoceros-hide) we will soon make them all believe together'.[34] He considered they ought to be happy to embrace Christianity at his command.

During the following two-and-a-half years Livingstone wrote that he

continued to profess to his people his full conviction of the truth of Christianity, and in all discussions on the subject he took that side, acting at the same time in an upright manner in all the relations of life. He felt the difficulties of his situation long before I did, and often said, 'O, I wish you had come to this country before I was entangled in the meshes of our customs!'[35]

The one particular custom which conflicted with the Bible was that of having many wives. Sechele had a problem with polygamy which perpetually plagued him. Although by no means uxorious he had married many wives and could not

---

[32] Blaikie, p 77.
[33] M T p 16.
[34] *Ibid*, p 17.
[35] *Ibid*.

free himself from them without appearing to be ungrateful to the parents who had done so much for him in his adversity.

As soon as Mary was settled in her new home David proceeded to visit Mokhatla, the chief of a large section of the Bakhatla.

On his way he was surprised at the unusual density of the population, giving him the opportunity of 'addressing the immortals on their eternal destiny at least once every day'.[36] Chief Mokhatla was eager to receive the missionary, but said that an arrangement must be made with the Dutch Commandant. This involved some delay.

While labouring at Chonuane, Livingstone undertook two treks eastward in order to establish churches and leave 'native agents' to evangelise further. These treks brought him into contact with the Dutch frontier farmers who resided in the red, rocky soil of the Magaliesburg Mountains. Although very friendly and polite towards the missionary, they were suspicious of his involvement with the local tribes. To them he was a 'serious British spy' who had come to cause strife among the settlers.

Early in 1846 Mary gave birth to a bonny boy, Robert Moffat Livingstone, and 1847 saw her pregnant again. Albeit an added strain on their stringent existence, she none the less chose to travel with her husband, and they journeyed on to the areas known today as Potgietersrus and Rustenburg.

They had a second interview with Krieger, the Dutch Commandant, but Livingstone's hopes of leaving a teacher with the tribe diminished as the Dutch were highly suspicious of the British.

The frontier farmers were at that time a self-contained community who had lived in isolation and had not changed their ways since leaving Europe in the seventeenth century. 'The views which the farmers held were those that had been

---

[36] D L to A Tidman 17/03/1844 in Mssny. Corr., p 95.

entertained by Dr Samuel Johnson, by John Newton and men of their day. To all these the Negro was a lower type of man . . .'[37] This attitude was also held precisely by the seventeenth-century Englishman, Puritan, Cavalier and Roman Catholic.

John Newton confessed that he never enjoyed sweeter communion with God than when on his way to and from the Gold Coast with cargoes of wretched beings, lying fettered and festering in the ship's hold beneath his feet. Yet this prosperous trafficker in human flesh could, and did, write with perfect sincerity the song 'Amazing Grace' and the hymn beginning:

How sweet the name of Jesus sounds
In a believer's ear!
It soothes his sorrows, heals his wounds,
And drives away his fear.[38]

Frontier farmers were a strong biblically-based people whose view of the African was derived from the Pentateuch. The heathen were accursed, in the position of the uncircumcised Philistine, outside the covenant, to be subdued and exploited rather than to be approached in friendship or even tolerated. (This view of the Christian among the Dutch settlers was to change in time and in about 1898 the Dutch Reformed Church of the Orange Free State began missions in the countries now known as Zambia and Zimbabwe.)

Another great problem in Chonuane was the long drought, a further test of Livingstone's faith, for rain fell on tribes without a missionary. The people needed no invitation to put two facts together.

We like you [said one uncle of Sechele] as well as if you had been born among us; you are the only white man we can become familiar with; but we wish you to give up that everlasting

---

[37] Macnair, p 95.
[38] 'The Golden Stool' Edwin W Smith, p 103 in Campbell, p 114.

preaching and praying; we cannot become familiar with that at all. You see we never get rain, while those tribes who never pray as we do obtain abundance.[39]

The drought continued and Agnes Livingstone, their second child, was born into very trying times. It became so dry that the decision was made to move; this time to the banks of the Kolobeng River, which was approximately forty miles to the north west of Chonuane. Within one year of moving and building they were on their way again. Three new homes built in five years was a huge undertaking. Perseverance and self-sacrifice became a way of life, and as a family they were committed to long hours of preaching.

After one year with the Bakwains no conversions had occurred 'yet real progress had been made ... Sabbath is observed so far that no work is done ... and hunting is suspended'.[40]

Despite Sechele's interest in the gospel, Livingstone would not recognise his or his tribe's professed interest in Christianity or repentance unless the fruits of such were seen for many years. Sechele was the chief rain-maker for his tribe and in the first season for rain he remained firm having 'unbounded confidence in his own powers'. The heavens remained dry.

The Livingstone house was said to be the reason why no rain came and they were requested to permit it to be sprinkled with medicine. To this they 'had no objections, provided the stuff did not smell badly, yet no rain came. The crops were lost'.[41]

Disenchanted with witchcraft, Sechele told David Livingstone: 'You shall never see me at that work again'.[42]

They lived at Kolobeng for four years, their mission house

[39] M T p 23.
[40] D L to A Tidman 17/03/1847 in Mssny. Corr., p 102.
[41] *Ibid*, p 103.
[42] *Ibid*.

standing on a little rocky eminence over the river. Livingstone persuaded the tribesmen to build a canal and dam in exchange for his labour in assisting to build a square house for their chief. They also erected a school under his supervision. Said Sechele, 'I desire to build a house for God, the defender of my town, and that you be at no expense for it whatever'.[43] Two hundred of his people were employed for this work.

A typical day in the life of the Livingstone household was being up with the sun, having family worship, breakfast, going to school, then working in the fields, or whatever was required. After a two-hour break at midday, manual labour continued for David while Mary taught in the school. At five o'clock in the evening he would go into town to give lessons and talk to anyone who showed interest. Once the cows were milked a meeting followed, and then a time of prayer in Sechele's house.

First a temporary house was built and in July 1848 they moved into their new home, after being 'a year in a little hut through which the wind blew our candles into glorious icicles (as a poet would say) by night, and in which crowds of flies continually settled on the eyes of our poor little brats by day'.[44]

He dwelt often on the dissension at Mabotsa and wrote to Dr Bennett saying, 'I often think I have forgiven, as I hope to be forgiven; but the remembrance of slander often comes boiling up, although I hate to think of it. You must remember me in your prayers that more of the Spirit of Christ may be imparted to me'.[45]

Livingstone was in the habit of preaching to the natives, his favourite topics being the love of Christ, the Fatherhood of God, the resurrection and the last judgement.[46] Dr Moffat

---

[43] Blaikie, p 85.
[44] *Ibid*, p 86.
[45] *Ibid*.
[46] *Ibid*, p 94.

saw Livingstone's preaching as highly effective. It was simple, scriptural, conversational and held the attention of the people. David wrote to his father telling him:

> For a long time I felt much depressed after preaching the unsearchable riches of Christ to apparently insensible hearts; but now I like to dwell on the love of the great Mediator, for it always warms my own heart, and I know that the gospel is the power of God—the great means which He employs for the regeneration of our ruined world.[47]

Livingstone needed to remain strong in his faith for trial after trial beset him. One trial was the drought. Others were to follow, yet his heart remained uncomplicated. A few excerpts from his diary in 1848–1849 read:

> May 20, 1848—Spoke to Sechele of the evil of trusting in medicines instead of God. He felt afraid to dispute on the subject, and said he would give up all medicine if I only told him to do so. I was gratified to see symptoms of tender conscience. May God enlighten him!

> July 10—Entered new house on 4th curt*. A great mercy. Hope it may be more a house of prayer than any we have yet inhabited.

> Sunday August 6—Sechele remained as a spectator at the celebration of the Lord's Supper, and when we retired he asked me how he ought to act with reference to his superfluous wives, as he greatly desired to conform to the will of Christ, be baptised, and observe His ordinances. Advised him to do according to what he saw written in God's Book, but to treat them gently, for they had sinned in ignorance, and if driven away hastily might be lost eternally'.[48]

The following day Sechele made an outward, public confession of this conversion by handsomely pensioning off his supernumerary wives and sending them to their families. He

---

[47] D L to Neil L 5/07/1848 *ibid*, p 94.
[48] *Ibid*, p 91.
  * Possibly Livingstone's abbreviation of 'current', ie the current month.

retained only one. 'She,' said Livingstone, 'was about the most unlikely subject in the tribe ever to become anything else than an out-and-out greasy disciple of the old school.' Again and again he had seen Sechele send her out of church to put her gown on and 'away she would go with her lip shot out, the very picture of unutterable disgust at his new-fangled notions'.[49]

Sept 1—Much opposition, but none manifested to us as individuals. Some, however, say it was a pity the lion did not kill me at Mabotsa. They curse the chief (Sechele) with bitter curses, and these come from the mouths of those whom Sechele would formerly have destroyed for a single disrespectful word. The truth will, by the aid of the Spirit of God, ultimately prevail.

Oct 1—Sechele baptised; also Setefano.

Nov—Long for rains. Everything languishes during the intense heat; and successive droughts having only occurred since the Gospel came to the Bakwains, I fear the effect will be detrimental. There is abundance of rain all around us. And yet we, who have our chief at our head in attachment to the gospel, receive not a drop. Has Satan power over the course of the winds and clouds? Feel afraid he will obtain an advantage over us, but must be resigned entirely to the Divine will.

November 27—O Devil! Prince of the power of the air, art thou hindering us? Greater is He who is for us than all who can be against us. I intend to proceed with Paul to Mokhatla's. He feels much pleased with the prospect of forming a new station. May God Almighty bless the poor unworthy effort! Mebalwe's house finished. Preparing woodwork for Paul's house.[50]

The drought was bad: trees started to die, the corn crop failed again, together with the vegetables. The Kolobeng River had 'dwindled down to a dribbling rill' and was useless for

---

[49] Johnson, p 80.
[50] Blaikie, p 92.

irrigation. A year later it dried up completely. Less than two inches of rain had fallen in two years. Livingstone measured the temperature at three inches under the soil and found that it was 130°F at midday.

The Livingstones followed in the footsteps of John the Baptist and ate locusts and honey. The former being 'the most constipating food I ever ate', wrote Livingstone. 'They taste just like the vegetables on which they subsist . . . the wild honey has the very opposite tendency, the two combined form one of the best kinds of foods the Bakalihari have'.[51]

The situation became desperate. Enormous frogs, which when cooked look like chickens, joined the menu. Meanwhile, three months after his baptism, Sechele was still standing up to his people's taunts and appeared to be making good progress.

A bell-man, a tall gaunt fellow, was employed to collect the people for the service.

> Up he jumped on a sort of platform, and shouted at the top of his voice, 'Knock that woman down over there. Strike her, she is putting on her pot! (for cooking). Do you see that one hiding herself? Give her a good blow. There she is—see, see, knock her down!' All the women ran to the place of meeting in no time, for each thought herself meant. But, though a most efficient bell-man, we did not like to employ him.[52]

The tribes were not the only folk resisting Livingstone. The frontier farmers were also opposed to native teachers of the gospel and even threatened to destroy any tribe that welcomed the preachers.

On 16th December 1848, Livingstone wrote in his diary:

> Passed by invitation to Hendrick Potgeiter. Opposed to building a school . . . Told him that if he hindered the Gospel the blood

---

[51] D L to Sir Risdon Bennett 30/06/1843 in Chamberlin, p 55.
[52] Blaikie, p 78.

of these people would be required at his hand. He became much excited at this.

Dec 17—Met Dr Robertson of Swellendam. Very friendly. Boers very violently opposed (to native agents) . . . Went to Pilanies. Had large attentive audiences at two villages when on the way home. Paul and I looked for a ford in a dry river. Found we had got a she black rhinoceros between us and the wagon, which was only twenty yards off. She had calved during the night—a little red beast like a dog. She charged the wagon, split a spoke and a felloe with her horn and then left. Paul and I jumped into a rut as the guns were in the wagon'.[53]

Sadly, though, by March 1849 Livingstone saw 'symptoms of pregnancy' in Mokokon, one of Sechele's former wives. He had gone back to her, Sechele confessed, twice. The blow to Livingstone was devastating. Sechele made no excuses and gave him an honest account of what had happened. Worried and wounded, Livingstone wrote to Moffat, 'The confession loosened all my bones. I felt as if I should sink to the earth, or run away . . . no one except yourselves can imagine the lancinating pangs'.[54]

Sechele repented. He told Livingstone that he was deeply sorry and wanted to obtain forgiveness. Livingstone took stern scriptural measures to discipline him, but he could not help acknowledging that Sechele's lapse had 'required no effort such as going to another man's wife . . . He had been so accustomed to their customs, it was like his ordinary food'.[55]

He also learned that Isak, son of one of his native teachers, Paul, had been regularly committing adultery and as a result another man's wife fell pregnant. Both Paul and Mebalwe had

---

[53] *Ibid*, p 92.
[54] D L to R Moffat 11/04/1849 in Fam. Lett. II, p 30.
[55] *Ibid*.

kept this from the missionary, allowing folk to laugh at Livingstone for not knowing.

He sent Sechele a note: 'My heart is broken. First Isak, then you. I can no longer be a teacher here'.[56]

Livingstone, hurt and hungry for souls who would turn and follow their Saviour, started to look northwards to where people lived and died not having ever heard the gospel.

Kolobeng as a mission station had suffered dreadfully through physical and spiritual drought. Livingstone wrote to London, 'Instead of quiet and comparatively well observed Sabbaths, it is quite common to see pack oxen laden with meat, or crowds of women burdened with locusts, returning home on that sacred day'.[57]

Livingstone came to the conclusion that he should cross the Kalahari desert and carry the gospel to the heathen. The necessity to move from Kolobeng became apparent as the drought persisted. The Bakwains split as some followed Sechele in search of good soil and superior defences against attack from the settlers, while others opted for settling in the north. Would Livingstone again move and build another home, school and church or leave them with one of his teachers to shepherd them and move north?

The missionary wrote:

> God in His good Providence had opened up for us an extensive region largely populated. I think that there can be no doubt but that it is our duty to follow in the path He has indicated, although that involves separation from the people for whom I have laboured for nearly six years and of whom I indulged many sanguine hopes. I have much affection for them, and though I part from them I do not relinquish the hope that they will yet turn to Him to whose mercy and love they have often been invited. The seed of the living Word will not perish.[58]

---

[56] D L to R Moffat 4/05/1849 *ibid*, p 42.
[57] D L to A Tidman 26/05/1849 in Mssny. Corr., p 127.
[58] P J, p 2.

While he felt God was leading him to the north across
the Kalahari desert where no white man had yet crossed
and lived, what would be the toll on him and his fragile
family?

Dr Livingstone and his family

6

The Search for a New Station

Livingstone decided to move forward. An invitation came for him to visit Chief Lechulatebe who lived on the edge of Lake 'Ngami, an area neither previously seen nor visited by a white man.

On 1st June 1849 Livingstone set out with two other Europeans, Mr Oswell and Mr Murray, who had been introduced to him by Colonel Steele. Mr Oswell undertook to defray the entire expense of the guides; a huge relief as the missionary and his family battled financially. The purpose for travelling was to head for Lake 'Ngami with the doctor. A firm friendship developed between Livingstone and Oswell. In fact Livingstone remarked, 'He was the best friend we ever had in Africa.'

A neighbouring chief, Sekomi, secretly wished the expedition to fail, lest he lose his monopoly of the ivory. He remonstrated with them for rushing ahead to a certain death, but Livingstone reassured him saying, 'No fear, people will only blame our own stupidity'.[1]

Sekomi then sent two of his men ahead to spread rumours among the people that the expedition was out to plunder them. His plans miscarried. Half way, one of the men was attacked by fever and died. The natives thought it a judgement and, seeing through Sekomi's sly reasoning, gradually became quite friendly to the party.

---

[1] Blaikie, p 82.

Progress was slow, as they could only march in the cool of the morning and evening. The wheels of the wagons often sank deep in the loose sand as the oxen strained to pull their heavy load.

Water was scarce and a very valuable commodity in the country. It was always carefully hidden by the bushmen to preserve it from any wandering band who might take it by force. Livingstone's method of conciliating the bushmen and gaining their favour was by sitting down quietly and talking to them in a friendly way until the precious fluid was brought forth. He knew that threats or domineering would be to no avail.

On one occasion Mr Oswell 'happened to spy a Bushwoman running away in a bent position in order to escape observation. He, thinking it to be a lion, galloped up to her. She thought herself captured, and began to deliver up her poor little property, consisting of a few traps made of cords'.[2] When Livingstone explained that they only wanted water and would pay her if she led them to it, she then walked briskly before the horses for eight miles. At their destination, Nchokotsa, a brackish water hole, she was rewarded with meat and a good supply of beads. On seeing the latter, she burst into a merry laugh.

In the setting sun, as the sweltering heat subsided, they saw the first of many salt pans. One was about twenty miles in circumference and the sun cast a beautiful blue haze over the white encrustations and caused it to look like a lake. Oswell threw his hat up in the air at the sight and shouted a huzza which made the poor bushwoman and Bakwains think him mad.

Livingstone too was convinced it was Lake 'Ngami. They did not know it lay still more than 300 miles distant. The waves danced, and the shadows of the trees were reflected in

---

[2] M T, pp 61–62.

such a perfect manner that the cattle, horses, dogs and even Hottentots whose thirst had not been sufficiently slaked, hastened towards the deceitful pools. Only a break in the haze dispelled the illusion.

These mirages continued to plague the party until they were finally rewarded upon reaching the Zouga River on 4th July. From then on they did not have to worry about water, for the river, after many miles, joined Lake 'Ngami.

Livingstone was first and foremost a missionary, preaching whenever he had the opportunity. In writing to Arthur Tidman he told him: 'I hope to be permitted to work as long as I live beyond other men's line of things and plant the seed of the gospel where others have not planted. But every excursion for that purpose will involve separation from my family for periods of four or five months'.[3]

He knew the challenge of the Great Commission issued by Christ was to preach the gospel. He was also fully aware of the sacrifice of his family while sowing the seeds of the Saviour's saving grace. Indeed he later regretted not playing with his children when he was at home with them as they had rapidly grown up away from him in his absences. It was a hard decision to make and one of anguish not only for himself but also for the family.

He was aware of his responsibility to those in Kolobeng, and he told Tidman that the Christian work there would be maintained by native teachers during the times of his absence.

On 1st August 1849 they arrived at Lake 'Ngami which, from local reports, was so large that it took three days to go round it.

Lechulatebe, a young chief, gave them a warm welcome, but withdrew his support once he heard that Livingstone wanted to meet Paramount Chief Sebituane, who lived 200 miles further north. He feared that the Europeans would

---

[3] D L to A Tidman 3/09/1849 in Mssny. Corr., p 133.

supply fire-arms to his neighbour, thus increasing the chance of attack from Sebituane. Livingstone would not be deterred. He worked many hours up to his waist in crocodile-infested water trying to make a raft out of some rotten wood. Only later did he realise how many crocodiles abounded there and was amazed that one did not attack him.

The rainy season was about to commence and Oswell suggested they return the following year with a boat. In agreement they returned home to Kolobeng via the Zouga River, where flourishing, green, gigantic trees made a sharp contrast to the dry, parched desert.

Livingstone enjoyed sailing in their innovative canoes which were hollowed tree trunks. He wrote to his friend Watt and said of the Bakoba that they 'are a fine frank race of men, and seem to understand the message better than any people to whom I have spoken on Divine subjects for the first time'.[4]

The missionary's active mind was already considering a 'navigable highway into a large section of the interior' and posed the question in the same letter, 'Who will go into that goodly land? Who?'

Livingstone knew where his heart lay and in a letter to his parents wrote: 'I am a missionary, heart and soul. God had an only Son, and He was a missionary and physician. A poor, poor imitation of Him I am, or wish to be. In this service I hope to live, in it I wish to die'.[5]

In a letter to Freeman he wrote:

I cannot help earnestly coveting the privilege of introducing the Gospel to a new land and people. When I heard the new language and saw a few portions of the people, I felt that if I could be permitted to reduce their language to writing, and perhaps translate the Scriptures into it, I might be able to say that I have not lived in vain.[6]

[4] Blaikie, p 102.
[5] D L to his parents 5/02/1850 in Blaikie, p 125.
[6] D L to the Revd J J Freeman 9/01/1850 in Mssny. Corr., p 142.

The siting of the lake and river was communicated to the Royal Geographical Society in extracts from Livingstone's letters to the Missionary Society and to his friend and former traveller, Captain Steele. Recognition was given to the other men as well, and in 1849 the Society voted him a sum of twenty-five guineas 'for his successful journey, in company with Messrs. Oswell and Murray, across the South African desert, for the discovery of an interesting country, a fine river, and an extensive inland lake'.[7]

This journey had hitherto defeated many other explorers who were sent out by the Geographical Society or had come on their own initiative in search of ivory.

The gift was a welcome bonus to a family who struggled so desperately for finance. It was awarded by Queen Victoria, so the Scot was compelled to review his criticism of former years as to the destination of the nation's money. He wrote to his parents, telling them, 'It is from the Queen. You must be very loyal, all of you. Next time she comes your way, shout till you are hoarse. Oh you Radicals, don't be thinking it came out of your pockets! Long live Victoria!'[8]

As soon as the rainy season was over Livingstone set out again. This time in April 1850, not wanting to be parted from his family despite the risk of fever, he took Mary and their three children, together with Mebalwe and Chief Sechele. Sechele was eager to visit Chief Sebituane, who had saved his life when an infant. The party crossed the Zouga River at its lower end and proceeded along its northern bank, hacking a path for the wagons through the dense vegetation. Losses through oxen falling into pits (dug by tribesmen for trapping game) were heavy, but the Bayeiye kindly took away the camouflage canopy covering the pits when they knew of their approach.

---

[7] Blaikie, p 102.
[8] D L to his parents 4/12/1856 in Blaikie, pp 103–104.

Near the confluence of the Tamanakle River they heard that the tsetse fly abounded—a small insect, a little larger than a house fly. The tsetse fly feeds on blood and in the process may transmit serious diseases to man and domestic animals. Its bite was fatal to oxen and a decision was made to recross the Zouga to try and avoid them. This was a laborious undertaking.

They also learned that a party of English hunters were all laid low by fever. Hurrying, they traversed sixty miles before reaching the malaria-stricken men. Sadly, one man, Mr Alfred Rider, an experienced artist, died before their arrival. The Livingstones nursed the two survivors, Wilson and Edwards, who perked up under Mary's caring hand and the doctor's wise treatment with quinine.

The trek continued, but not without a further set-back. The children were seized with malaria. Then followed the servants. Mary was pregnant and, fearing the worst, Livingstone decided to turn back. He met up with Oswell who was hunting on the Zouga, and they returned together to Kolobeng. Oswell was a keen, adept hunter whose skill was much talked about. If the locals wished to flatter Livingstone, they would say to him: 'If you were not a missionary you would be just like Oswell; you would not hunt with dogs either'.[9] He had been known to kill four large old male elephants in a day, and the value of ivory would be 100 guineas. A considerable amount, as that represented Livingstone's salary for the entire year.

They covered the weary 600 miles back to Kolobeng, where their fourth child, Elizabeth Pyne Livingstone, was born. Sadly the sickness prevailing among the Bakwains took hold of her and, after bearing up under it for a fortnight, she ceased struggling. As David wrote to their friend, Benjamin Pyne, 'She was taken away to see the King in His beauty and the

[9] M T, p 76.

blessed land. We hope to follow her thither. It is wonderful how soon the affections twine round a little stranger'.[10]

The loss affected the Livingstones greatly who 'felt quite desolate without her—"she was very beautiful, had fine blue eyes and was very strong"'.[11] All the other children had the disease but recovered.

They received yet another shock, for Mary Livingstone had an attack of a mysterious serious illness, accompanied by paralysis of the right side of her face. Rest was essential for her, so David decided to take them the 270 miles to Kuruman. There Mary gradually recovered and Livingstone tried to persuade his father-in-law to operate on him and cut out the troublesome large uvula from the back of his throat. For some time this had irritated him while he was preaching. Moffat went so far as to make a pair of scissors for the purpose, but his courage failed him.

The death of the child and illness of the mother were both charged to the missionary's account and he was asked if the 'loss of one child etc., etc. was not enough to satisfy him'. This was said to him by people whom he esteemed and caused him to search his heart, motives and ambitions. He told Tidman in a letter that he would prefer to teach his own children than send them away; furthermore the distances to other tribes he wanted to reach made him 'appear more as a traveller than a missionary'.[12]

He was also conscious that some of the brethren did not hesitate to tell the natives that his object was to obtain the applause of men. This bothered him, for he sometimes questioned his own motives, though he reassured himself that in the main it was for the glory of him to whom he dedicated his all. He told Tidman: 'I never anticipated fame from the

---

[10] D L to B Pyne 4/12/1850 in Chamberlin, p 142.
[11] *Ibid.*
[12] D L to A Tidman 17/10/1851 in Mssny. Corr., p 189.

discovery of the Lake. I cared very little about it. But the sight of the Tamunakle, and the report of other large rivers beyond, all densely populated, awakened many and enthusiastic feelings'.[13]

The Livingstones had time to talk over their future, and where most men would have accepted they must settle, every rebuff reinforced this missionary's resolve and widened his vision. Always there arose some challenging sentence such as, 'I shall open up a path into the interior or perish,' and soon greater plans were shaping themselves in his indomitable heart.

Chief Sebituane was expecting them. He had despatched three detachments of his men with thirteen brown cows to Lechulatebe, thirteen white cows to Sekomi and thirteen black cows to Sechele, together with a request to assist the white men to reach him.

This generous act softened Chief Sekomi's heart. He even furnished Livingstone with a guide on their third journey. This commenced in April 1851 and despite much criticism his family accompanied him, as the doctor did not want to be separated from them.

He wrote to his sister on 28th April 1851 saying:

> Fever may cut us all off. I feel much when I think of the children dying. But who will go if we don't? Not one. I would venture everything for Christ. Pity I have so little to give. But He will accept us, for He is a good master. Never one like Him. He can sympathise. May He forgive, and purify and bless us.[14]

Such was the faith and almost fanatical disregard for his life and the lives of his family for the cause of Christ. He told Tidman in a letter:

> We have an immense region before us. Thousands live and die without God and without hope, though the command went forth of old, 'Go ye into all the world and preach the Gospel to every

---

[13] *Ibid.*
[14] Blaikie, p 125.

creature.' It is a venture to take wife and children into a country where fever, African fever, prevails. But who that believes in Jesus would refuse to make a venture for such a Captain? A parent's heart alone can feel as I do when I look at my little ones and ask, shall I return with this or that one alive? However, we are His, and wish to have no interests apart from those of His Kingdom and glory. May He bless us and make us blessings even unto death.[15]

Oswell accompanied them, though the plan was that he leave them to settle, preferably on high ground, where they could establish a station. Livingstone continually acknowledged with gratitude the generous kindness Oswell bestowed upon them, and often in letters added a prayer that God would reward him and by his grace give him the highest of all blessings.

The party followed the now-familiar route, but beyond Nchokotsa no one knew the path. They had a bushman guide, Shobo, who escorted them across the desert where only low scrub in deep sand met their eyes. Not a bird or insect enlivened the landscape. Shobo wandered to all points of the compass, but to no avail—he was lost. On the morning of the fourth day he vanished altogether.

They continued in the direction they had last seen him. Livingstone was worried; the supply of water in the wagons had been wasted by one of the servants and

by the afternoon only a small portion remained for the children. This was a bitterly anxious night; and next morning, the less there was of water, the more thirsty the little rogues became. The idea of their perishing before our eyes was terrible; it would almost have been a relief to me to have been reproached with being the entire cause of the catastrophe, but not one syllable of upbraiding was uttered by their mother, though the tearful eye told the agony within. In the afternoon of the fifth day, to our inexpressible relief,

---

[15] D L to A Tidman 30/04/1851 in Mssny. Corr., p 171.

some of the men returned with a supply of that fluid of which we
had never before felt the true value.[16]

The guide returned and made out as if nothing was wrong.
Livingstone forgave him and his heart went out to the
bushmen. He wrote in his journal:

> What a wonderful people the Bushmen are! Always merry and
> laughing, and never telling lies wantonly like the Bechuana. They
> have more of the appearance of worship than any of the Bechuana.
> When will these dwellers in the wilderness bow down before their
> Lord? No man seems to care for the Bushman's soul. I often
> wished I knew their language.[17]

In the desert the problem was a lack of water. Along the rivers
the problem was tsetse fly and mosquitoes. The latter brought
malaria and it was frustrating to see the children covered with
bites. Livingstone wrote on one occasion that not a square
inch of whole skin was to be found on their bodies. How
much more could these little ones take? He couldn't leave the
family at Kolobeng as the station was threatened by attack
from the frontier farmers, and there were also innumerable
objections to Kuruman. Meanwhile, the search for Sebituane
continued. A guide, Chombo, volunteered and they pursued
their course, reaching the Chobe River which was infested
with tsetse fly.

One of Sebituane's chief men was sent to escort them, and
crossing the Chobe by canoe Livingstone and Oswell met the
great Chief Sebituane. He was a thin, wiry man of about five
feet ten inches in height and slightly bald. He gave them a
warm welcome, was a little flurried at first, but soon regained
complete self-possession.

Livingstone stated the object of his visit—'the preaching of
the gospel, their elevation in the scale of humanity, peace,

[16] M T, p 79.
[17] Blaikie, p 110.

and the avoidance of murder and the barter in slaves'.[18] This
was accepted, though a plea was made for guns to secure
peace against Sebituane's old rivals—the people of Mosilikatse
whom he had managed to defeat. The travellers were well-
fed and given a span of oxen to make up for all those lost by
the tsetse bites.

Livingstone held a service on the Sunday and Sebituane
attended. This was to be the only proclamation of the gospel
he would ever hear, for within the next week he was seized
with an inflammation of the lungs and died after a fortnight's
illness. Being a stranger, Livingstone feared to prescribe lest
in the event of his death, he would be blamed. The doctor
saw that he was dying and spoke a few words regarding
hope after death, but was checked by the attendants for
introducing the subject. He could only commend his soul to
God.

A warm friendship had been rekindled between the two
leaders which brought forth much sadness from the Scot when
Sebituane died. His death was also a great blow in another
sense. His influence covered a wide region and he had
promised to show it to Livingstone for him to select a suitable
locality for his residence. Livingstone would be able to work
in a land which had never heard the gospel of Christ being
preached.

Sebituane's daughter, Ma-Mochisane, succeeded him. From
her Livingstone received liberty to visit any part of the country
he chose.

Mr Oswell and he travelled in a north-easterly direction,
passing through a village, Linyanti, and on 4th August they
came to a magnificent river at Sesheke which the locals called
by the same name. It was in fact the Zambesi (today spelled
'Zambezi'). In his journal, Livingstone wrote: 'We thanked
God for permitting us first to see this glorious river. All we

---

[18] P J, p 16.

could say to each other was ... 'How glorious! How magnificent! How beautiful! . . .' In crossing, the waves lifted up the canoe and made it roll beautifully'.[19]

They persuaded an old man to take them out on the river in his dug-out canoe. The sight of the river, 300–400 yards wide, brought feelings of deep emotion from Livingstone, who admitted that he was close to tears. Only 'the old man who was conducting them across might have said "What on earth are you blubbering at? Afraid of these crocodiles, eh?" The little sentimentality which exuded was forced to take its course down the inside of the nose.'

The wide, swiftly-flowing water was certainly an impressive sight as animal, fish and reptile abounded, from wild game to the huge hippopotamus and cunning crocodile. He had heard of these reptiles above the great waterfalls situated about four days or eighty miles from the village of Sesheke. The waterfall was called 'Mosioatunya' or 'the smoke that thunders'. People told Livingstone about the noise it makes which can be heard at a considerable distance and the spray that can be seen ten to fifteen miles off. Livingstone's hopes for a navigable highway into the interior of Africa took hold. Traders and missionaries could come up as far as the falls. Slavery would then not pay, as commerce would take the place of this trade in humans for cloth, guns and beads. The slave-trade was still making inroads into Africa and only began on the Sesheke in 1850, when a group from the Mambari tribe came to Sebituane carrying vast quantities of cloth and guns, in exchange for boys of about fourteen years of age.[20]

The rainy season was about to begin, yet Livingstone had not discovered a healthy locality. 'The whole of the country of Sebituane is unhealthy.' He wrote that he 'was at a loss

[19] *Ibid*, pp 38–39. (He was obviously unaware of Silva Porto's discoveries.)
[20] D L to A Tidman 17/10/1851 in Mssny. Corr., p 183.

what to do, but will not give up the case as hopeless. Shame upon us missionaries if we are to be outdone by slave traders!'[21]

The more he thought, the more the missionary became convinced that if 'Christian missionaries and Christian merchants can remain throughout the year in the interior of the continent, in ten years the slave dealer will be driven out of the market'.[22]

Sadly the party turned back southwards on 13th August 1851. Although much had been accomplished regarding exploration, the desire of his heart had not been realised. None the less, the man of stone would not be moved into cancelling his vision. He would return after the rains.

As the wagon wheels turned slowly southwards, Mrs Livingstone's pregnancy would not wait—a son was born whom the proud parents named William Oswell Livingstone, after their fine friend and fellow explorer.

On the 18th, Thomas had an attack of malaria. They moved to higher ground while he battled with three successive attacks in only a fortnight. Livingstone realised that his family, already suffering the hardships in Africa, could not endure prolonged exposure while he searched for a new mission station.

The missionary's aim was still the same— 'We ought to preach the gospel. Some will believe and some will reject. If we are faithful we shall stand in our lot in the latter day and hear the sentence which will wipe away all tears from our eyes'.[23]

The pressure upon him to care for his family was great. He kept with him in his journal a letter from Mary Moffat, his mother-in-law. (It was evident from this that he pondered deeply his duty not only to God, but also to his family.) The letter remonstrated with him in the strongest terms for taking his wife and family with him exploring.

---

[21] Robertson, p 85.
[22] D L to A Tidman 17/10/1851 in Mssny. Corr., p 185.
[23] P J, p 45.

Travelling was taking its toll on Mary who wrote to her mother prior to the latest trek, expressing her dismay at winding her 'weary way to the far interior'. Her mother, who respected Livingstone, pleaded with him not to expose them to the cruelty of exploration, to mention 'nothing of the indecorousness of it. A pregnant woman with three little children trailing about with a company of the other sex, through the wilds of Africa, among savage men and beasts! Had you found a place to which you wished to go and commence missionary operations, the case would be altered'.[24]

Livingstone had taken his family and subjected them to cumbersome and irksome conditions as he was sure he would find a site for a station.

All true faith has in it an element of venture, and in this man the element was strong. Trusting God he could expose even the health, comfort and welfare of his wife and children. He was convinced that it was his duty to go forth with them and seek a new station for the gospel in Sebituane's country. This being true, God would take care of them, and it was 'better to trust in the Lord than to put confidence in man'.

The burden for solitary souls and the love for his family tore at his heart. He wrote: 'No one more than the African needs the humanizing influence of the gospel of Christ. Having this message to deliver to these lost souls, we can go anywhere in safety'.[25]

For Livingstone, the finger of God pointed him northwards. He had a great aversion to the common impression that the less success one had the stronger was one's duty to remain. Too many missionaries were only too ready to settle down and make themselves as comfortable as possible; whereas the great need was for men to move on, to strike out into the

[24] Mary Moffat to D L in PJ, p 71.
[25] D L to A Tidman 17/10/1851 in Mssny. Corr., p 187.

regions beyond. To go into all the world and preach the gospel to those who had not received it, rather than to those who had already heard the message of eternal salvation over many years yet shown no fruit.

So sure was he of his need to move to the north that he wrote to the directors saying, 'So powerfully convinced am I that it is the will of our Lord I should, I will go, no matter who opposes; but from you I expect nothing but encouragement. I know you wish as ardently as I can that all the world may be filled with the glory of the Lord'.[26]

He proposed that another missionary, Mr Ashton, be placed among the Bamangwato, a people who were in the habit of spreading themselves through the Bakalahari, and thus form a link between himself and the brethren in the south. His plans were generally approved by the directors who also had recommended that he should complete a dictionary of the Sichuana language.

Livingstone, however, had another problem—that of finance. The Livingstones had been as economical as possible, but they could not survive on his meagre salary. Oswell's generosity kept them from time to time, but they were still overdrawn against the account which the Society kept of their expenditure. Exploration and living in the interior were expensive. The cost of transport was phenomenal.

On reaching Kolobeng they found the station sadly deserted. The Bakwains had moved to Limaue. They saw Sechele who came down the following day and gave Livingstone an ox—a valuable gift in his critical circumstances.

Livingstone wrote in his journal: 'I have much affection for them. Though I pass from them I do not relinquish the hope that they will yet turn to Him to whose mercy and love they have often been invited. The seed of the living Word will not perish'.[27]

---

[26] Blaikie, p 123.
[27] *Ibid*, p 122.

They parted company as the Livingstones continued on to Kuruman for a short three-week stay and in January 1852 proceeded to the Cape.

The decision had been made. Livingstone would find and build a home. In the meanwhile his family would return to Britain. There the children would be educated and Mary would be relieved of the stress of living in Africa. If they stayed in Kuruman she would be continuously harassed and hampered by rumours of her husband's health and welfare.

Reaching Cape Town on 16th March 1852 the Livingstones received a cool reception— many missionaries were regarded as unpatriotic, and feelings ran high as the 'Caffre war' raged.

Their clothes were not only old and rather tattered, but much out of fashion. Their friend Oswell had arrived earlier and presented them with £170, a huge amount of money, saying that they had as good a right to the money from shooting elephants as he had. Concerning Oswell, Livingstone wrote in his journal: 'God bless and preserve him. O divine Love I have not loved thee strongly, deeply and warmly enough'.[28]

Livingstone at long last had his uvula excised which, he wrote, 'I hope will enable me more freely to preach unto the gentiles the unsearchable riches of Christ'.[29]

After a month in Cape Town, on 23rd April 1852, Mrs Livingstone and the four children—Thomas, the eldest who was only six, William, Robert and Agnes—bade a sorrowful goodbye to their father. It was a sad moment, especially not knowing when they would meet again. Mary Livingstone was full of fears. She hardly knew Britain and had grown dependent on her strong-minded husband.

David realised his responsibility as a father to the children. He was passionately attached to his wife and family, and he

---

[28] PJ, p 80.
[29] *Ibid.*

knew that to a great extent he was losing his children. He wrote a letter to Tidman:

> The act of orphanizing my children, which now becomes painfully near, will be like tearing out my bowels, for they will all forget me. But I feel it is a duty to Him who did much more for us than that. His command is, 'Go ye into all the world and preach the gospel to every creature.' Forbid it, that we should ever consider holding a commission from the King of kings a sacrifice . . .[30]

As the boat set sail on 23rd April 1852, the forlorn family waved goodbye with tearful eyes. Livingstone reflected upon his love for his lady and tried to busy himself as loneliness threatened to envelop his heart. He still had a mighty mission to accomplish for his Creator.

Meanwhile, during their absence from Kolobeng, an insidious crime was perpetrated.

------

[30] D L to A Tidman 17/03/1852 in Mssny. Corr., pp 194–195.

7

In His Service, Sowing Seeds of Salvation

Livingstone was now in his fortieth year of age and the days that followed were among his hardest. Surrendering his wife and children for the cause which lay heavily on his heart was to be a recurring conflict in his life.

One consolation at this depressing time was the friendship of Sir Thomas Maclear, Astronomer Royal at the Cape, who gave him further instruction on the accurate recording of positions and the drawing of maps. A firm friendship developed and later Livingstone's accurate records were highly spoken of.

Livingstone longed to leave civilisation and commence his commission, but much was still to be procured. He found it difficult to adjust to speaking English and even 'felt rather at a loss with the stairs, and much disposed to turn round and come down as one descends a ladder'.[1]

Funds were scarce and the authorities were hesitant to comply with his request for ammunition lest it reach hostile tribesmen. Finally his order was granted. However, Cape Town's suspicions were partly justified; he did give a lot of powder and lead to the Makololo, but they used it on game as they were too far north to engage the Dutch.

Livingstone also ran into trouble by accusing the Colesburg postmaster of overcharging postage from Kuruman. The

---

[1] D L to Robert Moffat 2/04/1852 in Fam. Lett. II, pp 167–168.

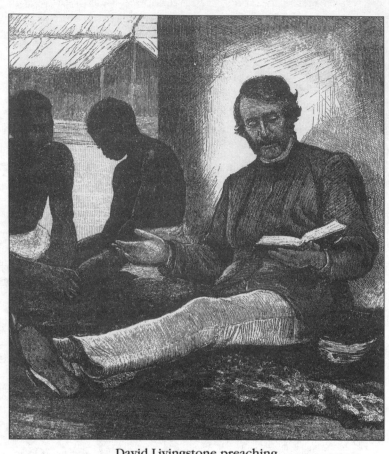

David Livingstone preaching

official took this personally and retaliated with a threat of action for defamation of character. The miserable affair resulted in Livingstone having to settle it out of court with the payment of £13.

The doctor missed his family. He wrote to his wife:

My Dearest Mary, How I miss you now, and the dear children! My heart yearns incessantly over you. How many thoughts of the past crowd into my mind! I feel as if I would treat you all much more tenderly and lovingly than ever. You have been a great blessing to me. You attended to my comfort in many many ways. May God bless you for all your kindnesses! I see no face now to be compared with that sunburnt one which has so often greeted me with its kind looks. Let us do our duty to our Saviour, and we shall meet again. I wish that time were now. You may read the letters over again which I wrote at Mabotsa, the sweet time you know. As I told you before, I tell you again, they are true, true; there is not a bit of hypocrisy in them. I never show all my feelings; but I can say truly, my dearest, that I loved you when I married you, and the longer I lived with you, I loved you the better ... Let us do our duty to Christ, and He will bring us through the world with honour and usefulness. He is our refuge and high tower; let us trust in Him at all times, and in all circumstances. Love Him more and more, and diffuse His love among the children. Take them all round you, and kiss them for me. Tell them I have left them for the love of Jesus, and that they must love Him too, and to avoid sin, for that displeases Jesus. I shall be delighted to hear of you all safe in England ...[2]

A few days later he wrote to his daughter Agnes, who was then five years old.

My Dear Agnes, This is your own little letter. Mamma will read it for you, and you will hear her just as if I were speaking to you, for the words which I write are those which she will read. I am still at Cape Town. You know you left me there when you all

---

[2] D L to Mary L 5/05/1852, *ibid*, p 182.

went into the big ship and sailed away. Well, I shall leave Cape Town soon. Malatsi has gone for the oxen, and then I shall go away back to Sebituane's country, and see Seipone and Moriye, who gave you the beads and fed you with milk and honey. I shall not see you again for a long time, and I am very sorry. I have no Nannee now. I have given you back to Jesus, your Friend, your Papa who is in heaven. He is above you, but He is always near you. When we ask things from Him, that is praying to Him; and if you do or say a naughty thing ask Him to pardon you, and to bless you, and to make you one of His children. Love Jesus much, for He loves you, and He came and died for you. Oh how good Jesus is I love Him and I shall love Him as long as I live. You must love Him too, and you must love your brothers and Mamma, and never tease them or be naughty, for Jesus does not like to see naughtiness. Good-bye, my dear Nannee.[3]

He preached while in Cape Town, but did not enjoy it as he felt more at home speaking Sichuana. One of the texts for his sermons was, 'Why will you die?' A question he posed to himself more than his congregation perhaps realised.

He arranged to take with him a native trader, George Flemming, whom Livingstone believed to be an emancipated slave; his duty was to introduce lawful traffic in order to supplant the slave-trade.

His overladen wagon with ten scrawny oxen edged its way out of Cape Town on 8th June 1852. He was too poor to provide better. This expedition was to make him famous and remain one of the most remarkable in the world's history. He was forty years of age and in good health.

He would face many trials and temptations at the end of which he could say, 'I have drunk water swarming with insects, thick with mud, putrid from rhinoceros' urine and buffalo's dung.'[4] He would live for months on basic food the natives provided and learn to overcome diseases as well as distances,

---

[3] D L to Agnes L *ibid*, p 183.
[4] Macnair, p 137.

being driven by his indomitable personality and fearless faith. The tribes acknowledged his strong personality and yielded to him because he used persuasion, not force, to accomplish his God-given goals. Though he would battle against loneliness and depression his resolve to win through would remain unbroken. Words such as 'try again' and 'all will come well in the end' were hallmarks of his character.

Livingstone had made enemies, one of whom was Commander Potgeiter. The Bakwains heard of intentions to molest the missionary and decided to defend him with their blood.[5] This Livingstone discouraged, but they remained adamant in their support for him.

The going was not easy and the missionary reached Griqua Town on 15th August and Kuruman a fortnight later. The most unexpected delay was due to the fact that the enormous weight of the wagon told on one of the wheels and 'down came the elegant Dutch vehicle'. The delay probably saved his life.

Had he not been delayed he would have reached Kolobeng in August. This was when 600 colonists and many natives attacked the mission station.

The Boers, with good reason, suspected Livingstone was supplying arms to Sechele and other independent chiefs on their western border. In 1849 the Transvaal government called for the missionary's release from Kolobeng and the following year ordered Sechele to prevent Europeans from travelling north along the road. When in 1852, by the Sand River Convention, the British renounced all jurisdiction of the north of the Vaal and recognised Transvaal's independence, the farmers decided to crush Sechele. They accused Livingstone of supplying some guns—a charge he never bothered to contradict —thus giving the Dutch further cause for concern.

---

[5] D L to W Thompson undated, though it appears to be late July/early August 1852 in Mssny. Corr., p 209.

On 28th August 1852, 600 whites under Commandant
Scholtz appeared before Durriawe. After attempting media-
tion, the burgers advanced on schedule two days later. In the
vicious bloody battle they lost three white men, a number of
African auxiliaries and took many captives.

Livingstone wrote a detailed letter to his wife:

. . . The Boers gutted our house at Kolobeng; they brought four
wagons down and took away sofa, table, bed, all the crockery,
your desk (I hope it had nothing in it—have you the letters?),
smashed the wooden chairs, took away the iron ones, tore out
the leaves of all the books, and scattered them in front of the
house, smashed the bottles containing medicines, windows, oven-
door, took away the smith-bellows, anvil, all the tools—in fact
everything worth taking: three corn-mills, a bag of coffee for
which I paid six pounds, and lots of coffee, tea, and sugar, which
the gentlemen who went to the north left; took all our cattle and
Paul's and Mebalwe's. They then went up to Limaue, went to
church morning and afternoon, and heard Mebalwe preach! After
the second service they told Sechele that they had come to fight,
because he allowed Englishmen to proceed to the North, though
they had repeatedly ordered him not to do so. He replied that he
was a man of peace, that he could not molest Englishmen, because
they had never done him any harm, and always treated him well.
In the morning they commenced firing on the town with swivels,
and set fire to it. The heat forced some of the women to flee, the
men to huddle together on the small hill in the middle of the town;
the smoke prevented them seeing the Boers, and the cannon killed
many, sixty Bakwains.[6]

This attack incensed Livingstone who complained bitterly
about it, and wrote in the same letter:

'They often expressed a wish to get hold of me. I wait here a
little in order to get information when the path is clear. Kind
Providence detained me from falling into the very thick of it. God

---

[6] D L to Mary L 20/09/1852 in Blaikie, pp 132–134.

will preserve me still. He has work for me, or He would have allowed me to go in just when the Boers were there. We shall remove more easily now that we are lightened of our furniture. They have taken away our sofa. I never had a good rest on it. We had only got it ready when we left. Well, they can't have taken away all the stones. We shall have a seat in spite of them, and that too with a merry heart which doeth good like a medicine . . .[7]

He made a formal representation of his losses, both to the Cape and British authorities, but never received a farthing in compensation.

Livingstone was to many an embarrassment and the term *Kaffir Boetie* (Kaffir-lover) was frequently applied to him, though this Livingstone took as a compliment, for it showed the blacks how committed he was to them.

This attack the doctor also took to mean a measure of judgement upon the tribe, for they had heard the word of God and made the gospel the 'butt of their ridicule. The Lord has seen it. When the bell was rung for school or service the whole of the children of the town were accustomed to run down to the church and commence a noisy game with a long rope just at the door.'[8]

The attack on the mission was to linger on in Livingstone's mind and many years later in 1929 General Smuts in his address at Edinburgh on 21st November said:

I once took the opportunity to discuss the matter with President Kruger, and his explanation of the differences which arose between the Boers and Livingstone was that Gordon Cumming—another of your errant countrymen—had supplied the border tribes with rifles and ammunition in exchange for ivory, and the Boers, finding the natives armed, concluded—erroneously—that Livingstone had done so, and treated him accordingly.[9]

[7] *Ibid.*
[8] P J, pp 90–91.
[9] Macnair, p 141.

This dark deed decided Livingstone's future. He became more determined to beat a path into the interior. He declined the Society's offers for a fellow missionary to accompany him on his rough travels. Had Moffat accepted, however, Livingstone would eagerly have taken him.

Further delay was caused by a sudden shortage of native staff who decided not to travel, fearing for their lives. Finally, however, after much persuasion and prayer, a party was assembled.

In a sombre and sad mood Livingstone surveyed his future and shortly after setting out penned:

> Am I on my way to die in Sebituane's country? Have I seen the last of my wife and children? The breaking up of all my connections with earth, leaving this fair and beautiful world and knowing so little of it? I am only learning the alphabet of it yet; and entering on an untried state of existence . . . Oh! if Jesus speaks one word of peace, that will establish in thy breast an everlasting calm! O Jesus, fill me with Thy love now, and I beseech Thee accept me, and use me a little for Thy glory. I have done nothing for Thee yet, and I would like to do something. O do, do, I beseech Thee, accept me and my service and take Thou all the glory . . .[10]

The company departed from Kuruman on 14th December 1852 and took a westward detour in order to avoid Boer raiders. It was familiar country and much of it beautiful, and prior to reaching the Chobe River, just south of Sinyati, travel had been pleasant and easy. Then the going changed rapidly for the worse. The land was waterlogged and the vegetation rank. The rains, just over, had been unusually heavy and every water-course was like a small river. Some of these contained great holes made by elephant, and into one of these the wagon slid, the pole broke and the wagon nearly upset.

In addition to that disaster which occurred on 1st April,

---

[10] 28th December 1852, P J, pp 97–98.

fever had plagued most of the staff. Only Livingstone and Kibacoe remained well until the latter hurt his leg. It festered and the doctor was called to care for the injured.

Livingstone reminded himself that 'we are not forgotten by God's good providence. Our Redeemer will not forget our work in His service. May He guide so that our efforts result in His glory.'[11]

Despite the rains Livingstone frequently had to go off in search of water himself. This did not worry him providing his health remained, and in an instance of faith he recorded in his journal:

> If God has accepted my service then my life is charmed till my work is done. And though I pass through many dangers unscathed while working the work given me to do ... Death is a glorious event to one going to Jesus ... There is something sublime in passing into the second stage of our immortal lives if washed from our sins. But O to be consigned to ponder over all sins with memories excited, every scene of our sinful lives held up as in a mirror before our eyes, and we looking at them and waiting for the day of Judgement.[12]

He also had much time to reflect on what he considered to be tempting God. He felt it was not the 'encountering of difficulties and dangers in obedience to the promptings of the inward spiritual life ... but the acting without faith, proceeding on our own errands with no previous convictions of duty and no prayer for aid and direction'.[13]

This same day he, in the seclusion of his journal, penned this prayer to the Lord: 'Purify my motives, sanctify all my desires. Guide my feet and direct my steps so that the Great and Glorious Jesus may be glorified.'[14]

---

[11] 27th March 1853, *ibid*, p 106.
[12] 4th April 1853, *ibid*, p 108.
[13] 17th April 1853, *ibid*, p 111.
[14] *Ibid*.

As they progressed, bushmen were employed to help navigate and pursue a course through the Chobe River which had burst its banks. Often Livingstone and a guide would paddle off on the pontoon to look for openings, dodging crocodiles which surreptitiously slid cautiously into the water and hippopotami which were notorious for overturning boats.

Livingstone had shown his remarkable powers of endurance by penetrating reeds so high that it was impossible to see more than a few feet ahead. Progress was achieved by putting a staff against the reeds and pressing against it with all their might, the serrated edges of the reeds cutting and irritating the skin as they persevered.

On one particular day they found themselves on a river, the banks thick with impenetrable reeds, no exit could be found and they had resigned themselves to a long cold night in the dug-out canoe, when suddenly they saw some people. The tribesfolk who were ignorant of boating looked in bewilderment at 'two men coming along the water on a bag'. To them they 'had fallen out of a cloud'. 'All stood gazing in mute astonishment; Livingstone called out to them 'Why do you stand there gazing, come here and help me to lift it out.' Some of them recognised the doctor and laughed with delight at his sudden appearance from the Chobe river.'[15]

Livingstone's determination to persevere astounded even the bushmen. Earlier one of them, discouraged, took out his dice and, after throwing them, said that God had told him to go home. Livingstone asked him to show the command. He threw them again, but the opposite result followed. 'He remained and was useful,'[16] for when lions had chased the oxen off, he recovered them.

The party continued to make their way to Chief Sekeletu, stopping on Sunday—the day of rest—to preach and recuperate.

[15] 29th April 1853, *ibid*, p 122.
[16] M T, p 170.

On that Sunday 15th May 1853, Livingstone preached twice to about sixty attentive people. He was also given presents of corn, nuts and honey by the chief who had eagerly awaited his arrival.

Seven days later, in another village, the evangelist awoke to a beautiful sight of game feeding close to the wagon. Over 100 people turned out to hear the white man, who was aware that a foundation stone of faith had to be laid. 'For the elements of Divine knowledge require to be communicated before an idea can be formed of the Christian system'.[17]

On the same day the doctor decided:

I will place no value on anything I have or may possess, except in relation to the Kingdom of Christ. If anything will advance the interests of that Kingdom, it shall be given away or kept only in reference to whether giving or keeping will most promote the glory of Him to whom I owe all my hopes in time and eternity. May the grace and strength sufficient to enable me to adhere faithfully to this resolution be imparted to me, so that in truth, not in name only, all my interests and those of my children may be identified with His cause.

I will try and remember always to approach God in secret with as much reverence in speech, posture and behaviour as in public. Help me Thou who knowest my frame and pitiest as a Father his children.[18]

The journal was also filled with observations of temperatures, animals, flora, fauna, as well as meticulous sightings which he carried out with the sextant. This was done at the request of the Missionary Society who took a keen interest in their evangelist and explorer.

Finally on Monday 23rd May 1853, Linyanti's whole population of between 6,000 and 7,000 people turned out en masse to see the wagons in motion.

---

[17] Sunday 22nd May 1853, P J, p 134.
[18] *Ibid*, p 135.

Chief Sekeletu, a good-natured nineteen-year-old, expressed joy at seeing Livingstone return. He confided in the missionary and took him aside to explain how he had come to be chief since Sebituane's plan was to place his sister, Ma-mochisane, in the chieftainship. She abhorred her position, which entitled her to take husbands as chiefs did wives, a practice she detested, though not a Christian, and she abdicated in favour of the private life.

The young chief promised Livingstone that 'anything in his town or out of it, if in his power, would freely be given.'[19]

Sekeletu asked many sensible questions about Christianity and its connection with putting away wives.

After church the following day Livingstone explained the nature of a book and the use of letters. The chief feared that learning to read would change his heart and make him put away his wives. Much depended on his decision and Livingstone, knowing this, prayed that 'God would influence his heart to decide aright'.

The people seemed to receive ideas on divine subjects slowly. They would listen, but never conclude that the truths must become embodied in active life. This frustrated Livingstone, but he had learned to look to the sovereign hand of God in such circumstances.

Suddenly, on Monday 30th May 1853, the fever cast itself without mercy at Livingstone. He allowed the local doctors to treat him which they enthusiastically did, placing the doctor's head under a blanket over a steaming pot to which they added herbs. 'After being stewed in their vapour-baths, smoked like a red herring over green twigs,' Livingstone concluded that he could cure the fever more quickly than their method.

His treatment of '3 grains of calomel, 3 of quinine, 10 grs

---

[19] Tuesday 24th May 1853, *ibid*, p 141.

rhubarb, 4 grains of resin of jalap mixed with a little spirit',[20] became known as the famous 'Livingstone pill' or 'Zambesi Rouser' and was his specific for malaria.

He also took to using the thermometer on himself. 'The heat in the axilla over the heart and region of the stomach was in my case 100 degrees; but along the spine and at the nape of the neck 103 degrees.' (Commenting on this, Dr Millar, in the *British Medical Journal* March 1913, considered that Livingstone must have been one of the first to employ a clinical thermometer.)[21]

Once Livingstone had recovered from the worst of the malarial attack he proposed to Sekeletu that the area be investigated for high ground. The chief was not keen on Livingstone leaving him and so hesitated to give his approval, though after several days granted his request providing they would go together.

Leaving Linyanti in the last week of June, Livingstone and Sekeletu went with 160 attendants to explore the Barotse country, whose chief town, Naliele, lay about 300 miles to the north of Linyanti.

Taking Seshele on the way, the party reached Naliele in a little over three weeks, but without finding or hearing of any district in which settlers could be reasonably sure of immunity from the dreaded disease, malaria, as well as remain accessible to the tribes among whom they would work.

Livingstone had grown to appreciate the magnitude of the task before him and, in a prophetic statement, he wrote in his journal:

Discoveries and inventions are cumulative. Another century must present a totally different aspect from the present. And when we view the state of the world and its advancing energies in the light afforded by childlike or call it childish faith, we see the earth

[20] *Ibid*, p 149.
[21] Gelfand, p 9.

filling with the knowledge of the glory of the Lord, aye all nations seeing His glory and bowing before Him whose right it is to reign. Our work and its fruits are cumulative. We work towards another state of things. Future missionaries will be rewarded by conversions for every sermon. We are their pioneers and helpers. Let them not forget the watchmen of the night, we who worked when all was gloom and no evidence of success in the way of conversion cheered our path. They will doubtless have more light than we, but we served our Master earnestly and proclaimed the same gospel as they will do.[22]

Those words show an incredible, almost uncanny, foresight into the future, for such is happening in Africa today.

On their journey up the river they came upon Mpepe, who was the rival candidate for the chieftainship. He favoured the slave-traders with Sekeletu's cattle and formed a plan to be head of the Makololo. The basis of his plan was to kill Sekeletu the next time they met.

Livingstone and the chief were unaware of this plot and in the afternoon's confusion avoided the confrontation on the road. However, the rivals had an *indaba* (meeting) in a hut and Mpepe intended to murder him there, except that the missionary foiled his plan. They were inside the hut and Livingstone, feeling tired, asked Sekeletu where he should sleep, to which the chief replied, 'Come, I will show you.' As they rose together the explorer unconsciously shielded the chief's body from the assassin's blow.

Sekeletu became aware of the plot and immediately sent some persons to seize his would-be assailant and, under cover of darkness, had him speared.

This created further unrest as the chief's faithful followers fled to the Barotse and, it being inadvisable for them to go there during the commotion, the chief and the doctor returned to Linyanti.

---

[22] Sunday 19th June 1853, P J, p 168.

A short while later they stopped at another village where Sekeletu, after a confrontation with Mpepe's father and the head man of the place, ordered they be executed. Suddenly in front of Livingstone's shocked eyes the men were seized and axed to death. Their bodies were taken by canoes into the middle of the river and fed to the crocodiles.

The executions happened too quickly for Livingstone to intervene and the shocked man showed his anguish in expostulations to the chief and others; and posed the question in his journal: 'Who will stop the stream of human blood which has flowed for ages in these dark places if we with our great instrument the Gospel do not?'[23]

Livingstone made contact with Senor Porto, a Portuguese explorer/slave-trader, and when they met on 12th August 1853, Livingstone saw the large company of slaves with him, a sight which horrified and haunted him. The strong tribes captured weaker villagers in order to sell them as slaves to Arabs. Also, the Islamic beliefs of the Arabs were being infiltrated to the tribes with whom they had dealings.

The clink of the chains binding the poor victims had a harrowing effect on Livingstone. Skinny children perishing of hunger caught his eye and haunted his heart as defenceless they were dragged along in despair.

On the following Sunday the missionary preached to a very large audience, most of whom had never heard the gospel before. They were remarkably attentive, though they lapsed into their heathenism straight afterwards. What disturbed the doctor was that they would cover themselves and everybody else with greasy animal fat and enjoy smoking wild hemp or *Cannabis sativa* (marijuana).

Nevertheless, the doctor remained patient, persevered and continued looking to Christ.

His letters to his children revealed much of his zeal for

---

[23] *Ibid*, p 201.

138   DAVID LIVINGSTONE

God. In one he clearly outlined the gospel message of salvation:

> If your sins and your naughtiness are not forgiven, blotted out by Jesus, then you will go away into Hell when you die, like the rich man of whom we read in the Bible. Mamma will read it to you. But if we love and pray to Jesus with our hearts, then when we die He will take us to His home. He takes those to His home whose sins are forgiven, and He came down to this world to die for us. Why should He die for us? We have sinned, and we ought to be punished; but He came down and stood in our place, and our punishment was that by which He died, our sins were all laid on Him. Now every one who asks of him receives pardon, forgiveness of sins, because Jesus suffered the punishment already. O how much we ought to love and thank such a kind Saviour as Jesus has made Himself for us. I have separated myself from you all, my dear children, and from Mamma whom I love very much too, in order to please Jesus and tell sinners who never heard of Him about His love.
>
> Kiss Mamma and Zouga for me, and each other too. Pray for me also. I pray for you all every day.[24]

But where was Livingstone to live? The country was fertile enough, rich in food-producing plants and animals, but the heavy rains and floods were a serious handicap in establishing a settlement for the Livingstone family, whom he hoped would soon join him.

This preliminary exploration decided Livingstone to pursue forthwith his intention of seeking a means of communication, if possible, with the west coast. His desire to develop a link between the interior and the coast has been seen by many as that of an enthusiastic explorer.

There was something of the explorer in him certainly, but it was secondary to his over-riding need 'to do the will of the Father'. In September 1853 Livingstone turned down a chance

---

[24] D L to Robert, Agnes and Thomas Livingstone in Fam. Lett. II, pp 191–192.

to visit the great Mosioatunya region where the magnificent waterfalls were, because he felt it was not his duty to travel there as the 'vicinity of Mosilikatse rendered it impossible for Makololo or any other tribe to reside there'.[25] Though Livingstone would be safe from the Mosilikatse because of the connection between the great tribe and Livingstone's father-in-law, there was still friction between the tribes, hence Livingstone's hesitation.

Again he preached and noted in his diary:

> A quiet audience today. The seed being sown, the least of all seeds now, but it will grow a mighty tree. It is as if it were a small stone cut out of a mountain, but it will fill the whole earth. He that believeth shall not make haste. Surely if God can bear with hardened impenitent sinners for 30, 40 or 50 years, waiting to be gracious, we may take it for granted that His is the best way. He could destroy His enemies, but He waits to be gracious. To become irritated with their stubbornness and hardness of heart is ungodlike.[26]

The Muslims 'professed the greatest detestation of the Portuguese "because they eat pigs", and disliked the English, "because they thrash them for selling slaves"'. Livingstone ventured to voice his views in defence of the victims, but to no avail.

In a letter to the Missionary Society he expressed his shock and concern over slavery. He told Tidman that he thought of going westward in the company of Antonio da Silva Porto, a slave merchant, but the sight of gangs of poor wretches in chains at the stockade influenced his decision to proceed alone, lest he, by associating with da Silva Porto, be accused of giving his consent to the slave-trade. He wrote: 'I have not, I am sorry to confess, discovered a healthy locality. The whole of the country of Sebituane is unhealthy . . . I am at a loss what

---

[25] D L to A Tidman 24/09/1853 in Mssny. Corr., p 253.
[26] 25 September 1853, P J, p 235.

to do, but will not give up the case as hopeless. Shame upon us, if we are to be outdone by slave traders'.[27]

Despite the difficulties he persevered, the fever taking a toll. His comment was, 'We must brave the fever. It is God not the Devil, that rules our destiny'.

The now rather skinny Scot also battled with the discouragement brought about by preaching to an unrepentant, heathen crowd. On 13th October he wrote in his journal:

Missionaries ought to cultivate a taste for the beautiful. We are necessarily compelled to contemplate much moral impurity and degradation. We are so often doomed to disappointment, we are apt to become either callous or melancholy. Or if preserved from these, the constant strain on the sensibilities is likely to injure the bodily health. On this account it seems necessary to cultivate that faculty for the gratification of which God has made such universal provision. See the green earth and blue sky, the lofty mountain and verdant valley, the glorious orbs of day and night and the starry canopy with all their celestial splendour, the graceful flowers so chaste in form and perfect in colouring. The various forms of animated life present, to him whose heart is at peace with God through the blood of His Son, an indescribable charm. He sees in the calm beauties of nature such abundant provision for the welfare of humanity and animated existence, there appears on the quiet repose of earth's scenery the benign smile of a father's love. The sciences exhibit such wonderful intelligence and design in all their various ramifications, some time ought to be devoted to them before engaging in missionary work. The heart may often be cheered by observing the operation of an ever present intelligence, and we may feel that we are leaning on his bosom while living in a world clothed in beauty and robed with the glorious perfections of its maker and preserver. We must feel that there is a Governor among the nations who will bring all His plans with respect to our human family to a glorious consummation. He who stays his mind on his ever-present, ever-energetic God will not

[27] D L to A Tidman 24/09/1853 in Mssny. Corr., p 250.

fret himself because of evil doers. He that believeth shall not make haste.[28]

In a letter to his father and other relations the Christian wrote:

> The conversion of a few, however valuable their souls may be, cannot be put in the scale against the knowledge of the truth spread over the whole country. In this I do and will exult. As in India, we are doomed to perpetual disappointment, but the knowledge of Christ spreads over the masses. We are like voices crying in the wilderness. We prepare the way for a glorious future in which missionaries telling the same tale of love will convert by every sermon.
>
> I am trying now to establish the Lord's Kingdom in a region wider by far than Scotland. Fever seems to forbid, but I shall work for the glory of Christ's Kingdom, fever or no fever.[29]

In early November, George Flemming and the driver bade the doctor farewell. They returned to Kuruman and the Cape, whereas Livingstone planned to find a path through the interior to Loanda on the west coast of Africa. The prayer in his journal on the 8th was: 'May God in mercy permit me to do something for the cause of Christ in these dark places of the earth. May He accept my children for His service and sanctify them for it. My blessing on my wife. May God comfort her.'[30]

Livingstone was prepared to die for what he knew to be right. He left his diary with Sekeletu, together with his wagon, oxen and a few meagre belongings.

Mentally, the missionary was sound, but malaria had already weakened him. Physically he was in no condition to commence this critical course.

---

[28] Thursday 13th October 1853, P J, p 244.
[29] D L to his parents and daughters 30/09/1853 in Fam. Lett. II, pp 227–8.
[30] P J, p 295.

8

From Linyanti to Loanda

Mary Livingstone and the youngsters braved the bitter chill of Blantyre, Scotland. The weather was in sharp contrast to the Kalahari. She stayed with her husband's parents, who had moved to a tiny house in Hamilton. It was not easy for Mary to live with the rather austere Mr Livingstone, not to mention the children who, for the first time in their lives, experienced cramped living conditions. Sadly his meddling in the affairs of Mary and the children caused them to leave after six months.

From Hamilton they lived a wretched nomadic existence, moving from Hamilton to Hackney, then to Manchester and Kendal. Finally they spent some months at Epsom. Sometimes they stayed in rented rooms, or with friends Mary's father had made during his last visit to England between 1839 and 1843.

It was not easy, though she was supported by the Society, and Mary longed for her husband to return. In his absence, with the pressures that confronted her like the strange style of living in a new country, she took to drinking.

Two years passed with hardly any letters. Her loneliness became the harder to bear, for she did not have a vision and her family and friends were far from her.

David, who took problems in his stride, was oblivious to Mary's sufferings and those of the children. The couple had agreed in support of his work to be parted for two years, but time stretched and the delay doubled.

In retrospect, it is easy to give advice and criticism, in particular to David whose vision to bring Christ to the heathen adversely affected their marriage.

Meanwhile, across the miles, the missionary planned to open up a route from the interior to the coast. In a letter to his father and family at Hamilton he wrote: 'So very sure am I that I am in the path which God's providence has pointed out, as that by which Christ's Kingdom is to be promoted, that if the Society should object, I would consider it my duty to withdraw from it'.[1]

His mind was set: an opening must be made for commerce and Christianity to flow freely into the interior. Sekeletu was eager to share in the adventure, but the elders of the tribe objected. One difficulty was that Livingstone was in bad health, subject to fits of giddiness, and the natives feared that if he died on the way they would be blamed for allowing him to go among unknown enemies.

To meet this objection and absolve the tribe from possible blame, Livingstone left his diary and a written explanation with the chief.

Twenty-seven porters were lent to him free of charge. His equipment, due to the meagreness of his funds, was totally inadequate for a journey so arduous. Three muskets for his carriers, a rifle and a double-barrelled smooth bore gun for himself, was all they had. His men carried their spears, but to show their purpose was peaceful, shields were left behind. Since the expedition would depend for food on what could be shot, the ammunition was carefully packed and divided into small bundles to guard against any possible large loss. A small amount of biscuits, tea, coffee and sugar were the only provisions. Packed in a roughly square tin canister were spare shirts, trousers and shoes to be used when they reached civilised life. He also carried a 'magic lantern' with biblical

---

[1] D L to Neil L 30/09/1853 in Blaikie, p 150.

scenes painted on glass slides to assist him preach and a few simple instruments for geographical observations. The only books that went with him were an almanac, some nautical tables and his indispensable Bible. All he had for sleeping was a small tent just sufficient for one person, a sheepskin and a horse blanket.

Medical supplies were also taken, but one of the servants who returned to Kuruman had stolen a large amount of medical stores and ammunition. Livingstone did not notice the theft till after they had gone. He wrote in his journal: 'This loss cripples me sadly, and I feel the loss of the medicines severely, for having been seized by a quotidian intermittent of great severity I have not the medicines which in combination have always proved effectual in cutting it short'.[2]

This had a major effect on the missionary who, in continual ill health, descended into fits of depression. None the less, in commencing the journey he was optimistic. He added stoically, 'I had always found that the art of successful travel consists in taking as few impedimenta as possible since much luggage excited the cupidity of the tribes'.[3] This comment was true—to a certain extent—but the supplies were dangerously insufficient.

When one looks at later explorers, such as Stanley, the necessity for huge teams carrying many stores is seen, for he rarely travelled with fewer than 200 porters. Poverty alone can explain the risk Livingstone took. Undoubtably had he been more comfortably furnished he would not have suffered so lamentably. But a man of Livingstone's character, even though he counted the cost, would not have cancelled the campaign, but rather run the risk of exercising his faith in Christ.

The explorer wrote a letter to Tidman prior to his journey telling him:

[2] A J, p 4.
[3] Macnair, p 155.

I am again through God's mercy and kindness quite recovered from the effects of that disease. I think I am getting rid of intermittent fever too, and, if spared, will impart some knowledge of Christ to many who never before heard His blessed name. There are many and very large tribes in the direction in which we go. All are sitting in darkness and the shadow of death. I hope God will in mercy permit me to establish the gospel somewhere in this region, and that I may live to see the double influence of the spirit of commerce and Christianity employed to stay the bitter fountain of African misery.[4]

This fountain was of course the sickening slave-trade. The barbaric nature of Africans selling fellow Africans to Arabs and other nationalities was a scourge he would encounter again. The slave-traders criss-crossed the continent in search of new specimens. In late August Livingstone met two Arabs who had made an epic journey from the island of Zanzibar, from there on to Angola, and then recrossed the continent to Mocambique (today it is known as Mozambique). A formidable journey, yet they marched on oppressing any opposition. They were neither interested in the welfare of the people nor in opening up the interior for commerce.

Livingstone took detailed descriptions and diligently documented longitudes and latitudes incorporating the rivers, lakes and landmasses. His skill also lay in settling the suspicious hearts of the chiefs he encountered on his travels. As H M Stanley noted long afterwards 'mildness of speech was the great secret which had carried him successfully through'.[5]

This solitary Scot was to show himself to be a prodigy of patience in dealing with savage souls; though, as he was only human, fever often brought on frustration which got the better of him. He strove to become a man of fearless faith and he

---

[4] D L to A Tidman 8/11/1853 in Mssny. Corr., p 257.
[5] Ransford, p 85.

had always believed that 'if we serve God at all, it ought to be done in a manly way'.[6]

On 11th November 1853, at the age of forty, Livingstone left Linyanti and on the 19th he and his men embarked on borrowed dug-out boats on the Zambesi at Sesheke, and the chief, being mindful of their needs, transmitted messages to all the headmen en route to furnish them with supplies. This many did according to their ability, supplying cattle, beads, fat and other presents. Two pairs of elephant tusks were also given to test the market in Loanda and bring back goods for the chief.

The expedition rose before five in the morning and as the dawn broke, the sun drank up the dew, while coffee was made for the whole party. The servants then loaded the canoes while the principal men enjoyed their coffee, before stepping into the canoes. The men paddled vigorously, occasionally scolding each other loudly. At about eleven they would land, eat any meat left over from the previous night, or eat a biscuit and some honey and drink water. The heat was oppressive and Livingstone endured it the best he could croached under an umbrella. Sometimes they reached a sleeping place two hours before sunset. Coffee and a biscuit or a piece of coarse bread made from corn represented the main meal of the day, unless they were fortunate enough to make a kill. Livingstone suffered so much from the fever that he was unable to sight his weapon.

He took pleasure in making detailed notes about birds, plants, flowers and fish. One variety of the latter was 'a striped fellow having the most formidable row of teeth outside his lips [which] sometimes leaps into the canoe'.[7] This was none other than the tremendous tiger fish.

The magnificent river impressed Livingstone. Often more

---

[6] Robertson, p 88.

[7] A J, p 6.

than a mile broad and adorned with many islands which, like the banks, housed thick vegetation. He wrote: 'The beauty of the scenery of some of the islands is greatly increased by the date-palm, with its gracefully curved fronds and refreshing light green colour . . . the lofty palmyra towering far above'.[8]

Sand banks often slowed their travel, as did the occasional rapid. They kept to the sides of the river in order to avoid possible contact with hippo who favoured the middle and were notorious for crushing canoes, much to the glee of the crocodiles who waited, with cold appraisal, for their next meal.

Throughout the latter part of December the doctor was ill with fever, but he forced himself to continue travelling. The narrow, wooden, dug-out canoe became a nightmare for the man whose heart raced uncomfortably and who vomited regularly. Further shivering or sweating and painful diarrhoea made the journey very demanding and debilitating.

He longed for Sundays—days of rest. One journal entry read: 'Sunday 19th—sick all Sunday, and unable to move. Several of the people were ill too, so that I could do nothing but roll from side [to side] in my miserable little tent, in which, with all the shade we could give it, the thermometer stood upwards of 90 degrees'.[9]

By the end of the first week of January 1854, Livingstone realised it would not be long before they would have to leave the canoes and go on foot. Several tribes through whose territories they travelled had many women under-chiefs. It was at the village of one such lady of the Balonda tribe that Livingstone was thwarted. This formidable female, Chief Nyamoana, decided to detain the doctor longer than his intention. She refused him permission to travel further by canoe, her reason being that if a bad cataract did not stop

---

[8] M T, p 212.
[9] Sunday 19th February 1854, A J, p 88.

him the extremely aggressive tribe called the Balobale certainly would. Livingstone remained unperturbed, for he knew she wanted to visit her brother, Shinte, the Paramount Chief of Balonda. Nyamoana was backed by her daughter Manenko, who observing Livingstone's firmness, decided to work on his guides and servants, and soon had them thoroughly scared of being butchered. Finally, Manenko refused permission for the canoes to be loaded. Livingstone, seeing no need to pursue his plan, submitted—to the relief of his men. Manenko was amused by his irritation and, placing a hand on his shoulder, 'put on a motherly look saying, "Now my little man, just do as the rest have done."'.[10]

The irony of having to obey the wishes of a young woman smeared with fat and red ochre and covered by a mass of ornaments and charms, did not escape him. The missionary described her condition as one of 'frightful nudity' and deplored the thin strip of leather only a few inches across which attempted to hide her genitals.

Finally on 11th January the party set off to Shinte's town, accompanied by a drummer who would beat his drum so as to warn people that a person of importance was coming. Wrote Livingstone, 'Manenko was accompanied by her husband and her drummer; the latter continued to thump most vigorously, until a heavy drizzling mist set in and compelled him to desist'.[11] Manenko marched on at a formidable pace. Few of the men could keep up with her, particularly Livingstone who had succumbed to another attack of fever. The rain fell in torrents and the doctor had to resort to travelling on ox-back, the indomitable Manenko walking by his side, keeping up a lively conversation.

Progress was slow as they plodded through the dense jungle while the men worked with axes to cut through the

[10] M T, p 279.
[11] *Ibid*, pp 281–2.

thickly-entwined creepers and undergrowth. The light was dim and the damp gloominess of this dark green world did nothing for the morale of Livingstone's men. He had severely scolded them, for he had no knowledge of their dreams telling them to go back.

All suffered from want on this journey and a meagre diet of manioc roots or tapioca did not help. In the forests there were man-made beehives for attracting the bees. They were full of honey, yet the missionary would not allow them to be tampered with.

On 15th January they arrived outside Shinte's town in the pouring rain and had to wait while the normal procedure of exchanging messages took place before entering the town. This took till noon the following day.

The village stood in a pleasant green valley with a limpid brook running through it. The town was embowered with trees and the mud huts were well built, with square walls—the first Livingstone had seen. The streets were straight and each hut had its patch of ground, in which tobacco, sugar cane and bananas were carefully cultivated in a small fenced enclosure of upright poles.

The next morning Livingstone was up and ready to meet Shinte by eight o'clock. He was informed that Shinte had been employed during the night in passing from the court of one wife to another till the morning dawned. 'Solomon,' he concluded, 'must often [have] been in a similar predicament with his outrageous female establishment'.[12]

Shinte was the first substantial ruler Livingstone had come across since leaving Sekeletu. A thousand men were present at the welcoming ceremony. Behind Shinte (who was adorned with a checked jacket, a scarlet kilt and many beads) were a number of musicians, several Mambari and two Portuguese

---

[12] A J, pp 51–52.

half-castes. Shinte stared at Livingstone, for he was the first white man he had ever seen.

Livingstone stated his reason for visiting—that of commerce and Christianity. He had to speak through an interpreter and much was lost. However, the outcome was favourable.

At a later meeting Shinte sent Livingstone a small girl. When he refused, a larger one was fetched on the understanding that size, not morality, was the problem. Again she was politely returned. Later, under cover of darkness, Shinte came to Livingstone's tent.

> Then, closing the tent, so that none of his own people might see the extravagance of which he was about to be guilty, he drew out from his clothing a string of beads and the end of a conical shell, which is considered, in regions far from the sea, of as great value as the Lord Mayor's badge is in London.

He hung it around Livingstone's neck and said, 'There, now you have a proof of my friendship'.[13]

Livingstone was touched by his generosity, but was still depressed to note the barbaric sale of people to the Mambari or Portuguese.

The fever tore at his health and morale, and often rendered him unfit to preach. Under such stress Livingstone searched his heart and reassured himself in his journal:

> This age presents one great fact in the Providence of God. Missions are sent forth to all quarters of the world; missions not of one section of the church but of all sections, and from nearly all Christian nations. It seems very unfair to judge the success of these by the number of conversions which have followed. These are rather proofs of the missions being of the right sort ... The fact which ought to stimulate us above all others is, not that we have contributed to the conversion of a few souls, however valuable these may be, but that we are diffusing a knowledge of Christianity throughout the world ... future missionaries will see

---

[13] M T, p 301.

conversions follow every sermon. We prepare the way for them. May they not forget the pioneers who worked in the thick gloom, with few cheering rays to cheer except such as flow from faith in God's promises. We work for a glorious future which we are not destined to see, the golden age which has not been but will yet be. We are only morning stars shining in the dark, but the glorious morn will break—the good time coming yet.

The present mission stations will all be broken up . . . our duty is onward, onward, proclaiming God's Word whether men will hear or whether they will forbear. A few conversions shew whether God's Spirit is in a mission or not. No mission which has His approbation is entirely unsuccessful. His purposes have been fulfilled if we have been faithful . . . And many missions which He has sent in the olden time seem bad failures. Noah's preaching was a failure. Isaiah thought his so too. His fellow priests and prophets were such a set of tippling bardies, how could the cause prosper? These drunken billies, every place smelling like the forecastle of a passenger steamer the first rough night by the vomiting of these greedy dogs. Poor Jeremiah sitting weeping salt tears over his people, everybody cursing the honest man, and he ill pleased with his mother for having borne him among such a set of ne'er-do-wells as could one day thrust him into a filthy muddy dungeon and the next ask him to prophesy to them, though they fully intended to do the opposite of what he should say. And Ezekiel's stiff-necked rebellious crew were no better. Paul said, 'All seek their own, not the things of Jesus Christ' and he knew that after his departure grievous wolves would spring up, not sparing the flock.

Yet the cause of God is still carried on and on to more enlightened developments of His will and character, and the dominion is being given by the power of commerce and population unto the people of the saints of the Most High. And this is an everlasting Kingdom, a little stone cut out of a mountain without hands which shall cover the whole earth. For this time we work. May God accept our humble imperfect service.[14]

---

[14] A J, pp 57–59.

Livingstone tried to preach with the aid of the slide lantern. The result was hardly encouraging. One picture was of Abraham about to slaughter Isaac. 'The Balonda men remarked that the picture was much more like a god than the things of wood or clay they worshipped.' Livingstone explained that this man was the first of a race to whom God had given the Bible.

> The ladies listened with silent awe; but when I moved the slide, the uplifted dagger moving towards them, they thought it was to be sheathed in their bodies instead of Isaac's. 'Mother! mother!' all shouted at once, and off they rushed helter-skelter, tumbling pell-mell over each other, and over the little idol-huts and tobacco-bushes.[15]

They could not get one of them back again.

The task of explaining that the lantern itself was not supernatural proved too difficult. The Balonda had already been told by the Mambari that English cloth, as did white men, came out of the sea. These stories, together with Livingstone's matches, hairbrush and lantern, made him appear as a magician— an impression that his mention of the Son of God coming down to earth and dying for their sins did not dispel.

Furthermore, the idea that 'words' could be contained in writing was even more baffling. When the explorer wrote up his journal, crowds often collected around him to watch the strange process.

Ten days passed before the missionary and his party were able to take to the road again, much time having been wasted negotiating for guides and provisions. One further hindrance was the fermented mead the people consumed, which left them stupefied as they sprawled out in stertorous slumber at all hours of the day.

---

[15] M T, p 298.

The rains continued incessantly, causing Livingstone chronic discomfort; rusting everything metallic, covering his clothes with mildew and rotting his canvas tent. 'Never did I endure such drenching,' he wrote to Thompson. 'If we could march I got on very well, I don't care much for fatigue, but when compelled to stand still by pouring rains, then fever laid hold with his strong fangs on my inner man, and lying in a little gypsy tent with everything damp or wet was sore against the grain'.[16]

They followed the course of the Leeba River until clear of Shinte's country and entered the flat Lobale region where they proceeded to the village of Chief Katema, near the shores of Lake Dilolo.

Eight bearers and guides accompanied him under Chief Shinte's orders. They were also given provisions, but a constant diet of manioc porridge was not exactly nutritious. A bond developed between Livingstone and his loyal followers. He was touched by their faithful attention to his needs.

At night the plan was to pitch the little tent with the main fire lit four to five feet in front of it. Each individual knew the space he had to occupy in relation to the door of the tent and fire. Livingstone's space for sitting and eating was directly in front of the door. One man took his station to Livingstone's right and another to his left. These were the eating, sleeping and cooking places so long as the journey lasted.[17]

At the first broad stream they came to his men, not knowing he could swim, expressed their fears on his account and 'pointing to an ox they cautioned "Now hold on fast by the tail, don't let go"'. Livingstone intended to follow the injunction, but tail and all went in so deep he thought it better to strike out alone for the bank. Just as he reached it he was

---

[16] D L to W Thompson 14/05/1854 in Mssny. Corr., pp 260–261.
[17] A J, p 17.

encouraged to see a universal rush had been made for his rescue. 'Their clothes were all floating down the stream, and two of them reached him breathless with their exertion'.[18]

Katema gave the party a friendly welcome and fed them well. His laughter warmed Livingstone's heart, as did his willingness to open up a trade route to the coast, though he remained bored when Livingstone preached. None the less, they parted good friends, Livingstone laden with goods.

Less agreeable was the fact that they needed guides to allay the suspicions of other tribes. These guides took them to villages they did not want to visit and the party was often detained. From then on food was no longer given as gifts, but had to be paid for. Since Livingstone's party had little to exchange they often went hungry. The natives frequently asked for *hongo* (payment) for the right to pass through their territory. The demand was usually for a tusk, gun, ox or, ultimately, a slave. The slave-trade had undermined usual standards of honesty and fair play, and fines were often extorted by vile methods. On one occasion a knife was planted on one of his men and cloth demanded as recompense. Soon all his beads and cloth had gone, and Livingstone was reduced to parting with his shirts.

Gradually the forests thinned out, but the rains had flooded the valleys they crossed, and morale waned as the rain and incessant drenching continued. Often Livingstone encountered idols, though he noticed that 'they do not love them as Christians love Christ. They fear them, and betake themselves to them only when in perplexity or danger'.[19]

They finally came upon the Chiboque people who filed their teeth into points and many had straws thrust through the cartilage of their noses. They were as hostile as they looked and were firmly entrenched in the slave-trade.

---

[18] D L to W Thompson 14/05/1854 in Mssny. Corr., p 261.
[19] A J, p 48.

Another time Njambi, a Chiboque chief, had his men surround Livingstone's encampment. Their object was evidently to plunder them of everything. The missionary's men seized their spears while the opposition brandished their swords, spears and guns. Livingstone, in spite of his weakness and fever, responded with the same courage he so often showed. He calmly seated himself, placed his double-barrelled gun across his knees, and invited the chief to be seated also.

The Chiboque claimed that one of the explorer's entourage had spat at them. After this incident was explained to be an accident, the usual demands for a man or ox were made. Livingstone would rather have died than part with one of his men. Finally a demand was made for a gun and still the Scot refused. His followers, whose nerves were starting to crack, begged him to give some shirts and they would surrender their beads. This he did offer, but to no avail; any attempt at a settlement made the greedy tribe demand more. Tension among the tribes took its hold, a shout was raised by the armed party, and a rush made at Livingstone with a brandishing of arms. One young man made a charge at his head from behind, but Livingstone quickly brought round the muzzle of his gun to the attacker's mouth and he retreated.[20]

In the excitement, some of Livingstone's men crept round behind the chief and his headmen and were able to threaten them with their spears. In this more advantageous position Livingstone asked again why they wanted to shed blood when all he wanted was to pass peacefully on his way. He was constantly conscious that if the Chiboque used their guns he would be the first target. 'But,' as he said later, 'I was careful not to appear flurried and, having four barrels ready for instant action, looked quietly at the savage scene around.'[21]

Finally both parties agreed to live longer and an ox was

[20] M T, pp 339–342.
[21] Ibid, p 342.

given as a gift if the Chiboque would provide anything asked for. The tribe did not keep to their word but enjoyed the ox. No lives being lost, Livingstone continued his journey.

Livingstone became frustrated with the fierce fever that ravaged him as well as useless guides who kept demanding goods before continuing. The explorer would rather have travelled by compass and sextant, but his followers were adamant that guides were necessary.

Superstition ranked high among the natives and the shrewd Scot turned it to his advantage on one occasion. Tired of losing their good oxen to mean chiefs he discovered that 'they would not take some which had their tails docked; they thought that this was medicine in them. When I learned this "Hallo, off with the tails of the whole of them"'.[22]

During tense scenes Livingstone felt no fever, but when they were over the energy exerted took its toll. Some days after the narrow escape a mutinous spirit began to emerge in some of his followers, who demanded to be treated on the same level as Livingstone's head men. The missionary listened to their grievances and pressed the party onwards so that an ox could be slaughtered at a village. The next morning the lead mutineer and his party engaged in a noisy rubbing of a goat's skin he had purchased. Despite the sick doctor's requests for him to desist he rebelliously continued threatening the leader's authority. Livingstone put his head out of the tent and asked again, only to receive an impudent laugh. Suddenly he seized a double-barrelled pistol and darting forth put them to flight. Livingstone informed them that he would not kill outright, but he who would not obey would have a limb broken on the spot.

Order was swiftly restored. However, more trials would test the tenacity of the travel-weary team. Another chief challenged Livingstone with extortionate requests. A settlement was reached; Livingstone gave him a shawl and two

---

[22] D L to Robert Moffat 19/05/1854 in Fam. Lett. II, p 244.

bunches of beads for some yams, a goat, fowl and meat. The chief seemed pleased. The following day, however, the cunning chief renewed his demands. This, in Livingstone's weakened state, was a day of torture. Weary, Livingstone wrote:

> After talking nearly the whole day we gave the old chief an ox, but he would not take it but another. I was grieved exceedingly to find that our people had become quite disheartened, and all resolved to return home. All I can say has no effect. I can only look up to God to influence their minds that the enterprise fail not, now that we have reached the very threshold of the Portuguese settlements. I am greatly distressed at this change, for what else can be done for this miserable land I do not see. It is shut. O Almighty God, help. Help, and leave not this wretched people to the slave-dealer and Satan. The people have done well hitherto. I see God's good influence in it. Hope He has left only for a little season. No land needs the Gospel more than this miserable portion. I hope I am not to be left to fail in introducing it'.[23]

Sickness and depression heavily taxed the weary Christian. Obstinate fever had reduced him to a skeleton, while the pelvic bones rubbing on his hard bed 'cause sores on the parts lain on, and those chafed by the wet pad in riding are one scab from abrasion'.[24]

Once, when he was riding in the rain, his ox went off at a plunging gallop, the bridle broke and Livingstone came down heavily on the crown of his head. The ox then gave him a kick on the thigh, 'shewing plainly there is no love lost' between them.

Strength and sinew strained, they continued slowly, still hundreds of miles from the sea. All they needed to do was take up the gauntlet, cross the Quango River and they would be in friendly Portuguese territory.

On 30th March 1854, so weak from fever and hunger that

---

[23] Tuesday 23rd March 1854, A J, p 114.
[24] *ibid*,p 112

his men had to lead him to prevent his falling, Livingstone looked down from the high land upon the wide valley through which the broad Quango wound its way, surrounded by lush, green, dark, fertile forest to the north west. The sight was invigorating and it stirred his heart. Yet the coast was nowhere to be seen.

They continued, only to encounter a major problem on the banks of the Quango. On 4th April, the chief of the Bashinje refused permission for them to cross in his canoes unless a man, an ox or a gun was given, adding that otherwise they must turn back.

The chief finally fancied Livingstone's blanket. The weary wanderer had parted with all of his clothes, save those he stood up in, his razors, spoons, beads and cloth. To give this up meant that the sick man would suffer even more during the damp darkness of the night; the tent being rotten through and only fit for scrap. It was either the blanket or a man. Livingstone would not give a man away as a slave; he would rather risk his health.

Livingstone declined to give up his blanket until they were all on the other bank. This was not accepted. Tension mounted and the atmosphere became almost tangible as the explorer tried to regroup his men into a position of safety.

How much more pressure could Livingstone take? He had committed his way to God and to him he looked for strength, security and a safe passage for his men.

His prayers were answered, for suddenly a Portuguese patrol in search of beeswax made its appearance and gave them protection. The timing was nothing short of miraculous. Livingstone and his men hurried on, shots rang out above their heads as the angry chief protested. No one was injured. The young Portuguese Sergeant of Militia, Cypriano di Abreu, provided them with food for the four or five days it took to reach Cassange, a trading station. There Livingstone arrived in a pitiful state, his clothing just rags and his body a bag of bones. The commandant and officials were amazed at seeing the skinny Scot and his faithful followers. After hearing his story, Captain Neves not only entertained him in his own house and clothed him from head to foot, but also freely furnished food for his famished followers. A grateful Livingstone wrote in his journal: 'I was naked and he clothed me. May he find mercy of the Lord in that day.'

The same welcome and ungrudging assistance was given by the Portuguese all the way down the coast—surprisingly as Livingstone was a British subject and it was Britain who had stopped the slave-trade through a military blocade. The slave-trade had been a major source of income to the Portuguese in the area and a severe slump followed.

Strengthened by good food and care Livingstone and his team made steady progress from Cassange, and by the end of the first week of May they had travelled another 200 miles to Ambaca, the next Portuguese settlement of any size.

Livingstone preached to them and set about learning the language, which he was later to master, but he did not stay long for he was eager to complete the final 150 miles and reach Loanda. Letters would surely be awaiting his arrival.

Shortly before leaving he had a relapse of fever and his followers became increasingly apprehensive that he would sell them as slaves and return to Scotland. He managed to reassure them and they persevered, though twenty miles outside Loanda Livingstone's health reached its lowest ebb. He did not have enough strength to stay more than ten minutes on the ox at a time. He was also suffering from chronic dysentery. For twenty days Livingstone was too sick even to write in his journal. His sturdy servants carried the desperate and dying man the last few miles into Loanda, where they arrived on 1st May 1854.

In Loanda he was taken in by Mr Edward Gabriel, who was Her Majesty's Commissioner for the Suppression of the Slave-Trade in Loanda. After a good meal and wash he was put to bed. 'Never shall I forget,' said he, 'the luxuriant pleasure I enjoyed in feeling myself again on a good English couch after six months sleeping on the ground.' Mr Gabriel rejoiced that Livingstone fell soundly asleep almost immediately.

Who would have thought that the resilient missionary would rest, recuperate and then attempt to return to the Makololo, retracing the rugged route which had so nearly ruined him?

9

The Weary Wanderer Treks from Coast to Coast

The sea air and comfortable clean conditions aided Livingstone's slow convalescence, though for a while he lay on the brink of death. It was again by the hand of God that two British warships, engaged in suppressing the slave-trade, entered the harbour. The ship's doctor, Mr Cockin, prescribed and made up pills of opium, opium suppositories, calomel and quinine. The treatment was successful and by August Livingstone was able to take the Makololo aboard a British warship, the 'Pluto'.

This was an unforgettable experience, for they had never seen anything larger than a dug-out. The ship's cannons were fired in their honour and within a short while they were pleading for Livingstone to obtain one to fire at the Matabele. Seeing the support that was afforded Livingstone in ships and weapons, the humble missionary 'rose rapidly in their estimation'.

The Pluto's captain was a Commander Norman Bedingfield. A firm friendship developed, though within two years Livingstone would wish that he had never met the man.

Disappointment lay in the fact that no letters were awaiting his arrival. None the less, Livingstone set to work and wrote up his journals as well as corresponding with his family, friends and the Society.

The Acting Governor-General, the Bishop of Loanda, received him and his whole party formally and gave warm support to the idea of opening up the interior to commerce.

Mr Gabriel, at his own expense, attired the Makololo in robes of striped cotton cloth with red caps for the auspicious occasion. He had also kept a wise and friendly eye on them during Livingstone's illness and found work for them so they were able to buy goods for themselves.

Livingstone was offered a passage to England, but he refused as he felt he had to take the men back. If he left them to their own ends and they perished, Sekeletu would not forgive him. Furthermore, a route to the coast still had to be established as the forests made wagon travel impossible. Livingstone would have to explore the Zambesi. This was a bitter decision for him to make as his wife and family needed him; he had already been away two years.

Fame had found the explorer. The Geographical Society awarded him their highest honour—their gold medal. The Astronomer-Royal at the Cape, Mr Maclear, commended his sightings and in a letter to Livingstone wrote telling him, 'You have accomplished more for the happiness of mankind than has been done by all the African travellers hitherto put together'.[1] Despite such acclamation, Livingstone felt it his duty to return to the Makololo at Linyanti. He wrote to Mary explaining the situation in detail—a healthy locality for a mission, within walking distance of as many people as possible, still had to be found. Furthermore, the delay would help the children to learn more if they remained in Britain. He had no idea of the ordeal she was experiencing.

Livingstone sent his letters and copies of his journal to England and made preparations to return to Chief Sekeletu. Another year had passed, but still the same question hung over his heart: 'Can the love of Christ not carry the missionary where the slave-trade carries the trader?' In writing to Robert Moffat he said, 'I never have had the shadow of doubt as to the propriety of my course, and wish only that my exertions

---

[1] Blaikie, p 168.

may be honoured so far that the Gospel may be preached and believed in all this dark region'.[2]

They departed on 20th September 1854, fully laden with goods they had bought with the tusks, as well as gifts, from a colonel's uniform, cloth and beads to a horse and saddle for Sekeletu. A Dutchman gave Livingstone ten young cattle and the merchants also provided Livingstone's men with clothing and muskets. Livingstone was now forty-one years of age.

Within a month they were a hundred miles inland. Livingstone had the offer of European company, but turned it down. His proposed companion had been an Austrian botanist, Dr Walweitch, but Livingstone felt that although the botanist would accompany him, the work would still fall on his shoulders. Furthermore the Austrian had an irritable temperament.[3]

Livingstone was delayed at Golungo, for some of his men became ill and the horse, too, was sick. In addition, shortly after his arrival, Senhor Castro developed an attack of fever, as did Dr Walweitch. This delayed Livingstone's departure. As one patient rallied the other incurred a relapse and it was only on 4th December that the party, without Dr Walweitch and also without the horse, for it had died, moved forward.

The next major stop was Ambaca, a two-hour walk beyond the Quango River. There he stayed in the commandant's house where, while asleep, he was attacked by tampans (venomous ticks). Within a short while the doctor was down with fever. As a result of his malady he deduced correctly, and for the first time on human record, that the bite of the tampan may be followed by fever.[4]

Not to be thwarted, they were soon on the move again and

---

[2] Blaikie, pp 151–152.
[3] African Journals, p 151, Vol 1.
[4] Gelfand, pp 91–92.

reached Pungo Andongo on 13th December 1854. He stayed with Colonel Pires in whose home he fell to the fever which delayed him, and where he received news that the ship, 'Forerunner', had gone down off Madeira and all the passengers but one had drowned. Had Livingstone chosen to return, he might very well have been on that ship. As it was he had sent on it all his journals and a profuse number of letters.

Patiently he had to rewrite all his journals and letters before moving on. Only on 1st January 1855 was he fit enough to travel. Finally he reached Cassange twenty-eight days later, but the continual rain and wet conditions brought the fever back.

Here they waited for the last opportunity of receiving mail from England. If a ship had landed at Loanda a runner could speedily catch up with the retinue. It was over two years and still no news from his family. Letters arrived on 12th February, just national news which made him anxious, but still no word from his family. The Crimean War was at a critical stage. He could not wait, he had to move on.

He left Cassange on 16th February, but again was delayed the following day for many of the crew came down with what could have been bilharzia. After three days they forced themselves on.

They had little difficulty in crossing the Quango River after managing to barter the ferryman down from thirty yards of cloth to six. Livingstone and many of his men were weak with fever, but to remain motionless in such damp conditions only aggravated their suffering.

On 16th March 1855 fever again overpowered the forlorn figure and he was forced 'to lay by for eight days tossing and groaning all the time'. While this ill he compiled another letter to Mary, pouring out his heart with regard to the slave-trade. One agent had

two chains full of women going to be sold for ivory . . . These women are decent-looking women, as much so as the decent run of Kuruman ladies, and were caught lately in a skirmish the Portuguese had with their tribe and they will be sold for about three tusks each. Each has an iron ring round the wrist, and that is attached to the chain, which she carries in the hand to prevent it jerking and hurting the wrist . . . it is only by the goodness of God in appointing our lot in different circumstances that we are not similarly degraded, for we have the same evil nature, which is so degraded in them to allow of men treating them as beasts. I long for the time when I shall see you again. I hope in God's mercy for that pleasure. How are my dear ones? I have not seen any equal to them since I put them on board ship. My brave little dears! I only hope God will show us mercy. . .[5]

Still weak from the fever a nasty incident occurred. One of his headmen struck another headman on the mouth while bargaining for a piece of meat. Livingstone's 'principal men paid five pieces of cloth and a gun as an atonement; but the more they yielded, the more exorbitant he became and he sent word to all surrounding the villages . . . As their courage usually rises with success', Livingstone resolved to yield no more and departed. In passing through a forest they were startled by a body of men rushing after them. They began by knocking down the burdens of the men at the end of the procession, and several shots were fired, each party spreading out on both sides of the path. Livingstone fortunately had a six-barrelled revolver and with this in his hand, forgetting the fever, he staggered along the path with two or three of his men and encountered the chief. The sight of the six barrels gaping into his stomach with Livingstone's 'ghastly visage looking daggers at his face, seemed to produce an instant revolution in his martial feelings, for he cried out, 'Oh! I have only come to speak to you, and wish peace only'. Mashauana had hold of him by the hand and found him shaking'.[6] They examined the chief's gun to find that it had been discharged, despite his confession of wanting only peace.

[5] Blaikie, p 173.
[6] M T, p 445.

The pale doctor ordered everyone to sit down and demanded to know their intentions. The chief wanted only peace, but refused to leave lest Livingstone shoot him in the back. To this the missionary, his fearless faith rising, demonstrated that he was not afraid of the cowardly chief and turning, mounted his ox and took his departure from the turbulent tribesmen.

The people were not generally receptive to his preaching. In fact Livingstone had earlier come across tribes, like one sect called Quifombos, where 'each must present the heart of a human victim to his god. Hence, when bodies are found with the heart taken out, it is said a Quifombo has done it'.[7]

Another cult Livingstone noted was the Empaccaseiros. This he described as being similar to Freemasonry. They had a 'grand master at Cambambe, and another at Massangano. When the former dies twenty men are sacrificed, on the death of the latter, four'.[8] The men in the Empaccaseiros are all good hunters and chosen by the chiefs. 'The initiation is somewhat like the Bechuana circumcision, but they go through many more observances, one of which is passing through fire ... They know each other in all the tribes by certain words and obtain relief from the other thereby'.[9]

As sickness sapped his strength Livingstone suffered spiritually. After being attacked again by the Chiboque, and seeing much idolatry, his hope for the immediate conversion of many waned. At such a time he wrote: 'How painful is the contrast between the inward gloom and the brightness of the outer world, between the undefined terrors of the spirit and the peace and beauty that pervades the scene around'.[10]

---

[7] A J, p 170.
[8] *Ibid.*
[9] *Ibid.*
[10] M T, p 441 and Jeal, p 145.

Month followed month as they marched on in dull country over heavy, spongy ground, shadowed by dense, dripping forest. Night after night he lay down to sleep on a bed he made by dragging a quantity of earth up above the surface of the flood and laying grass on top.

> The bogs [wrote Livingstone] are exceedingly trying to both cattle and men. The surface is covered with a kind of thick wiry grass, which is rooted in clods and floating on soft slush. If one can manage to tread on these they bear him up but one often steps on the side instead of the crown and the foot slips off down ... The oxen found this much more difficult. They are always one or two feet in the mud and frequently all four, leaving them lying on their belly. So fatigued do they become by about quarter of a mile of this that they lie down disheartened and can be raised only by the people biting their tails.[11]

When not slushing through marshes, the thick forests presented a few problems of their own. On reaching Cabango on the banks of the Chihombo River, he was unable to write in his journal as, he'd received a blow to his eye from the branch of a tree while riding through the forest.

The infection soon cleared and after traversing many marshes, streams and frustrating forests they entered Shinte on 28th June 1855. They remained there several days before going down the Leeba by canoe. While they were proceeding down the river a female hippopotamus struck the canoe, lifting one half out of the water. The frightened occupants were soon knocked off their positions and they swiftly swam to the shore so as to avoid a confrontation with a crocodile.

By the end of July they were back in the Makololo country where they were rapturously received. The women came to meet them 'with their curious dancing gestures and shouts of "Lulliloos". They kissed the hands and cheeks of the different persons of their acquaintance and the whole commotion of

---

[11] Macnair, p 175.

the moving cavalcade raised such a dust that it was a relief
to reach the council room where the elders sat'.[12]

The following day, 23rd July 1855, a thanksgiving service
was held. 'The men decked themselves out in their best, for
all had managed to preserve their suits of European clothing,
which, with their white and red caps, gave them a rather
dashing appearance. They tried to walk like soldiers and called
themselves "my braves".'[13]

He maintained his meetings and on 5th August 1855 wrote
in his journal:

> A large audience listened attentively to my address this morning,
> but it is impossible to indulge any hopes of such feeble efforts.
> God is merciful and will deal with them in justice and kindness.
> This constitutes a ground of hope. Poor degraded Africa! A
> permanent station amongst them might effect something in time,
> but a considerable time is necessary. Surely some will pray to their
> merciful Father in their extremity, who never would have thought
> of Him but for our visit.[14]

Winter drew to a close and the trees and bushes which lined
the river began to bud and blossom in defiance of the heavy
haze which hung in the sky.

As they entered home territory the men were warmly
received. This raised their morale, which for months had
suffered while they slowly struggled through the troublesome
tribes, swamps and forests. At one stage the missionary nearly
had a mutiny on his hands when, for the second time, many
men refused to march. This was because they feared an attack.
An insubordinate individual was about to fire at a hostile tribe
against Livingstone's orders. The doctor saw this and quickly
rectified the situation by punching him on the head with his
pistol.

---

[12] M T, p 492.
[13] Blaikie, p 174.
[14] *Ibid*, p 175.

Thus they submitted and trekked on. Tense times were forgotten as they excitedly neared Linyanti, finally reaching their destination on 13th September 1855. They had been away two months short of two years.

The men who accompanied Livingstone soon boasted shamelessly about their experiences, talking about large ships that had eaten 'black stones' (coal). In their uniforms they 'excited the unbounded admiration of the women and children'.[15] Sekeletu was also pleased with his colonel's uniform and was thrilled that Livingstone had returned without losing one man (though one absconded).

The wagon was in good condition, just as he had left it, but more important there was mail. However, it remained to be collected from where it had been deposited on a little island close to the falls of Mosioatunya, one year ago. Many months prior, a party of Matabele had brought some packages from Mr Moffat to the south bank of the river. The Makololo imagined that the parcels were directed to Livingstone as a mere trick, in order to place witchcraft medicines on their hands. They consequently refused to touch them and it was only after the Matabele had left that they cautiously removed the parcels to the island, built a hut and left them there.

Livingstone eagerly visited the island, for he had not heard from his family for three years. 'Such a rush of thoughts and trembling emotions'[16] flooded his being as he unwrapped the old parcels. The news was already a year old, but at least he knew that up until then his family was safe and well.

The doctor stayed on a while in Linyanti to regain his strength, renew his acquaintance with Sekeletu and catch up on his correspondence and journal writing. He wrote to Mary explaining that he had written to her at every opportunity and was sorry that the letters had not reached her. Her letters

---

[15] M T, p 492.
[16] D L to W Thompson 13/09/1855 in Mssny. Corr., p 279.

to him had also miscarried, though he took comfort from such words as his mother-in-law, Mary Moffat, wrote.

My Dear son Livingstone, Your present position is almost too much for my weak nerves to suffer me to contemplate. Hitherto I have kept up my spirits, and been enabled to believe that our great Master may yet bring you out in safety, for though His ways are often inscrutable, I should have clung to the many precious promises made in His word as to temporal preservation, such as the 91st and 121st Psalms—but have been taught that we may not presume confidently to expect them to be fulfilled, and that every petition, however fervent, must be with devout submission to His will. My poor sister-in-law clung tenaciously to the 91st Psalm, and firmly believed that her dear husband would thus be preserved, and never indulged the idea that they should never meet on earth. But I apprehend submission was wanting. 'If it be Thy will,' I fancy she could not say—and, therefore, she was utterly confounded when the news came. She had exercised strong faith, and was disappointed. Dear Livingstone, I have always endeavoured to keep this in mind with regard to you. Since George [Fleming] came out it seemed almost hope against hope. Your having got so thoroughly feverished chills my expectations; still prayer, unceasing prayer, is made for you. When I think of you my heart will go upwards. 'Keep him as the apple of Thine eye', 'Hold him in the hollow of Thy hand'.[17]

Livingstone calmed her fears with his favourite texts, 'Commit thy way to the Lord and He shall direct your path,' and, 'Lo, I am with you always; even unto the end of this age'. For the future he took assurance from the text that 'the earth shall be full of the knowledge of the Lord'.

Livingstone was indignant at the 'so called Missionaries to the heathen, who never march into heathen territory, and quiet their consciences by opposing their do-nothingism to my blundering do-somethingism'.[18]

---

[17] Blaikie, p 176.
[18] *Ibid*, p 177.

Livingstone made himself heard among the heathen. On 14th October 1855 they had yet another service and the next day in his diary he wrote:

We had a good and very attentive audience yesterday, and I expatiated with great freedom on the love of Christ in dying, from His parting address in John 16. It cannot be these precious truths will fall to the ground; but it is perplexing to observe no effects. They assent to the truth, but 'we don't know', or 'you speak truly' is all the response. In reading accounts of South Sea Missions it is hard to believe the quickness of the vegetation of the good seed, but I know several of the men, and am sure they are of impeachable veracity. In trying to convey knowledge, and use the magic lantern, which is everywhere extremely popular, though they listen with apparent delight to what is said, questioning them on the following night reveals almost entire ignorance of the previous lesson. O that the Holy Ghost might enlighten them! To His soul-renewing influence my longing soul is directed. It is His word, and cannot die.[19]

The eight-week halt did the exhausted explorer immense good, not only physically. He said, 'In travelling the heart becomes benumbed. I feared much I was becoming a heathen myself, but a little rest has, thank God, quickened my spiritual feelings'.[20]

The relationship with Sekeletu progressed, though the missionary was disappointed to hear that in his absence the chief had conducted marauding parties against his neighbours. Livingstone sternly reprimanded him and the young leader listened without bearing any malice, and when the party was due to move eastwards he supplied above a hundred men. He also gave them ten slaughter cattle, three of his best riding oxen, stores of food and a right to levy tribes in submission to Sekeletu.

---

[19] *Ibid*, p 175.
[20] Macnair, p 181.

The chief did not want Livingstone to go, but appreciated the value of the venture. The last continent crossing to the coast was such a success that within days of Livingstone's return a party had to be despatched with more tusks for trade to Loanda.

The missionary still had high hopes of settling among the Makololo and his departure was made more bearable by the knowledge of his return with his wife, known by the locals as 'Ma Robert' (literally mother of Robert, their first child). In a letter to Arthur Tidman on 12th October 1855 Livingstone reported on inter-tropical Africa, its conditions and suggestions for future missionary development. Regarding the frustrating fever and formidable obstacles the man told Tidman, 'These privations, I beg you to observe, are not mentioned as if I considered them in the light of sacrifices. I think the word ought never to be mentioned in reference to anything we can do for Him who, though He was rich yet for our sakes became poor'.[21]

Livingstone realised the pressing, depressing shortage of missionaries, and surveying the scene soberly stated, 'Let the seed be sown, and there is no more doubt of its vitality and germination than there is of the general spring and harvest in the course of nature'.[22] Livingstone had located a position 'about the forks of the Leeba and Leeambye or Kabompo and river of the Bashukulompo as a most desirable central point for the spread of civilization and Christianity'. Though he wrote, 'I feel a difficulty as to taking my children there, without their intelligent self-dedication. I can speak for my wife and myself only. We will go whoever remains behind'.[23]

On 3rd November Livingstone and his 114 porters set out for the Zambesi. His plan was to follow the river right down

[21] D L to A Tidman 12/10/1855 in Mssny. Corr., p 293.
[22] *Ibid*, p 300.
[23] Blaikie, p 189.

to its mouth on the east coast, a journey of roughly 1,000 miles.

In late November, five years after he had first heard about the great falls east of Sesheke, the explorer and his entourage neared the falls of Mosioatunya or 'the smoke that thunders'.

Sekeletu and about 100 more followers set out to escort the men to Mosioatunya. They encountered a fearful thunderstorm one evening and in the pitch black night, men and beasts bumped into each other amid the blinding lightning and roaring rain. In the confusion the main party was not able to reach the advance guard and Livingstone had to lay down for the night on the cold soaking ground. 'He expected to spend a miserable night, but Sekeletu kindly covered Livingstone with his own blanket, and lay uncovered himself'. Such a simple act of genuine kindness touched Livingstone and caused his heart to cry all the louder, 'God grant that 'ere this time comes they may receive that gospel which is a solace for the soul in death!'[24]

The following day, reunited with the rest of the retinue, they rowed on in their dug-out canoes, passing sprightly tribesmen who adorned the stakes of their stockades with the skulls of the Matabele defeated by Sebituane. As the wide river meandered towards the rift where it would be rejuvenated, the canoes bobbed precariously. The long flat horizon was broken by a lovely, lofty column of vapour, rising several thousand feet above the river as it roared into a new life.

Crocodiles which crowded the banks suddenly slipped slyly into the water from where they surveyed the scene. The humorous grunt of the giant hippos could hardly be heard above the deep, distant murmur that rose from the depths of the earth and grew in volume until low tumultuous thunder throbbed continuously.

---

[24] M T, p 516.

White columns of vapour spray leaped energetically into the serene sky. The tops of the columns 'appeared to mingle with the clouds. They were white below, and higher up became dark, so as to simulate smoke very closely'.[25] Lush green vegetation adorned the banks and islands in sharp contrast to the dry dusty bush. Towering over all, while standing majestically 'the great burly baobab, each of whose enormous arms would form the trunk of a large tree, beside groups of graceful palms, with their feathery-shaped leaves depicted on the sky'.[26]

Half a mile from the falls Livingstone changed his canoe for a lighter one manned by natives well acquainted with the rapids who, availing themselves of the eddies and still pools caused by the jutting rocks, brought him to an island in the middle of the river and on the very edge of the lip over which the water rolls. It was a terrifying experience: 'At one time we seemed to be going right into the gulf but though I felt a little tremor I said nothing, believing that I could face a difficulty as well as my guides'.[27]

This was a perplexing sight to Livingstone for 'no one could perceive where the vast body of water went; it seemed to lose itself in the earth, disappearing into a transverse fissure only 80 feet wide'. Creeping with awe to the extremity of the island, he 'peeped down into a large rent which had been made from bank to bank of the broad Zambesi'.

Livingstone saw the falls as majestic, but was he perhaps that enamoured to find such an obstacle in a highway to the interior? That is probably how he partly described the falls and only afterwards did their magnificent mountain of mist finally make an impression.

It was later that he penned the powerful phrase, 'Scenes

---

[25] *Ibid*, p 519.
[26] *Ibid*.
[27] Macnair, p 183.

so lovely must have been gazed upon by angels in their flight'.[28]

The falls, so rugged in their beautiful brilliance, are one of the wonders of the world, yet only a few explorers had set sight on them. Many local natives believed them to be bewitched and kept away lest they annoy the god who revealed himself in the rainbow.

More than a mile of water suddenly surged and descended in a swirling mass; a spontaneous crescendo crashing against the solid basalt rock. Falling over 360 feet the water hit the ground with such force that vapour continuously rose as mist. The sun's rays transformed into the rainbow through the mist as the spray parted company with the water and the furious foam. Thereupon it rose high towards the heavens; the particles met again and dramatically descended as rain.

Livingstone later wrote *Missionary Travels and Researches in Africa* and in the book he named these waters the 'Victoria Falls' as a mark of respect for his Sovereign, Queen Victoria.

Dr Livingstone has often been accused of claiming for himself the credit of discoveries made by others; accused of writing as if he had been the first to traverse routes in which he had already been preceded by the Portuguese.[29] Possibly some areas in Livingstone's subsequent routes had already been traversed by a Portuguese traveller or two, but even so this should not reduce the credit due to him. He derived little, if any, benefit from their experience as they had mapped out the interior of Africa inconclusively. Furthermore, the missionary was not merely interested in being the first European to discover areas. Had he been so inclined he would have forged a path to the falls years earlier. His motivating

---

[28] M T, p 519.

[29] Senor Porto must have encountered the falls in his slave dealings. A Boer family is also believed to have seen the falls, but if so they died before informing the civilised world.

factor was first his work for Christ and secondly, as a means to promoting the gospel, commerce.

After a short stay at this scenic site they moved on. Slowly but steadily the eastward slog continued, often over ground which was far from favourable for walking. 'Pedestrianism,' said Livingstone, 'may be all very well for those whose obesity requires much exercise; but for one who was becoming as thin as a lath through the constant perspiration caused by marching day after day in the hot sun, the only good I saw in it was that it gave an honest sort of man a vivid idea of the treadmill'.[30]

Immediately east of the Victoria Falls the river loops to the south before flowing in a north-easterly direction. The explorer decided to travel north of the river cutting out the loop. This area was high, fertile and free from malaria— possibly the place to build a mission and trading station. The more he pressed on traversing the plateau the more convinced he became of the siting. It was cooler than the Zambesi valley, the area supported sizeable trees, and it seemed suitable for cattle.

He then came upon the Batoka (or Batonga), a tribe he found to be rather degraded and lacking in moral courage and self-respect. The women wore some clothing, but the men strolled around *inpuris naturalibus*. As Livingstone wrote, 'they have even lost the tradition of the "fig leaf"'. Although they were friendly and brought him gifts (they had never seen a white man before), their form of greeting did not liven Livingstone's heart. He wrote:

> They throw themselves on their backs on the ground, and, rolling from side to side, slap the outside of their thighs as expressions of thankfulness and welcome, uttering the words, 'Kina bomba'. This method of salutation was to me very disagreeable, and I never could get reconciled to it. I called out 'stop, stop! I don't

---

[30] Blaikie, p 180.

want that'; but they, imagining I was dissatisfied, only tumbled about more furiously, and slapped their thighs with greater vigour. The men being totally unclothed, this performance imparted to my mind a painful sense of their extreme degradation'.[31]

On hearing Livingstone's message, the villagers expressed their satisfaction as he 'directed their attention to Jesus as their Saviour whose word is "Peace on earth and good will to men"'.[32]

The missionary noted that 'none desire Christian instruction, for of it they have no idea. But the people are now humbled by the scourgings they have received, and seem to be in a favourable state for the reception of the Gospel'.[33]

The New Year saw the expedition rejoining the Zambesi and the frequent storms did not cause delay—unlike the west coast—as the temperature was warm and the drainage good. Mode of travel via canoes would have been the quickest and simplest, but Livingstone could not afford such luxuries so they continued on foot. (The canoes previously used were on loan from Sekeletu.)

At the confluence of the Loangwa and Zambesi, they came upon the remains of the Portuguese settlement, Zumbo, which lay derelict and deserted. The church was broken up and a disused damaged bell lay on its side among the stones. They encountered hostile tribes who refused to lend Livingstone and his men their canoes, and a heavy spirit settled upon them.

Livingstone realised that their very lives were in imminent danger, and for once this man of fearless faith succumbed to the worry that wrestled in his heart as he faced the full terror of the situation. He solemnly wrote in his diary:

14th January 1856—at the confluence of the Loangwa and Zambesi. Thank God for His great mercies thus far. How soon

---

[31] M T, pp 551–552.
[32] *Ibid*, p 553.
[33] *Ibid*, p 555.

I may be called to stand before Him, my righteous judge, I know not. All hearts are in His hands, and merciful and gracious is the Lord Our God. O Jesus, grant me resignation to Thy will, and entire reliance on Thy powerful hand. On Thy Word alone I lean. But wilt Thou permit me to plead for Africa? The cause is Thine. What an impulse will be given to the idea that Africa is not open if I perish now! See, O Lord, how the heathen rise up against me, as they did to Thy Son. I commit my way unto Thee. I trust also in Thee that Thou wilt direct my steps. Thou givest wisdom liberally to all who ask Thee—give it to me, my Father. My family is Thine. They are in the best hands. Oh! be gracious, and all our sins do Thou blot out.

Leave me not, forsake me not. I cast myself and all my cares down at Thy feet. Thou knowest all I need, for time and eternity. It seems a pity that the important facts about the two healthy longitudinal ridges should not become known in Christendom. Thy will be done! . . . They will not furnish us with more canoes than two. I leave my cause and all my concerns in the hands of God, my gracious Saviour, the Friend of sinners.

Evening—Felt much turmoil of spirit in view of having all my plans for the welfare of this great region and teeming population knocked on the head by savages tomorrow. But I read that Jesus came and said, 'All power is given unto me in heaven and in earth. Go ye therefore, and teach all nations—and lo, I am with you always, even unto the end of the world'. It is the word of a gentleman of the most sacred and strictest honour, and there is an end on't. I will not cross furtively by night as I intended. It would appear as flight, and should such a man as I flee? Nay, verily, I shall take observations for latitude and longitude to-night, though they may be the last. I feel quite calm now, thank God.[34]

In the morning the foreboding spirit intensified. Warriors from neighbouring villages reinforced those already present; women and children had been sent away. Only one canoe had been produced though many more were visible. At this critical moment the company looked to their leader. Livingstone

[34] Blaikie, p 181.

calmly ordered camp to be dismantled. Slowly, resolutely, he shepherded his porters to the bank and into the solitary canoe, first the goods, then the cattle and finally the men. Progress was slow and they were very vulnerable. Livingstone stood steadfast on the bank. At times the armed men crowded around him and he cautiously kept them amused with his watch, his mirror and his burning-glass. Then finally with the last man safe in the canoe Livingstone thanked the chief politely for his kindness and stepped aboard. The next day he sent back gifts.

About 500 miles from the mouth of the Zambesi the doctor decided upon another short cut. This entailed going overland and missing out the hilly region of Kebrabasa (today known as Cabora Basa). Upon reaching the Portuguese settlement of Tete Livingstone found out that rapids existed at Kebrabasa. He wrote: 'Had I known this previously, I certainly would not have left the river without first examining it'.[35]

This mistake was to plague Livingstone in months to come.

After the Portuguese had abandoned Zumbo, Tete became the most westerly settlement in Mocambique. Livingstone, upon reaching Tete in the first week of March 1856, was shocked to see so many slaves. Out of a population of 4,000 only 350 of the inhabitants were not slaves, and only thirty were true Portuguese.

The town was formed in the early sixteenth century on the false hope that gold and silver were easily obtainable. A failure of these minerals to abound encouraged the trade in humans, which in itself was not very lucrative as the west coast of Africa, from where the majority of slaves were sent, was closer to America.

The missionary stayed with the commander of the garrison, Major Sicard, whose kindness was very timely as a further attack of fever laid Livingstone low. This gave him, once he

---

[35] M T, p 604.

started to recuperate, time to catch up with his correspondence. One of the letters was to the King of Portugal whom Livingstone thanked for his people's kindness. However, the essence of it was to encourage the King to establish more commercial trading with the natives and discourage the slave traffic.

With the end in sight he wrote to Sir Roderick:

> I do not feel so much elated, by the prospect of accomplishing this feat. I feel most thankful to God for preserving my life, where so many, who by superior intelligence would have done more good, have been cut off. But it does not look as if I had reached the goal. Viewed in relation to my calling, the end of the geographical feat is only the beginning of the enterprise.[36]

In Tete it was decided that the many Makololo would be allocated land and live there until Livingstone returned within a year to take them home. At noon on 22nd April 1856 he bade farewell to Sicard and, with a small crew, canoed to Senna.

The team made rapid progress as the river was at its peak, though the explorer regretted he 'had not come when the river was at its lowest rather than at its highest'.[37] He would have then been able to obtain a more accurate assessment of the river with regard to it being a navigable waterway. He was, however, informed somewhat incorrectly by British seamen, Captain Parker and Lieutenant Hoskins, that it 'may be considered conclusive as to the capabilities of this river for commercial purposes'.[38] Livingstone believed that a small flat-bottomed steamer could be navigable throughout the year as far as Tete and there on by smaller vessels. Treacherous sand bars which move with the annual flow of the river were not taken into consideration; an oversight that cost them dearly in later years.

---

[36] D L to Sir Roderick Murchison, March 1856, in Blaikie, p 193.
[37] M T, p 656.
[38] *Ibid.*

They reached Senna on the afternoon of 27th April 1856. Wrote Livingstone, 'I thought the state of Tete quite lamentable, but that of Senna was ten times worse'.[39] Everything was in a state of stagnation and ruin. Law and order had dissipated, with rebel tribes even overruling the Portuguese garrison. They quickly moved on to Quillimane, but attacks of malaria became more severe and frequently Livingstone feared for his life. When he arrived at Quillimane on 25th May he was so sick he gave instructions for the sale of Sekeletu's ivory in the event of his death. However, news that warships had been calling at the mouth of the river to enquire of him stirred his spirit and the resourceful traveller rallied.

He set to work again writing letters, including one to Arthur Tidman, secretary of the Society, in which he detailed an outline of missionary stations which were urgently needed to reach those with 'superstitions—the mere wreck of a primitive faith floating down the stream of time'.[40] His feelings for the lost souls ran deep: 'We have still a debt of gratitude to Jesus on our own account besides, and there is no greater privilege on earth than, after having had our own chains broken off, to go forth to proclaim liberty to the captives, the opening of the prison to them that are bound'.[41]

Livingstone was also grieved to note that eight of the crew of H M Brigantine, 'Dart', including the commander and two officers, were lost on the sand bar at the mouth of the mighty river when they came to pick up the missionary. He wrote, 'I feel as if it would have been easier to have died for them, than to bear the thought of them all cut off from the joys of life on my account'.[42]

[39] *Ibid*, p 658.
[40] D L to A Tidman 23/05/1856 in Mssny. Corr., p 307.
[41] *Ibid*, p 308.
[42] *Ibid*, p 309.

There were letters waiting for him, but still none from his wife. They had gone astray and he had to wait six weeks before the 'Frolic' called. She brought abundant supplies, many letters, some from his family, and much-needed money. Among the letters was one that wounded him sorely. It was from Dr Tidman, on behalf of the London Missionary Society, who under extreme financial restraints, felt compelled to write to Livingstone. The letter began by expressing admiration for his magnificent efforts, but went on to say that their financial position prevented it from promising 'within any definite period to enter into any remote, untried and difficult fields of labour'.

This was a big blow to the fever-ridden and now 'down-trodden' man. It appeared to be revoking the promise given to him to press northwards from Kolobeng. Furthermore, it cast doubts on his efforts to find a healthy locality in which to build a mission station—exploration was not missionary work. Any suggestion that he was less a missionary than the 'dumpy' man in the long coat with a book under his arm hurt him. Had he not, in season and out of season, preached the Gospel? Had he not discovered a belt of land eastward of the Makololo country suitable for missionary enterprise?

The Mission directors might have been wiser to wait until Livingstone reached London, as in his tired and weak state he misconstrued their letter. None the less, the seeds of mistrust had been sown.

It was agreed that Livingstone set sail on the 'Frolic'. He bade farewell to his faithful followers, explaining to them what they must do should he die and assuring them that 'nothing but death would prevent my return'.[43] They replied, 'Nay, father, you will not die; you will return to take us back to Sekeletu,' and they promised to wait for him. Few men have ever commanded such love from their employees.

---

[43] M T, p 677.

Dr Livingstone decided after much pleading to allow Sekwebu to accompany him. Initially he tried to discourage by warning him that he would die in such a cold country as England. 'That is nothing,' Sekwebu remonstrated. 'Let me die at your feet'.[44]

The journey out to sea was in itself horrifying as the tender received blow after blow as the waves beat her down. Crashing through the tops of the high waves the rowing boat endeavoured to reach the ship, the men constantly bailing out water. Terrified, Sekwebu looked at Livingstone and cried, 'Is this the way you go? Is this the way you go?'[45] He had neither seen the sea nor even a big ship in his life. Finally he was hauled by rope onto the ship and became a favourite with the sailors. 'Sekwebu would often remark to Livingstone "Your countrymen are very agreeable and what a strange country this is, all water together." He also said that he now understood why I used the sextant'.[46]

Livingstone, for thirteen years since his arrival in Africa, had hardly spoken English, and the latter three-and-a-half years not at all. Such disuse of his native tongue made him 'feel sadly at a loss' with the crew.

The journey, however, proved too much for Sekwebu who became seized with fear and wanted to die rather than be tormented by such foreign and claustrophobic surrounds. The officers proposed to secure him by putting him in chains, but Livingstone would not agree, knowing that 'the insane often retain an impression of ill treatment'; chains were to them slavery. In Mauritius Sekwebu refused to go on shore and tragically one evening in a fit of insanity 'he tried to spear one of the crew then leaped over-board and, though he could swim well, pulled himself down hand under hand, by the

---

[44] *Ibid*, p 681.
[45] *Ibid*, p 682.
[46] *Ibid*.

chain cable'.[47] Before Livingstone's eyes the man disappeared into the dark depths of the ocean. This shock was followed by another; the Scot was to learn that his father had succumbed to sickness and had died. The journey continued, giving him time to recover both physically and mentally as he looked forward to seeing his family.

However, another serious scene was to befall the ship. The engine shaft snapped and the 'Frolic' was nearly wrecked on an island near the bay of Tunis. But 'most providently a wind sprung up and carried them out of imminent danger'. Disembarking at the bay of Tunis Livingstone proceeded via another vessel, reaching England on 9th December 1856. They docked in Dover where a new door opening to Livingstone would present further hardships and a degree of strife. For the moment he longed to be with his family and wife, though they were not there to meet him.

[47] *Ibid*, p 683.

David Livingstone and his daughter Agnes, 1857

10

Fickle Fame Fans its Flames

The ship docked at Dover, not Southampton, so upon reaching London Livingstone rushed by train to greet his wife and well-wishers waiting for him at Southampton. Here he was a celebrity; his name was known throughout the country and his exploits for Christianity and civilisation captivated many hearts.

No doubt the times were propitious. The recent war in Crimea had brought credit to a few. In India troubles were brewing, at home the country was depressed. Britain needed their own hero, someone who had succeeded against uncommon odds. A man of the people, who owed help to no one, but had won his way through diligence and dogged determination. There was much, too, in his very look; a hardy somewhat emaciated figure. His story was written plainly on his face, with deep lines telling a tale of suffering and a tanned complexion that showed the effects of exposure. Furthermore, his hesitant English speech revealed his solitude among another culture.

Other travellers had been equally brave, but no other British subject had ventured so far into the interior, nor had anyone mapped so explicitly its places, peoples and prominent insects, animals, fauna and flora. His patient, persevering heart in winning the honour and support of uncivilised tribes was amazing.

Mary Livingstone gave her husband a welcome bathed in love and a longing never to be parted from him again.

She penned her thoughts down on paper as a poem for
him.

> A hundred thousand welcomes, and it's time for you to come
> From the far land of the foreigner, to your country and your home.
> Oh as long as we were parted, ever since you went away,
> I never passed a dreamless night, or knew an easy day.
>
> Do you think I would reproach you with the sorrows that I bore?
> Since the sorrow is all over, now I have you here once more,
> And there's nothing but the gladness, and the love within my heart,
> And the hope so sweet and certain that again we'll never part.
>
> A hundred thousand welcomes! How my heart is gushing o'er
> With the love and joy and wonder thus to see your face once more.
> How did I live without you these long long years of woe?
> It seems as if 'twould kill me to be parted from you now.
>
> You'll never part me, darling, there's a promise in your eye;
> I may tend you while I'm living, you will watch me when I die;
> And if death but kindly lead me to the blessed home on high,
> What a hundred thousand welcomes will await you in the sky!
>
> Mary[1]

In a letter to her daughter, Mary Moffat tried tenderly to
prepare her heart for the sorrow she would have in bidding
farewell to her children. As for her thoughts of David she
commented in a motherly manner, 'Now, with a little rest
and relaxation, having youth on his side, he might regain all,
but I cannot help fearing for him if he dashes at once into
hardships again. He is certainly the wonder of his age.'[2]

Dr Moffat's congratulation to his son-in-law was full of
fatherly wisdom:

> The honours awaiting you at home would be enough to make a
> score of light heads dizzy, but I have no fear of their affecting
> your upper storey, beyond showing you that your labours to lay

---

[1] Blaikie, p 199.
[2] M Moffat to M Livingstone, *ibid*, p 200.

open the recesses of the vast interior have been appreciated. It will be almost too much for dear Mary to hear that you are verily unscathed ... you have succeeded beyond the most sanguine expectations in laying open a world of immortal beings, all needing the gospel.[3]

Praise poured in and within several days, on 15th December, the Royal Geographical Society held a special meeting to welcome him. Many of his previous friends from Colonel Steele and Mr Oswell to Sir Roderick, who chaired the meeting, attended. His geographical discoveries were acclaimed, his honour more so by keeping his word to his bearers to escort them back into the interior. Livingstone replied that he was only doing his duty as a Christian to open up the interior to Christendom and that the enterprise would never be complete till the slave-trade was abolished and the whole country opened up to commerce and Christianity.

The next day the London Missionary Society held a reception for him. Lord Shaftsbury, a steadfast believer in Christ, was in the chair. Livingstone was warmly welcomed and God praised for his leading in Livingstone's life. A special word was shared by Lord Shaftsbury for Mary.

That lady was born a Moffat, and she became a Livingstone. She cheered the early part of our friend's career by her spirit, her counsel and her society. Afterwards, when she reached this country, she passed many years with her children in solitude and anxiety, suffering the greatest fears for the welfare for her husband, and yet enduring all with patience and resignation, and even joy, because she had surrendered her best feelings, and sacrificed her own private interests to the advancement of civilization and the great interests of Christianity.[4]

Openly Livingstone commended and promoted the Society, who were relieved that publicity would aid their work in

---

[3] R Moffat to D L, *ibid*, p 201.
[4] *Ibid*, p 204.

distant lands. Sadly the Society in 1855 had an overdraft of £12,000 which rose to £13,000. The missionary was tired of labouring under tight restraint and believed the Society to be no longer backing him in his vision to establish mission stations in the interior. In retrospect one can sympathise with both the Scot and the Society.

While in Quillimane Livingstone had written to Sir Roderick Murchison, explaining his dilemma and sowing the seeds for alternative support.

> I suspect [he wrote] I am to be sent somewhere else, but will prefer dissolving my connection with the Society and follow out my own plans as a private Christian. This is rather trying, for, the salary being professedly only a bare subsistence (100 pounds per annum), we have in addition the certainty of education for our family and some provision for our widows . . . Should I be unable to return I hope you will direct the attention of travellers to developing the rich resources of the country.[5]

Murchison responded to this appeal for help and did everything in his power to see that Livingstone became financially independent.

Livingstone, however, was keen to see his family and as soon as the initial engagements were completed travelled to Hamilton. His father's empty chair deeply affected him as it was then his absence was truly felt. 'The first evening,' wrote one of his sisters, 'he asked all about his illness and death. One of them remarking that after he knew he was dying his spirits seemed to rise, David burst into tears. At family worship that evening he said with deep feeling—"We bless thee O Lord, for our Parents; we give thee thanks for the dead have who died in the Lord." '[6]

At first Livingstone proposed that his stay in London should

[5] D L to R Murchison 5/08/1856, *Zambezi Journals of David Livingstone*, Vol 1, p xviii in Jeal, p 167.
[6] Blaikie, p 207.

only be a few months in order to return to Quillimane before the unhealthy season set in. However, upon receiving an assurance from the Portuguese government (which was never fulfilled by them) that his men would be looked after, he prolonged his stay.

He set to work on convincing his fellow countrymen that Christianity and commerce were the keys to civilisation. The expanding middle class courted his ideas as they suited many of their new religious ideals. These folk had quickly discovered that Christian virtues could easily be exchanged for business virtues, thinking an exemplary home and a weekly confrontation with the Maker would produce rewards in this life and the next. Further guilt could be assuaged by the occasional charity. The meek little missionary fitted the bill.

On 5th January 1857 Murchison had arranged a meeting to inaugurate a testimonial fund for Livingstone. Deciding more could be done he wrote that evening to Lord Clarendon, the British Foreign Secretary, suggesting that the services of the man who could speak more African languages than any other European be employed by the government.

Livingstone, perhaps somewhat reluctantly, continued to urge the Society on a course of establishing mission stations in the interior; one on the Batoka Plateau and the other to the south with the Matabele. The Livingstones would reside at the station near the Makololo and the Moffats with the Matabele.[7] This was agreed to by the Society on 22nd January and the Society's General Meeting on 14th May which proposed the mission be under the charge of Dr Livingstone.

Little contact was made between the Society and Livingstone, but a fund was established to finance two stations. The doctor had now entered into a new sphere, that of writing, and early in 1857 he set to work on a book. He sometimes worked in the house of a friend, but generally in a London or suburban

---

[7] LMS Board minutes 12/01/1857 in Jeal, p 168.

lodging, invariably with his children about him. He relished the time with his children, often taking them for walks and romps in the woods.

Livingstone never liked to walk in the streets for fear of being mobbed as did once happen in Regent Street when he had to take refuge in a cab. For the same reason it was awkward for him to go to church.

One person with whom the family stayed was Sir Risdon Bennett who was impressed at 'how strong was his attachment to his own family . . . and how entirely he had retained his simplicity of character . . . his love for Africa, and confidence in the steady dawn of brighter days for its oppressed races, were unbounded'.[8]

They also stayed with Frederick Fitch of Highbury New Park who, in a letter to William Blaikie, told him that

> Dr and Mrs Livingstone were much attached, and thoroughly understood each other. The Doctor was sportive and fond of a joke, and Mrs Livingstone entered into his humour . . . In society both were reserved and quiet. Neither of them cared for grandeur; it was a great trial to Dr Livingstone to go to a grand dinner. Yet in his quiet way he would exercise an influence at the dinner-table.[9]

He often used to rise early, have a cup of tea and set to work with his writing.

Despite his commitment to the book, many public engagements had to be fulfilled, as it was considered an honour to have him grace the tables of the well-to-do. He enjoyed intelligent company and he and Mary regularly attended private dinner parties.

The Prince Consort and some of the younger members of the Royal family interviewed the missionary, and in May he

[8] Blaikie, pp 211–212.
[9] *Ibid*, p 213.

was presented with the Freedom of the City of London, though Hamilton had been first to grant him this honour.

The same month Livingstone ventured to approach the government offering his services and on the 22nd he wrote to Lord Clarendon stating his devotion to further work in Africa, and how his future efforts would benefit trade and the enhancement of his country's good name. He outlined a policy which he thought would not offend or encroach upon the rights of Portugal. He went on to say, 'I do not intend to accept gratuity from my former employers, the London Missionary Society. I venture to accept such a salary as your Lordship may seem suitable, should you approve of my suggestions and think me worthy of employment in a public capacity'.[10]

Livingstone at that stage had not resigned from the Society, who understood he was going to be their representative in the interior on a mission station. The doctor, rather deceitfully, had not informed them. He had a bigger vision which he believed the Society could not cope with.

None the less, the Missionary Society continued raising funds for the two Missionaries and plans for development were slowly formulated. Tidman, the Secretary, was however wary of such a grand venture.

Livingstone's large book *Missionary Travels and Researches in Southern Africa* was published by John Murray and released on 10th November 1857. Twelve thousand copies were printed in the first edition and before long were sold out, whereby they found themselves with orders for thirteen 13,800.[11] He lavishly gave many copies away to those who had offered him a hand of friendship when he needed it most. Within a short while the publication was a best-seller; his open honesty and humour were appreciated by the people.

---

[10] D L to Lord Clarendon, May 1857, in Campbell, p 244.
[11] Blaikie, pp 213–214.

More pressing engagements flooded his diary, while he became more determined to be financially independent. In a letter to Sir Thomas Maclear he wrote: 'I am not yet fairly on with the Government but am nearly quit off with the Society though I don't mean to be a whit less a missionary than heretofore.'[12]

It hurt him to receive complaints about his ministry. Years earlier he had gone to Africa with the impression that virtually instantaneously souls would be won for the Lord. He found the actual case to be different. Livingstone learned, like many other early missionaries, that they were called by the Creator to be sowers of seed and not reapers of harvests, and the further inland the harder the hearts were to the gospel.

Psalm 126 had a deep significance: 'Those who sow in tears shall reap with joyful shouting. He who goes to and fro weeping, carrying his bag of seed, shall indeed come again with a shout of joy, bringing his sheaves with him'.[13]

These men and women were, in God's purpose, to prepare the hearts of the people to receive the good news, and Livingstone came to see himself as one such pioneer. During the sixteen years, he had done much to bring the knowledge of Christ to tribes that had never heard of him—no missionary in Africa had ever preached to so many tribes. In a few instances he had been successful in being an instrument in turning men from darkness to light. Many critics said he only had one convert. He did have a few more than Chief Seshele; a man, Setefano, was baptised with Seshele, though little is known of him. It should also be noted that Livingstone only regarded a man as truly converted once he had made a confession of his faith and walked without major sin for several years.

Through the generosity of his publisher, John Murray, Livingstone made a small fortune on the book. More than

---

[12] D L to Sir Thomas Maclear 13/05/1857 NAZ reference 665–673.
[13] Psalm 126:5–6.

half he poured into a Zambesi expedition, supported further missionaries and with the remainder he bought a home in Hamilton for his family and provided for his children's education.

But still the critics continued their allegations. In answer to one lady's critical comment regarding his calling as a missionary Livingstone replied:

> Nowhere have I ever appeared as anything else but a servant of God, who had simply followed the leadings of His hand. My views of what is missionary duty are not so contracted as those whose ideal is a dumpy sort of man with a Bible under his arm. I have laboured in bricks and mortar, at the forge and carpenter's bench, as well as in preaching and medical practice. I feel that I am 'not my own'. I am serving Christ when shooting a buffalo for my men, or taking an astronomical observation, or writing to one of His children who forget, during the little moment of penning a note, that charity which is eulogised as 'thinking no evil'; and after having by His help got information, which I hope will lead to more abundant blessing being bestowed on Africa than heretofore, am I to hide the light under a bushel, merely because some will consider it not sufficiently, or even at all, missionary? Knowing that some persons do believe that opening up a new country to the sympathies of Christendom was not a proper work for an agent of a Missionary Society to engage in, I now refrain from taking any salary from the Society with which I was connected, so no pecuniary loss is sustained by anyone.[14]

Such a gesture would surely have given the Society reason to believe he would not remain longer with them. Livingstone also knew the value of publicity and publically he supported the Society, as well as his greater vision—that of seeing Africa set free.

After the book was released Livingstone moved through the

---

[14] D L to Miss Mackenzie 3/10/1857, NAZ reference 704–711, also in Blaikie, p 216.

country attending meetings and giving addresses. In August he addressed the British Association for the Advancement of Science in Dublin, the following month in Manchester and then in Glasgow, where he was presented with the Freedom of the City, together with a testimonial of £2,000. He was admitted as an Honorary Fellow of the Faculty of Physicians and Surgeons. In all his speeches he clearly gave the glory to his Lord and Saviour. 'My great object was to be like Him— to imitate Him as far as He could be imitated'.[15]

In another speech he said that poverty and hard work were often looked down upon—he did not know why—for wickedness was the only thing that ought to be a reproach to any man. And in another address he invited the folk to accept God's offers of mercy to them in Christ and give themselves wholly to him. 'To bow down before God was not mean; it was manly'.[16]

He never lectured for a fee and often gave away the money that was given to him. On one occasion he was offered £30 for speaking; this he proposed be put towards a coffee-room on the plan of French cafés where men, women and children might go instead of whisky-shops.

In Edinburgh he kept to a tiring schedule and despite the honour of the Freedom of the City he was growing weary of public speaking. He then moved on to Oxford and Cambridge. In the Senate House in Cambridge he addressed a very large audience. The last part of his lecture was an earnest appeal for missionaries. He said:

For my own part, I have never ceased to rejoice that God has appointed me to such an office. People talk of the sacrifice that I have made in spending so much of my life in Africa. Can that be called a sacrifice which is simply paid back as a small part of a great debt owing to our God, which we can never repay? . . . It

[15] Blaikie, p 221.
[16] *Ibid*, p 223.

is emphatically no sacrifice. Say rather it is a privilege. Anxiety, sickness, suffering, or danger, now and then, with a foregoing of the common conveniences and charities of this life, may make us pause, and cause the spirit to waver, and the soul to sink; but let this only be for a moment. All these are nothing when compared with the glory which shall hereafter be revealed in, and for us. I never made a sacrifice. Of this we ought not to talk, when we remember the great sacrifice which He made who left His Father's throne on high to give Himself for us.

And in a strange, prophetic utterance he continued:

I beg to direct your attention to Africa: I know that in a few years I shall be cut off in that country, which is now open; do not let it be shut again! I go back to Africa to try to make an open path for commerce and Christianity; do you carry out the work which I have begun? I LEAVE IT WITH YOU![17]

The last sentence, a loud cry from the heart, pierced many men's hearts. From that meeting men were later to go forward into the ministry.

Livingstone favoured 'a Consulship to the Makololo and other Central African tribes' which would enable him to do all he wished 'for both them and English commerce'.[18] Confident, he tendered his resignation in December to the London Missionary Society. Whether it was wise for Livingstone to detach himself from missionary service and become a government official with a purely secular commission may be doubted in view of later events.

He valued his appointment in February as H M Consul at Quillimane for the east coast of Africa south of Zanzibar. It had financial as well as prestigious blessings. Besides, he liked the hat as well, and was to make the black peaked cap with gold braiding his standard head-dress.

---

[17] *Ibid*, pp 225–226.
[18] D L to R Murchison 15/04/1857, *Zambezi Journals* Vol 1, p xxiii in Jeal, p 171.

David Livingstone before the Zambesi expedition. Note the
consular cap

Plans were cemented for the Zambesi expedition—Livingstone was to have six European assistants, besides many naval men who would join the party from time to time, and the government was generously prepared to equip the party. However, learning to cope on his previously meagre budget of £100 caused him to make the mistake of over-economy. He bought an inferior paddle-steamer of shallow draught. Livingstone still expected the Society to build a mission station and Tidman, caught in a dilemma, decided to send a missionary in May, having been let down by Livingstone.

As his stay in Britain drew to a close the doctor was invited to have a private audience with the Queen.

> Livingstone told Her Majesty that he would now be able to say to the natives that he had seen his chief, his not having done so before being a constant subject of surprise to the children of the African wilderness. He mentioned to Her Majesty also that the people were in the habit of inquiring whether his chief was wealthy; and that when he assured them she was very wealthy, they would ask how many cows she had.[19]

A banquet was given for the Livingstones prior to their departure and amid all the pomp and ceremony Livingstone turned the gaze of the public to his wife. He declared:

> It is scarcely fair to ask a man to praise his own wife, but I can only say that when I parted from her at the Cape, telling her that I should return in two years, and when it happened that I was absent four years and a half, I supposed that I should appear before her with a damaged character. I was, however, forgiven. My wife, who has always been the main spoke in my wheel, will accompany me in this expedition, and will be most useful to me. She is familiar with the languages of South Africa. She is able to work. She is willing to endure, and she well knows that in that country one must put one's hand to everything. In the country to which I am about to proceed she knows that at the missionary's

[19] Blaikie, p 235.

station the wife must be the maid-of-all-work within, while the husband must be the jack-of-all-trades without, and glad am I indeed that I am to be accompanied by my guardian angel.[20]

One of the greatest sacrifices was having to leave the children behind with their grandmother in order for them to finish their schooling. Almost daily the doctor would write a few lines to the children, urging them to take Jesus for their friend. In a letter to Tom he wrote:

> My dear Tom—I am soon going off from this country, and will leave you to the care of Him who neither slumbers nor sleeps, and never disappointed any one who put his trust in Him. If you make Him your friend He will be better to you than any companion can be. He is a friend that sticketh closer than a brother. May He grant you grace to seek Him and to serve Him. I have nothing better to say to you than to take God for your Father, Jesus for your Saviour, and the Holy Spirit for your sanctifier. Do this and you are safe for ever. No evil can then befall you.[21]

The treasure which he had found and lived for was for him greater than anything else the world could offer. His prayer was that his children would also come to know Christ.

As the ship 'Pearl' edged out of Liverpool late on the night of 12th March 1858 a snowstorm sprinkled flakes on the faces of those on the docks. Livingstone was embarking on an expedition which would sear his spirit.

---

[20] *Ibid*, p 237.
[21] *Ibid*, p 240.

Charles
Livingstone

Dr John
Kirk

Thomas
Baines

11

The Zambesi and Shire; Sickness and Sensitive Spirits

Livingstone was forty-five years of age and this expedition was to prove to be the most exacting of all. He had under his command six European assistants; more had been suggested, but he refused them. Commander Bedingfield, the Royal Navy Officer whom Livingstone knew from Loanda, was to prove the first problem. Dr John Kirk, MD, a young man of twenty-six, went as botanist and physician and Richard Thornton as geologist. Also Thomas Baines, a middle-aged man with varied and wide experience, to act as artist and store-keeper, and George Rae, a Scottish ship's engineer. Finally, Charles Livingstone made up the team. His function was vague, but it was hoped that his skills in cotton growing as well as photography would be put to use. An interesting combination of men who were to suffer much under malaria and the torrid heat of the Zambesi.

The journey was initially rough and many were seasick. However, Livingstone noted that Mary had another reason other than the stormy seas to be ill; she was 'affected with the nine months complaint'. After pondering the matter he decided that she and their son, Oswell, should disembark at the Cape. This they did on 21st April 1858.

The reception at the Cape was warm, for Livingstone's missionary and exploratory exploits were held in admiration by many ambitious men. Moffat, however, was angry with his son-in-law for deceiving the Society and withdrawing from establishing the Makololo Mission. Furthermore, the doctor had encouraged Moffat's son, John, to leave the Missionary Society which had trained him to become an independent missionary. Livingstone had promised him a salary and a lump sum of £500 to help him get established, totalling £1,400. Livingstone did this to ensure that the Makololo would have a missionary should he, Livingstone, not go.

On 1st May 1858 the 'Pearl' departed from the Cape. On this occasion it was the doctor who left his wife at the docks as the ship set sail for the mouth of the Zambesi. David confided in a friend, James Young, that 'it was a bitter parting with my wife, like tearing the heart out of one. It was so unexpected.'[1]

Livingstone, the consul, set a high standard for himself and the men under his command. Once the expedition was underway he planned to have prayers every morning with the party, and each man was provided with a full, written portfolio outlining their duties.

Finally the ship arrived at the mouth of the Zambesi on 16th May 1858. All were well except for Dr Livingstone who was suffering from chronic diarrhoea. None the less, he set the team to work, for he did not want to remain in the malaria-infested delta longer than was necessary. Too many men had lost their lives there.

They moved the three sections of the 'Ma-Robert', the small eighty-foot paddle-steamer called after Mrs Livingstone's African name, by bolting the compartments together. A promising opening into the mouth of the Zambesi was investigated, but to no avail. The delta was a mass of sand bars and mangrove swamps which thrived in the murky, muddy water and high temperatures. After three anxious days the Kongone mouth was discovered and the 'Pearl', together with the 'Ma-Robert', found its way through.

While quinine was dealt out plentifully, the memory of the

---

[1] D L to James Young 10/05/1858 in Blaikie, p 248.

failure of the Niger expedition and the subsequent death of all stirred the Scot to find a passage to the Zambesi and up to Tete without delay.

Unfortunately, Livingstone had had little, if any, earlier training or experience in leading men. He was a solitary man who, though he enjoyed the company of certain friends, was aloof to many others. While a leader needs to be able to identify with his men and relate to their responsibilities in reinforcing the efforts of the team, Livingstone's iron will and incredible powers of endurance were paradoxically to prove counter-productive to the expedition, for he demanded of every man the same stamina and tenacity as he enforced on himself.

Livingstone had incredible patience with the natives, possibly because of cultural difference, but little time for Europeans of unequal disposition. His years alone had made him self-sufficient and disinclined to talk unless he had something specific to say. He was aware too of the critics, many of whom would love to see the expedition fail, and were wary of giving a consularship to a mere peasant Scot who had trundled about Africa for a few years.

The plan was to get everyone up to Tete in the 'Pearl' and from there travel by the smaller vessel to the Batoka Plateau, where the agricultural experiments were to begin. Unfortunately, the shallow river and shifting sand bars marred progress and it was decided to disembark on an island forty miles from the mouth of the river. Here, on Expedition Island as it was to be known, stores were deposited. A steel shed was erected and several men allotted to remain with the provisions while the rest of the team, after bidding farewell to the 'Pearl', took as much as possible up to Shupanga and Senna.

The country was in a state of war between the Portuguese and tribes led by a half-caste named Mariano and that, coupled with the high risk of fever, encouraged the men to move urgently upstream. Livingstone and the crew would have to

The 'Ma-Robert' on the Zambesi

navigate through the rather tense battle zone. To complicate matters the designated captain of the 'Ma-Robert' had resigned.

Commander Bedingfield felt he had command over Captain Duncan and his ship the 'Pearl'. This resulted in a rather heated clash in which Livingstone rebuked the former in front of everybody; Bedingfield resigned, but the consul persuaded him to stay. Character clashes continually arose between the trio, resulting in Bedingfield's resignation being accepted before the expedition was truly underway.

Livingstone now navigated the 'Ma-Robert', and on 15th June 1858 they met with the rebels who came on board. However, after hearing the English view on slavery they proposed not to hinder their progress. Henceforth they were recognised by both parties; although on a later occasion when they landed to greet the Portuguese they found themselves in the midst of a battle. As bullets shot past, Livingstone gave medical assistance to the Portuguese Governor who was suffering with fever, finally taking him on board the 'Ma-Robert' and up to Shupanga. This was the neighbourhood in which they were now labouring.

It was soon apparent that the 'Ma-Robert' was a dubious vessel. She consumed vast quantities of wood which they had to chop for one-and-a-half days to keep the vessel going for one day. The swift current of the Zambesi did not help matters, nor did the many sand bars upon which the vessel constantly stuck, and the sight of men dragging the hunk of metal with ropes was not uncommon. Furthermore, the boilers and cylinders were always giving trouble and the pipes were often blocked. The cramped, heated conditions frayed nerves and when it rained the roof leaked and all were saturated. But the 'wretched sham vessel', as Livingstone called it, was yet to display her greatest weakness. The hull was made out of thin steel which had not been properly tested and soon started to rust in a honeycomb of holes. The 'Old Asthmatic' had to be plugged up, to no avail, with clay and at night she would be beached upon a sand bar to prevent her sinking.

When 'Ma-Robert' took her first load, Kirk, Baines and Charles Livingstone were left on Expedition Island with a few Kuruman natives Moffat had brought to the Cape to join the expedition. By 9th July 1858 Baines took ill with contracted pupils, shivering and severe headache. Charles also succumbed to sickness and they battled under Dr Kirk's kind care for days, finally recovering before the 'Ma-Robert' returned on 19th July. Livingstone, who had not seen them sick, took a rather unsympathetic view of their state of health and urged them to keep active, for that he believed from experience in Angola to be the best form of action to take.

They reloaded the boat and quickly set off, Baines now accompanying Livingstone, Rae and Kirk. Baines was dropped off to guard the stores at Senna while goods were slowly moved up the Zambesi. Rae contracted the fever and suffered with it, but the 'Livingstone Pill' of quinine and a few other ingredients brought about a quick recovery.

The heat, claustrophobic conditions and fever aggravated working conditions, and friction soon developed between the men. Charles Livingstone was the trouble-monger, whose rather self-righteous attitude caused much unpleasantness. Sadly David constantly took sides with his brother which further isolated him from the hearts of the men with whom he worked.

Finally the 'Old Asthmatic' wheezed and spluttered her way into Tete on 8th September 1858, many months having been spent merely in moving supplies. Dr Livingstone went alone in the boat and 'no sooner did the Makololo recognise him, than they excitedly rushed to the water's edge. Some were hastening to embrace him, but others cried out, "Don't touch him, you will spoil his new clothes."'[2] They had remained for more than two years at Tete expecting him to return. Thirty had died of smallpox and six had been killed by an

---

[2] Zam. & Tribs., p 42.

unfriendly chief. They said to Livingstone: 'The Tete people often taunted us by saying, "Your Englishman will never return," but we trusted you and now we shall sleep'.[3]

Six months after the 'Pearl' had first anchored off the mouth of the Zambesi the whole party was united at Tete. Morale was low and Livingstone, in his determination to reach the interior, remained aloof to the diseases to which his men succumbed, believing activity to be the answer. This theory they took a dim view of; it may have worked with Livingstone, but they were not that enthusiastic. The consul's restless energy often made him a trying companion. Coupled with that he communicated very little and remained undeviating in all his plans. The more problems that perpetuated the more the pioneer plummeted into a pondering state of surliness, which Kirk was to describe as 'ever morose'.

The Governor of Tete welcomed the party and showed them exemplary kindness, though Livingstone was to remain firm in his attitude to slavery. Those slaves, however, who were in the direct ownership of the Governor and other Portuguese were generally well-treated. One native, Chibanti, told Livingstone that he had sold himself into slavery for he had no parents or relative to care for him. Thus

> he sold himself to Major Sicard, a notoriously kind master whose slaves had little to do, and plenty to eat. 'And how much did you get for yourself?' they asked 'Three thirty yard pieces of cotton cloth,' he replied; 'and I forthwith bought a man, a woman, and a child who cost me two of the pieces and I had one piece left.'[4]

He subsequently purchased more slaves and gradually opened up a business carrying ivory by canoe to Quillimane.

On 8th November 1858 Livingstone, Kirk and Rae set out in the 'Ma-Robert' to confront the next obstacle in their

---

[3] Blaikie, p 251.
[4] Zam. & Tribs., p 49.

path—the Kebrabasa rapids. They had left Charles, Thornton and Baines in Tete to recuperate from fever. After one-and-a-half days steaming, the Zambesi narrowed into a gorge thirty yards across and the current increased, reducing the 'Ma-Robert' to a few knots. Sheer black rocks rose formidably on either side of the river. The rugged mountainous region was an unfriendly sight.

They managed to negotiate through the first small rapid, but at the second the force of the current swung her bows round onto a rock, piercing her just above the water-line. There she stayed whilst Livingstone and Kirk set off the next day on foot over rough, rocky country to investigate upstream. The next rapids they encountered were worse, with a fall of eight feet in twenty yards at one section. Kirk calculated the current to be so great and eddies so strong that when the river was in flood no steamer could hope to pass up or down in safety. Livingstone believed that the river would burst its banks and as a result slow down. He so desperately wanted to establish a highway into the interior that at one stage he even contemplated blasting the rocks to create the waterway.

None the less, a full search of the rapids still had to be completed. They returned to the boat and then to Tete where no time was lost in gathering all the men, invalid or not, to explore the region. The party had to progress on foot; Baines and Thornton held the party up, together with Charles Livingstone, as understandably they were more interested in convalescing than clambering over scorching rocks. David's brother was the main offender, but favouritism prevailed and a further rift developed between Baines, Thornton and the consul. Eventually, Thornton and Charles were left behind.

The banks consisted of boulders covered with a black glaze, which made them slippery. The sun too was scorching; anyone who left his hand on a rock for more than a few seconds was badly burned, but Livingstone would not give in. Even his thermometer gave readings of 130°F.

The Makololo told Dr Livingstone they 'always thought he had a heart but now they believed he had none' and tried to persuade Dr Kirk to return, on the ground that it must be evident, in attempting to go where no living foot could tread, his leader had given unmistakable signs of having gone mad. All their efforts of persuasion, however, were lost upon Dr Kirk, as he had not learned their language and his leader . . . was not at pains to enlighten him.[5]

At one stage they thought they had passed the worst and could blast the rocks. Livingstone's spirits began to rise until, while travelling back, a member of the Makololo informed him of a fearful waterfall that lay further upstream as high as a tree. He listened in stunned silence and almost disbelief. Kirk volunteered to accompany Livingstone, and during the next few days the two men encountered the worst conditions imaginable. It was, as Livingstone put it, 'The hardest work he had ever done in his whole life.' Slippery rocks gave way to thick scrub which pulled and tore at their clothes, almost taunting them in their work.

On 2nd December 1858 they reached two rapids, but these did not fit the dramatic description given by the Makololo. Later that day, after clambering up an almost perpendicular cliff, the two men set eyes on a sorry scene. Below them was a waterfall thirty feet high. As water thundered over it the Scot, who had made it his life's ambition to open up a path into the interior, looked on. His heart sank as the shock seared his spirit. Only a few weeks earlier, on 1st September 1858, he had written in his journal:

We shall succeed, but I feel concerned about our companions down the river. The Lord look in mercy on us all. It is His work we are engaged in. The high position I have been raised to was not of my seeking. Nor was the eclat which greeted me at home a matter of my choice. I therefore commit all to the care and help

---

[5] *Ibid*, p 60.

of Him who has said, 'Commit thy way unto the Lord, trust also in Him, and He shall bring it to pass.' I do so from the bottom of my heart, and pleasant it is to cast one's cares on Him who careth for us. Lord, take Thou the guidance of all my affairs, and let them all tend to the promotion of Thy glory.[6]

His journal entry on 17th October 1858 carried some hope:

If we can blast away the rocks which obstruct the passage, how thankful I shall feel. It will be like opening wide the gates which have barred the interior for ages. Will the good Spirit of the Lord grant this honour unto us, His servants, of this expedition? If it is to promote the good of my fellow men, I will turn quarryman next.

End of November 1858—Things look dark for our enterprise. This Kebrabasa is what I never expected. What we shall do if this is to be the end of the navigation I cannot now divine, but here I am, and I am trusting Him who never made ashamed those who did so. I look back to all that has happened to me. The honours heaped on me were not of my seeking—they came unbidden. I could not even answer the letters I got from the great and noble, and I never expected the fame which followed me. It was Thy hand that gave it all, O Thou blessed and Holy One, and it was given for Thy dear Son's sake.

It will promote Thy glory if Africa is made a land producing the articles now raised only or chiefly by slave labour. O grant me the honour to begin the great work here, but whatever Thy Will may be, I do hereby submit to it as the best. Only punish me not as my grievous lack of service and unprofitableness deserve. Spare me, good Lord, spare me, whom Thou hast redeemed with Thy most precious blood. The good Lord look upon me. Thou hast raised me. I trust in Thee if Thou throwst me down. Spare me, dear Jesus. Dear Lamb of God, do not utterly despise the work of Thy hands. I am all the work of Thy hands.

December 3rd 1858—Came to a dead halt, urging everything we could think of to induce the guides to go on. They at last said

---

[6] Campbell, p 253.

they would go to die with me. The Makololo declared . . . that I had become insane surely, for they showed me the broken blisters on their feet in vain . . . To make it permanently available for commerce the assistance of a powerful Government is necessary, and a company of Sappers would soon clear out the channel.[7]

As the full realisation of the Zambesi being closed to him sunk in, Livingstone remained in a silent, sombre mood. The expedition to all intents and purposes had failed. Had God let him down after leading and guiding him so far?

In the Bible we read: 'God causes all things to work together for good to those who love God, to those who are called according to His purpose.'[8]

Livingstone certainly saw himself as God's chosen instrument to bring enlightenment to the cultures at the centre of the continent. Many of his critics would make light of the sense of direction and purpose he displayed yet, despite his many failings, he was prepared to be used by God for his glory.

Dr David Livingstone was for a time greatly depressed and disillusioned. However, the circumstances had one great benefit in that they forced him to turn north and lay bare to the world the arterial roads of the slave-trade. The man who was broken in spirit, unbeknown to himself, was to be one of God's great instruments in the decline of the sordid slave-trade.

Upon returning to Tete Livingstone made application to the government for a more suitable boat, and while awaiting an answer from London he decided to explore the Shire River in the hope of mapping the great lake which the natives said was the source of the Shire.

On 20th December 1858 the consul, Kirk and Rae left Tete and steamed to the mouth of the Shire. A beginning was made on this enterprise in January 1859 when the party succeeded

---

[7] *Ibid*, p 254.
[8] Romans 8:28.

in pushing up the Shire for 200 miles. Weeds hindered their progress, but they persevered before their progress was stopped by the rapids. These Livingstone named the Murchison Cataracts after Sir Robert Murchison.

The unrelenting strain on all concerned was not conducive to good humour and amiability. The 'Old Asthmatic' kept up her hunger for firewood, while the weak walls invited the water to pour in.

When Livingstone ordered another boat he told the new Foreign Secretary, Lord Malmesbury, 'We are all of the opinion that a steamer of light draught would pass the rapids without difficulty when the river is in full flood.'[9] This statement was not exactly true, and Livingstone probably feared the recalling of the expedition if results were not forthcoming. To obtain these, a boat capable of venturing through rapids was desperately needed. If the Shire was not navigable, Livingstone realised he would have to cancel the boat and disband the expedition.

Livingstone had enough data based on the information available from a Tete trader, Candido Jose da Costa Cardosa, to draw a basic map and ventured his life and the lives of his crew in opening up a new area. The year 1859 was to be a grand one for the Zambesi expedition, but it would not be without its problems.

On the Zambesi River natives had often run to the banks to gaze at the strange-looking boat, but on the Shire the locals were not so friendly. On several occasions poisoned arrows were fired at the steamer and warning shots were offered in return, while other crowds demonstrated that dues were required for passage. This change in attitude was one of the first noticeable fruits of the abhorrent slave-trade. The doctor was in no mood to endure the same problems he encountered in Angola and they pressed on until they reached the rapids.

---

[9] 17th December 1858, Kirk on the Zambesi, p 136 in Jeal, p 212.

The purpose of this visit was to do a reconnaissance of the river and let the locals see they were friendly. Occasionally Livingstone would venture ashore to make contact with the less aggressive folk. 'Long afterwards an old Chief recounted that as the "burning canoe" approached, he hid his warriors in the reeds ready to fire off a shower of arrows. But he relaxed when the Doctor stepped ashore, swept off his cap and smiled at him. "How," concluded the chief, "could I give the sign to kill a man who smiled?"'[10]

It is interesting to note Livingstone's views regarding peace and war. In reply to a question of that nature he quipped:

I love peace as much as any mortal man. In fact I go quite beyond you for I love it so much I would fight for it. You who in a land abounding in police and soldiery ready to catch every ruffian who would dare to disturb your pretty dwelling may think this language too strong, but your principles to be good must abide the test of stretching. Fancy yourself here . . . I can never cease wondering why the friends who sincerely believe in the power of peace principles don't test them by going forth to the heathen as missionaries of the cross. I for one would heartily welcome them from the belief that their conduct would have a good influence though it would never secure their safety.[11]

Though Livingstone as yet had never fired to kill any man, he knew that by merely having a weapon it would have a restraint on them.

The boat returned to Tete and plans were made to go on foot once the rapids were reached. Livingstone remained committed to the relationship he had with his Lord and Saviour, and journal entries in March depict such a love.

March 3rd, 1859—If we dedicate ourselves to God unreservedly He will make use of whatever peculiarities of constitution He has

[10] Ransford, pp 156, 158.
[11] D L to Joseph W Sturge 11/12/1858 in Chamberlin, p 268.

imparted for His own glory, and He will in answer to prayer give wisdom to guide. He will so guide as to make useful. O how far am I from that hearty devotion to God I read of in others! The Lord have mercy on me a sinner!

March 5th—A woman left Tete yesterday with a cargo of slaves (20 men and 40 women) in irons to sell to St. Cruz (a trader), for exportation at Bourbon. Francisco at Shupanga is the great receiver for Cruz. This is carnival, and it is observed chiefly as a drinking feast.

March 6th—Teaching Makololo Lord's Prayer and Creed. Prayers as usual at 9:30 am. When employed in active travel, my mind becomes inactive, and the heart cold and dead, but after remaining some time quiet, the heart revives, and I become more spiritually-minded. This is a mercy which I have experienced before, and when I see a matter to be duty I go on regardless of my feelings. I do trust that the Lord is with me, though the mind is engaged in other matters than the spiritual. I want my whole life to be out and out for the Divine glory, and my earnest prayer is that God may accept what His own Spirit must have implanted—the desire to glorify Him. I have been more than usually drawn out in earnest prayer of late—for the expedition—for my family—the fear lest's misrepresentation may injure the cause of Christ—the hope that I may be permitted to open this dark land to the blessed gospel. I have cast all before my God. Good Lord, have mercy upon me. Leave me not, nor forsake me. He has guided well in time past. I commit my way to Him for the future. All I have received has come from Him. Will He be pleased in mercy to use me for His glory? I have prayed for this, and Jesus Himself said, 'Ask, and ye shall receive,' and a host of statements to the same effect. There is a great deal of trifling frivolousness in not trusting in God. Not trusting in Him who is truth itself, faithfulness, the same yesterday, today, and for ever! It is presumption not to trust in Him implicitly, and yet this heart is sometimes fearfully guilty of distrust. I am ashamed to think of it. Ay; but He must put the trusting, loving, childlike spirit in by His grace. O Lord, I am Thine, truly I am Thine—take me—do what seemeth good in Thy sight with me, and give me complete resignation to do Thy will in all things.[12]

---

[12] Blaikie, pp 253–254.

By mid-March they were underway and the 'Old Asthmatic' wheezed and spluttered her way upstream. Hippopotami kept carefully out of the way, while the crocodiles frequently made a rush at the vessel as if to attack it and, coming within a few feet of her, just as suddenly sank like a stone to reappear further away with stealthy eyes surveying the scene. The crocodiles were very aggressive and on 21st March 1859 a woman was taken by one. The crew of the 'Ma-Robert' 'saw him dragging her up to a quiet spot to eat her. A relative, probably her mother, stood wailing at the bank.'[13]

As he surveyed the surrounding countryside, the consul saw the importance of colonising this region. Although he had no colour prejudice, he was a purposeful patriot, genuinely believing the British to be the salt of the earth. After all, they had a democracy which could not be matched and both the natives and immigrants would benefit by working alongside each other. Christian settlers would, he believed, lead the locals into a better economic life and higher ethical principles. His anxiety to establish such settlements was also inspired by the sickening sight of the slave-trade which would disappear with the onset of commerce.

Livingstone, with amazing insight, also knew the limitations of colonisation. He wrote in his Kolobeng notebook (1850–1853):

> With colonies it is the same as with children—they receive protection for a time and obey from a feeling of weakness and attachment; but beyond the time at which they require a right to think for themselves, the attempt to perpetuate subordination necessarily engenders a hatred which effectually extinguishes the feeble gratitude that man in any condition is capable of cherishing.

Though the dream for these colonies took hold of his heart, Livingstone could not convince those in Whitehall. They were

---

[13] *Zambesi Journals of David Livingstone*, Vol I, p 88 in Jeal, p 216.

unwilling to winch boats and families past cataracts into the dark continent.

Once the tin tub had made it to the Murchison cataracts, Livingstone and Kirk set off on foot in search of a small lake. They were now entering the country controlled by the Ajawa who acted as middle men for the Arab slave-traders. Livingstone now understood why the Manganja people along the banks of the river were aggressive and frightened. On 18th April 1859 they reached Lake Shirwa, which was roughly seventy miles long by thirty miles wide. This lake, he was informed, was but small in comparison to the great lake further north. Satisfied with what had been achieved, and determined 'rather to gain the confidence of the people by degrees than to explore', the doctor led his people back to the boat, passing close to the site of modern Blantyre.

They coaxed the 'Ma-Robert' back into the Zambesi and travelled down to the coast in order to see if any mail had been delivered. No ship lay at the coast, but they saw a customs house being built at the Zambesi mouth. A sure sign the Portuguese were closing the interior to foreign shipping.

They were back at Tete on 23rd June 1859 where tempers between Charles Livingstone, Baines and Thornton were indeed tense. Charles told his brother tales of Baines' thieving and Thornton's laziness.

The consul needed little encouragement to discharge Thornton. In a letter to Sir Roderick Murchison, Livingstone told him, 'Thornton has turned out insufferably lazy and so absolutely useless as a geologist that much against my will I have stopped his salary.' When Livingstone forced him to mine a coal shaft to check the ore deposit 'he did not know how to mine: lay in his tent all day and gorged himself with food . . . a disgrace to the expedition and English name'.[14] In addition, Livingstone did not take kindly to his 'sneers about

---

[14] D L to Sir Roderick Murchison 22/07/1859 NAZ L I 1/1/1 no. 1029–1036.

Scotchmen', and thus Thornton was duly handed a letter of dismissal. The young man had been in his early twenties when he joined the expedition and it was to prove, although harsh at the time, a good lesson in his life. Thornton showed a new spirit of enterprise by leaving the Zambesi and joining up with Baron von der Decken when they explored Mount Kilimanjaro.

Later Livingstone, encouraged by Thornton's new lease of life, was to invite him to rejoin the expedition. He accepted the offer and received back pay to the date of his dismissal, which no doubt helped to amend any hard feelings. Thornton was tragically to die a short while later.

Thornton's dismissal had been relatively simple compared to the saga with Baines, who was an experienced traveller, respected by many and with a good record. However, he possessed a phlegmatic character with regard to his store-keeping, which was understandable considering fever and the difficulty they had in monitoring stocks. Accusations of him misappropriating the expedition's paints and stores, already in short supply, were levelled by young Charles Livingstone. Sadly the doctor listened to his brother and was to make a big mistake.

David Livingstone, like his brother, suffered from moods of depression, and this had a great bearing on his action. Had he used more discretion and wisdom he would probably have seen that the men had suffered from fever during which time marauders could have made off with provisions. None the less, Baines was left with the stores and a strict letter from the consul when the party departed on 11th July 1859. In the letter Livingstone stated that he was prepared to overlook the misdemeanour providing Baines did not paint portraits of the Portuguese with expedition material or take them for rides in the whaler as Baines had previously damaged the boat. He was also to monitor the stores strictly.

Travel up the Shire was not easy. The 'Ma-Robert' took to entertaining more water in her bilges. The hot, humid conditions within the boat became an ideal breeding ground for rats, which appeared after dark creating havoc. They woke the weary travellers up by scampering across their faces and then burst into a loud laugh of He! He! He!. 'Every night they went fore and aft, rousing with impartial feet every sleeper, and laughing to scorn the aimless blows, growls, and deadly rushes of outraged humanity.'[15]

Scorpions, centipedes and poisonous spiders were frequently brought into the ship with the wood, and occasionally found their way into the beds. Fortunately in every instance they were discovered and destroyed before doing any harm. 'Snakes sometimes came in with the wood, but oftener floated down the river.' They were also found 'climbing on board with ease by the chain-cable, and some poisonous ones were caught in the cabin.'[16] A green snake also lived with them for several weeks, concealing himself behind the casing of the deckhouse in the daytime. As Livingstone wrote, 'To be aroused in the dark by five feet of cold green snake gliding over one's face, is rather unpleasant, however rapid the movement may be.'[17] Myriads of cockroaches also lived on the vessel, biting the sleeping men as well as devouring their food, flannels and boots. In vain they tried to eliminate them, but for every one killed hundreds seemed to take their place.

These conditions were prone to produce irritable passengers, but Livingstone was determined to continue. He had already asked for another vessel, but no news came as to its building progress. The first hundred miles of the 200-mile journey to Lake Nyasa took three weeks, and by the time the expedition members started to climb the Shire Highlands they were already exhausted and touchy. Livingstone's mood darkened with the dawning of the devastating destruction of the slave-

[15] Zam. & Tribs., p 151.
[16] Ibid.
[17] Ibid, p 152.

trade. When they passed through villages, the people ran into their huts, 'the children screamed in terror, and even the hens would fly away and leave their chickens'.[18] By the side of the path they would come across piles of slave-taming sticks. They were about eight feet long; the victim's neck was put into the V-shape of the top of the stick and a bolt secured it in place. Another slave would have to hold the other end until the victim was considered tame, then he was allowed to go into chains. Wrote Livingstone:

> My heart is sore when I think of so many of our countrymen in poverty and misery, while they might do so much good to themselves and others where our Heavenly Father has so abundantly provided fruitful hills and fertile valleys . . . But all is in the hands of the all-wise Father. We must trust that He will bring all out right at last.[19]

In the same letter to his daughter he urged:

> My dear Agnes, you must take Him to be your Father and guide. Tell Him all that is in your heart, and make Him your confidant. His ear is ever open, and He despiseth not the humblest sigh. He is your best friend, and loves at all times. It is not enough to be a servant, you must be a friend of Jesus. Love Him and surrender your entire being to Him. The more you trust Him, casting all your care upon Him, the more He is pleased, and He will so guide you that your life will be for His own glory.[20]

The dour doctor loved the Lord, though his problems, as with all humans regardless of their fame, were evident. He kept his thoughts private, alienating himself at the expense of his followers at a time when his men most needed support and encouragement. Fever further plagued the crew just when they needed much perseverance to tackle the Shire Highlands.

---

[18] D L to Agnes L 1/06/1859 in Blaikie, p 256.
[19] *Ibid.*
[20] *Ibid*, pp 256–257.

They finally reached the southern shore of Lake Nyasa, the second largest lake in Africa, on 17th September 1859. This area was already well-known to Arab slave-traders whose main routes passed just south of it.

The consul realised that Britain would have to move fast in order to annex this territory and move against the slave-trade. Livingstone wanted the people to be free physically as well as spiritually.

A Portuguese trader, Candido Jose da Costa Cardosa, had visited the region earlier, but he had neither claimed it for Portugal nor even mapped it conclusively. Thus the region was available to receive the stamp of a British Protectorate, though that in itself would take a lot, for in addition to the interests of the Arabs, the tribes were at war with one another and the Portuguese had lost their love for the doctor. They resented his outspoken remarks regarding their expanding involvement with the slave-trade since the blockade of Angola. Furthermore, they were not too partial to the British clambering over land they felt belonged to themselves.

Livingstone realised that to win the support of the British Government for the development of this region he would need to convince them that the Shire Highlands were the ultimate region to colonise and that the slave-trade was sufficiently horrific to warrant immediate action. In order to despatch his latest proposals he decided to return to the coast and await a vessel. Thus the party returned to the rusting 'Ma-Robert'.

The Baines issue still bothered Livingstone and he decided more drastic action was necessary, so he sent Kirk off with an official letter. His orders were to search Baines' goods for any stolen articles and to accompany him to the coast whereby, having been relieved of his duties, he would be discharged. This was embarrassing for Kirk, who found Baines to be rather 'a good-natured soul' who, when well, worked hard. Baines continually professed his innocence. Indeed Kirk had found nothing which could incriminate him, but such pleas fell on deaf ears. The engineer Rae was to accompany Kirk overland

and they would then use the smaller vessel to take Baines to the coast and also meet Livingstone prior to Baines' departure.

Livingstone was not a well man; he had haemorrhoids and these frequently bled. One note in his diary was that he had bled all night.[21] Such a condition was serious, yet he continued to demand a high standard from himself and his men. The 'Ma-Robert' reached Kongone on 10th November, but not until 3rd December was contact made with the 'Lynx', the ship delivering provisions. A few letters had been sent and Livingstone received these while waiting for the 'Lynx'. One letter was to inform him that they were 'blessed with a little daughter on 16th November 1858 at Kuruman. A fine healthy child.'[22] Anna-Mary was already a year old when Livingstone received the news.

Livingstone had ordered a boat and now that the 'Ma-Robert' was beyond being fixed by an engineer it was decided that Rae would return to Britain to oversee the new vessel's construction. Rae did not travel with Baines, but was dropped off at Mazaro from where he made his way to Quillimane. Disobeying Livingstone's instructions to take a passage via the Cape, the engineer went home by Aden and was shipwrecked, though he managed to survive.

Meanwhile at Shupanga, Livingstone was pleased to receive a little more mail. He learned that four British universities had combined to send out a mission to the Zambesi. However, there were no fresh orders from the government. Livingstone was not one to waste time waiting for orders to come from Britain, so he elected to travel back to the Makololo to return the men to their tribe.

In Tete the Portuguese were very cool towards the consul, who denounced his erstwhile friends as members of 'an utterly

---

[21] Diary, 14th October 1859, *ibid*, p 264.
[22] *Ibid*.

effete worn-out used up syphilitic race'.[23] Thornton was also back in Tete and, as mentioned earlier, Livingstone allowed him to rejoin the team as they prepared to move west into the interior on foot.

Charles Livingstone was not keen to travel and constantly had arguments with his brother, which to the others appeared to be mere temper tantrums. The consul, however, remained unmoved. He had decided to return to the Makololo.

[23] D L to W C Oswell 1/11/59 in Jeal, p 219.

12

The Missionary Returns to the Makololo

Temporary repairs were needed yet again to the launch, though it was clear she could not be kept afloat much longer.

Progress up river was not easy. The 'Ma-Robert' craved wood and the men were without fresh provisions. 'The slave-trade had done its work, for formerly all kinds of provisions could be procured at any point, and at the cheapest rate.' The expedition could not get anything by any means.

Optimistically, the doctor wrote in a letter to Mr Braithwaite, a good friend, 'It is well that God and not the devil reigns, and will bring His own purpose to pass, right through the midst of wars and passions of men'.

Stopping at Tete to drop off two sailors and collect provisions, the consul also installed a sugar mill for the locals. It was a gift from a Miss Whatley in Dublin and, though intended for Sekeletu, he did not receive it due to the physical barrier of the Victoria Falls and Kebrabasa rapids.

Final preparations for the journey were made. Land was obtained for the two sailors who would remain in charge of the expedition stores and on 15th May they made a start from Tete. In order to escape the extortion of the Banyai tribes, the party proceeded up the left bank of the river.

Those of the Makololo who worked on board the ship were not sorry that the steamer could not accompany them owing to the rapids. They had become heartily tired of cutting the wood that the insatiable furnace of the 'Old Asthmatic' required. One worker laughingly exclaimed in broken English,

'Oh, Kebrabasa good, very good; no let shipee up to Sekeletu, too muchee work, cuttee woodyee, cuttee woodyee: Kebrabasa good'.[1]

The party was led by David and Charles Livingstone and John Kirk. In looking to the future Livingstone was, as always, endeavouring to obey the injunction, 'Commit thy way to the Lord, trust also in Him, and He shall bring it to pass'.[2]

At the crossing of the Kafue River news reached the travellers of the arrival of the London Missionary Society in Matabeleland. It was reported to be prospering and this filled Livingstone with cheerful expectations of the corresponding mission to the Makololo. Little did the Livingstones anticipate the sad reality.

On every side, the sickness of the slave-trade stared the expedition in the face. Furthermore, the doctor was infuriated to hear that Portuguese slave-dealers had no scruples in sheltering themselves under Livingstone's own name and reputation, declaring that they had his authority to do their evil deeds. Sadness and suspicion soured the once-smiling faces.

Livingstone convinced the folk of his calling and was encouraged to continue. They rose about five each day as dawn appeared, had a cup of tea and a bit of biscuit; stowed away the cooking and sleeping utensils and all were on the path by sunrise. At about nine they stopped for break-fast, which generally consisted of heated-up leftovers from supper, and then continued for several hours. They averaged approximately six hours' travel per day at a leisurely pace.

Mid-afternoon they pitched the camp, hunted game for dinner and collected and studied specimens. A dozen fires were kindled nightly in the camp and the men would huddle together in conversation. At times animated political discus-sions sprung up and the amount of eloquence expended on

---

[1] Zam. & Tribs., p 173.
[2] Blaikie, p 268.

those occasions would keep the doctor amused. Each man had his own ideas on tribal government which he voiced and if agreed upon would be echoed by a loud 'e he', equivalent to the English 'hear, hear'.

It is believed that the souls of departed chiefs enter into lions and render them sacred. On one occasion, attracted by the buffalo meat, a lion crept close to the camp and roused all hands with its roaring. 'Tuba Mokoro, imbued with the popular belief that the beast was a Chief in disguise, scolded him roundly during his brief intervals of silence . . . "You are like the scavenger beetle, and think of yourself only. You have not the heart of a Chief; why don't you kill your own beef?" '[3]

They then threatened to send a ball through him if he did not depart. Prudently he kept in the dark, outside of the luminous circle made by the fires, where he did not like to venture. A little strychnine was put into a piece of meat and thrown to him. He soon departed and they heard no more of him.

The Englishmen struggled with the cooking. The cook would rarely make the maize meal properly and the raw meal would play havoc with their digestive system. On complaining, the Makololo called them 'mere water-porridge fellows'.[4]

They all slept under the stars unless a chief gave the headmen a hut to rest in. The fires were continually restored as they burned low and Matonga, one of the men, volunteered to take sole charge of the doctor's fire. For payment he received the heads and necks of all the beasts they killed. A profitable venture, especially when they encountered giraffe or even buffalo. But on days when only guinea-fowl were bagged for the pot he loudly complained.

The party soon established itself and the deserters, who preferred their women in Tete to traipsing all the way to

[3] Zam. & Tribs., pp 160–161.
[4] Ibid, p 170.

Sesheke, parted cowardly under dark rather than legally resign from the expedition.

On 7th June 1860 they emerged from the Kebrabasa hills into the lion-infested Chicova plains. Their fires burned brilliantly throughout the night to ward off any unwelcome visitors. Nothing unforeseen occurred and the party moved on.

Marching near the river afforded the men many opportunities to study the game, though tribes were in the habit of digging pitfalls to capture the animals. A sudden descent of nine feet is an experience not easily forgotten and scouts were sent forward to ask tribal folk to uncover them.

They would send presents to the paramount chiefs through whose areas they were passing. These were well-received and gifts exchanged. On one occasion they sent Chief Chikwanitsela a present, but were informed the next morning that he had a cough and could not come over to see them.

Indignant, one of Livingstone's party remarked, 'And has his present a cough too, that it does not come to us? Is this the way your Chief treats strangers, receives their present and lends them no food in return?'[5]

The only edible things they needed in the central plains were vegetables. Now and then they received a supply of sweet potatoes which allayed the uncomfortable craving that a continuous diet of meat and meal had induced.

The party met many tribes en route to Sesheke. One group was the Bawee, a people who live entirely naked, clothed only in a coat of red ochre paint. They were as friendly as they were naked and they felt no shame, nor could any feeling be aroused by laughing and joking at their appearance. The females had some form of clothing, but the men only really felt naked when a pipe was not in their mouths. Livingstone thought them 'perhaps the most inveterate smokers in the world. The pipe is seldom out of their mouths, and they are

---

[5] *Ibid*, p 193.

as polite smokers as any ever met with in a railway carriage. They did ask if we had any objection before lighting their pipes'.[6]

The Batoka tobacco was famed for its strength, and it was certainly very strong and very cheap: 'A few strings of beads will purchase enough to last any reasonable man for six months'.[7] Its strength caused the sole smoker in the party headaches, but this quality only increased its popularity.

The long march did the men much good. It certainly helped Livingstone to overcome his depression as he busied himself with the expedition, though the relationship with his brother became strained. Charles' criticism of David injured him and in compiling an assessment of Charles Livingstone he wrote: 'As an assistant he has been of no value. Photography very unsatisfactory. Magnetism still more so. Meteorological observations not creditable, and writing in the journal in arrears. In going up with us now he is useless, as he knows nothing of Portuguese or the native language. He often expected me to be his assistant instead of acting as mine'.[8]

Charles sulked, generally dragged his heels and occasionally muttered that his brother was 'no Christian gentleman' and that he was employed 'in the service of the devil'.[9] Such a spirit only increased further tension.

Meanwhile the travellers trekked on, and occasionally the party lost sight of one another in dense bush. Livingstone, unaware that he had separated from the party, stooped to pick up a specimen of the wild fruit marula. A rhinoceros took exception to his presence and with an angry snort dashed at the solitary scientist who, not seeing the rumbling rhino, carried on unawares. Strangely she stopped when only her

---

[6] *Ibid*, p 239.
[7] *Ibid*.
[8] *Zambesi Journals of David Livingstone*, Vol I, p 169 in Jeal, p 231.
[9] Jeal, p 232.

own length distant short of him. Startled, the doctor sprinted off. 'A branch pulled out his watch as he ran, and turning half round to grasp it, he got a distant glance of her and her calf still standing on the selfsame spot, as if arrested in the middle of her charge by an unseen hand'[10]

One cannot help but marvel at the many miraculous escapes members of the party had and see the protecting hand of the Lord upon their lives. As the angel arrested Balaam's donkey in Old Testament times, was not the raging rhino also held at bay by the hand of the Almighty?

The ways of the Lord are beyond understanding, for while he was protecting the men in the expedition, for their work was not complete, other fine courageous Christian families were laying down their lives in bringing the gospel to the dark regions. Had the doctor known, he would probably have hastened to their aid.

Sadly the missionary realised that the Portuguese who were engaged in the slave-trade were devoted to it and would never encourage those who sought its extirpation. Opening up the Zambesi had afforded Portuguese traders new facilities for conducting their unhallowed traffic.

In a letter to Mr James Young, Livingstone wearily wrote: 'I am tired of discovery when no fruit follows. It was refreshing to be able to sit down every evening with the Makololo again, and tell them of Him who came down from heaven to save sinners'.[11]

Halting at a Makololo village they were told that Mosilikatse's main town was a distance of one month away. They were heartened to hear 'that the English had come to Mosilikatse, and told the Chief that it was wrong to kill men; and he had replied that he was born to kill people, but would drop the habit'.[12] This was an amazing testimony of the friendship that

---

[10] Zam. & Tribs., p 215.
[11] D L to James Young 22/07/1860 in Blaikie, p 272.
[12] Zam. & Tribs., p. 221.

had been fostered between Mosilikatse, the great chief, and Robert Moffat, the fine missionary.

The march resembled a triumphal procession as the Makololo welcomed the itinerant missionary home. They entered and left every village adorned with gifts, amid the cheers of the inhabitants, the men clapping their hands and the women 'lullilooing', with the shrill call of 'Peace'. They all wanted the consul to protect them. To such requests, his invariable reply was that others had come and were coming to take his place to tell them more about the God who loved them.

Rumours had started to reach the party that the members from the London Missionary Society who were labouring among the Makololo had perished. At the Victoria Falls the vague assertions became definite information; nearly all the missionaries had fallen to the frightening fever.

This came as a blow to the doctor, who was held by many to be in some measure responsible, as he wanted the station established. The enterprise had been undertaken in reliance on his advice and close co-operation. He had pressed upon the Society the need to follow up, without delay, the influence he had acquired over the Makololo people.

Robert Moffat wisely, and with some prophetic insight, cautioned against the move of the three missionaries and their wives. The Lord's seasoned servant wanted Livingstone first to establish a base on high ground, move the tribes to the new locality and then introduce the missionaries. To claim prior right, in Moffat's own words, 'might prove fatal to some, if not all'.[13]

Moffat wanted to house the missionaries at Kuruman until Sekeletu and his people had moved to higher ground. Meanwhile, the Matabele chief was also keen to assist Moffat's son-in-law, David Livingstone, and sent a party of

---

[13] R Moffat to LMS 20/07/1855 in Campbell, p 268.

men to the Zambesi below the Victoria Falls to build some
large canoes for them. Sekeletu took this the wrong way and
despatched a contingent of warriors to drive them away. This
failed and, fearing the worst, suspicion sunk into the spirit of
this sensitive chief.

The London Missionary Society party thus ventured
forward to the disease-ridden district. Mr Helmore, with his
wife and four children, and Roger Price, with his wife and
one child, left Kuruman for Linyanti on 8th July 1859. Mail
despatched to the doctor informing him of their movements
sank off the Mocambique coast, thus creating a further
breakdown in communication.

After a long trying journey Helmore and Price expected to
meet Livingstone in Linyanti, but there was no sign of him
or news of his arrival. The chief was suffering from leprosy
and refused to remove himself or to allow the members of
the mission to move to a healthier site.

Helmore and Price made a gallant effort to commence work,
preaching in the open air under a hot, humid sun surrounded
by rank and steaming vegetation. They laboured faithfully for
the Lord, preaching life-giving news to the lost and dying in
Linyanti.

Two of the Helmore children succumbed to fever; then the
infant daughter of Mrs Price. Mrs Helmore followed suit,
together with her husband and Mrs Price, and yet only yards
away stood Livingstone's wagon, the canopy torn by weathering and time. It was a desolate-looking structure, but it
contained a medicine chest full of quinine and other drugs to
combat the virulent, malicious malaria. They failed to search
the wagon and sickness claimed six tragic lives out of a party
of nine.

After the burials Roger Price, discouraged and dejected,
together with the heartbroken Helmore orphans, headed back
across the Kalahari desert towards Kuruman.

But even as they departed, Sekeletu, riding in Helmore's
wagon which he had already appropriated, robbed them of

food, clothing and bedding. Ironically this was the same chief who still kept Livingstone's wagon and stores guarded and intact.

Chief Sekeletu was not keen on moving to high ground for the simple reason he feared Mosilikatse. Moffat had become a dear friend to Chief Mosilikatse and would do anything for him. Chief Sekeletu needed Livingstone, for he knew the ferocious chief would not attack a place where Moffat's son-in-law was living. The other missionaries could offer no similar guarantee.

While travelling from village to village, rumours of the death of the missionaries and the departure of survivors reached Livingstone. There was little point in hurrying, for the damage was done; yet he still wanted to investigate the news himself. He pressed on, deeper into the interior.

The party could see the mighty spray of the Mosioatunya twenty-one miles out[14] and they soon arranged a visit to the vertiginous falls. On 9th June their guide took them by canoe to the main island. His name was Tuba Mokoro, which translated means 'smasher of canoes', an ominous name, but he alone knew the waters of the chafing river. Talking was prohibited as they paddled their perilous course. Only Tuba was permitted to pass instructions to the paddlers. The passengers were admiring their skill when suddenly, as they 'were driving swiftly, a black rock, over which the white foam flew, lay directly in their path'. The pole was planted against it as readily as ever, but it slipped, just as Tuba put forth his strength to turn the bow off. They struck hard and took in water. Tuba seeing the danger shot the canoe into the side and baled out the water. Here it was explained that the accident was due to Tuba having no breakfast. Need it be said that they 'never let Tuba go without that meal again'?[15]

---

[14] Zam & Tribs., p 257.
[15] Ibid, p 253.

Stopping off at the main island, beneath spray-drenched fronds and ferns, they surveyed the spectacular scenery. They cautiously crept forward enjoying the cool water, and on reaching the lip they peered over the giddy height, when the wondrous and unique character of the magnificent cascade at once burst upon them. As the mighty Zambesi thundered past in a deafening roar, they marvelled at the sheer power in the confluence of air, water, energy and life. The ferocious Falls, turbulent as they are timeless, captivated the travellers.

They measured the depth of the rift 'by lowering a line, to the end of which a few bullets and a foot of white cotton cloth were tied'.[16] One of them lay with his head over a projecting crag and watched the descending calico, till, after his companions let out 310 feet, the bullet on the end rested on a sloping projection, probably fifty feet from the water below, the actual bottom still being further down. 'The white cloth now appeared the size of a crown-piece'.[17] This was incredibly accurate, as too were their measurements by sextant of the width and distance.

Writing from the Falls to Dr Moffat on 10th August 1860, Livingstone said: 'With great sorrow we learned the death of our much-esteemed friends, Mr and Mrs Helmore, two days ago. We were too late to be of any service'.[18]

They then purposed to move on 100 miles to Linyanti; but not before meeting Mr Baldwin, an Englishman from Natal who, guided by his pocket-compass alone, visited the Falls. This man was being held a prisoner by Mashotlane whom he had hired to ferry him across the river. Baldwin, in order to bathe himself, jumped in the river and swam ashore. Indignant, Mashotlane ordered his arrest.

---

[16] *Ibid*, p 253.
[17] *Ibid*.
[18] Blaikie, p 275.

The Victoria Falls

'If,' said Mashotlane, 'he had been devoured by one of the crocodiles which abound there, the English would have blamed us for his death. He nearly inflicted a great injury upon us, therefore, we said, he must pay a fine.' As Mr Baldwin had nothing with him wherewith to pay, they were taking care of him till he should receive beads from his wagon two days distant.[19]

Further problems had broken out with Charles who, while they were only a few days distance from Sekeletu, fell down a six-foot elephant trap. The young man lost his temper with the headman of the Makololo and kicked him with all his strength. David flew into an uncontrollable rage; the two brothers came to blows, while the headman nearly murdered Charles. Kirk then witnessed 'the most abusive filthy language ever heard in that class of society'.[20]

Of that incident Kirk recorded in his journal:

I trust that if I am sent on an overland trip, I may not have C.L. for a companion, for if he can break out and abuse, tearing with nails so as to draw blood and tear clothes, saying that his brother was serving the Devil, indulge in epithets such as 'the cursing consul of Quillimane', repeated over and over again, act before the men in such a way as to make them look on him as mad, which if I could only say that I thought he was, would be the most charitable thing I could do. But one who loses his temper so suddenly so as to change from joking to kicking with iron nailed boots the chief man sent by a proud powerful savage chief, ... is one on whom no reliance can be placed. Nothing but the high personal regard for Doctor [Livingstone] averted bloodshed in that case. The spear was poised and needed only a stroke of the arm to send it to the heart. I never expected so much moderation from savages'.[21]

---

[19] Zam. & Tribs., pp 260–261.
[20] Jeal, p 232.
[21] Kirk's Journal, p 310, *ibid*.

The expedition had reached the end of its tether, yet it still had to trek onwards while David Livingstone became increasingly estranged from his brother. Charles' curt, callous statements cut deeply into the doctor's spirit, inciting David to record in his journal the insults his brother had flung at him.

His trust in his brother betrayed, he sank slowly into himself. Other than his strong prayer life, his private journal became his only outlet, further enhancing his image as the solitary Scot.

Kirk bore the brunt of the battle bravely, restricting his opinions to his diary, and avoided Charles whenever possible. Though he could not draw close to the doctor, Kirk's respect for Livingstone and his relationship with the natives remained strong.

On 18th August 1860 they entered the new town of Sesheke, which was built on a site closer to the Falls than the old site Livingstone had visited. The young man who had shown so much promise was now a pitiful object. He had contracted some kind of leprous disease, and thinking himself bewitched, put a number of people to death, while living apart from the people in the wagon in sulky sickness and retirement. The country was suffering grievously and Sebituane's great Barotse empire was crumbling to pieces. Already vast sections of the Barotse and Batoka tribes had obtained their independence and the Makololo power was visibly being vanquished.

The missionary was deeply disappointed, yet the chief's personal attachment to his 'father' was as evident now as when Livingstone had departed. The consul and Kirk administered treatment to Sekeletu. Improvement was rapid as the chief responded to their lunar caustic and internal doses of hydrate of potash.

Sekeletu's mother travelled many miles to meet David. She had lost weight and, considering this to be unattractive, asked the doctor for 'the medicine of fatness'.[22]

---

[22] Zam. & Tribs., p 295.

Livingstone, wanting to see the graves of the missionaries for himself, pressed on to Linyanti. He found everything in his wagon intact, eroded only by the weathering of time and white ants. With gentle reproaches for not bringing Ma-Robert (Mrs Livingstone) and the children, they asked the Scot, 'Are we never more to know anything of them but their names?' They took the doctor to the graves of those departed and stood silently as he surveyed the solemn scene.

Staying only a short while, Livingstone bade them farewell, and the retinue returned via Sekeletu to retrace their steps to the coast.

Livingstone remained unwearied in his efforts to preach the gospel. In his journal entry dated 2nd September 1860 we read:

> On Sunday evening went over to the people, giving a general summary of Christian faith by the life of Christ. Asked them to speak about it afterwards. Replied that these things were above them—they could not answer me. I said if I spoke of camels and buffaloes tamed, they understood, though they had never seen them; why not perceive the story of Christ, the witnesses to which refused to deny it, though killed for maintaining it? Went on to speak of the resurrection. All were listening eagerly to the statements about this, especially when they heard that they too must rise and be judged. Lerimo said, 'This I won't believe.' 'Well, the guilt lies between you and Jesus.' This always arrests attention. Spoke of blood shed by them; the conversation continued till they said, 'It was time for me to cross, for the river was dangerous at night.'

> 9th September—Spoke to the people on the north side of the river—wind prevented evening service on the south.[23]

Livingstone noted that the tribes were spiritual. He stated:

> It is evident they believe that the soul had a continued existence; and that the spirits of the departed know what those they have

---

[23] Blaikie, p 276.

left behind them are doing, and are pleased or not, according as their deeds are good or evil; this belief is universal. The owner of a large canoe refused to sell it, because it belonged to the spirit of his father, who helped him when he killed the hippopotamus.[24]

The deaths of the missionaries, and Livingstone's realisation that the Makololo were disintegrating as a tribe, confirmed his conviction that his calling was to eradicate the slave-trade. The need was greatest in the Shire Highlands.

They left Sesheke on 17th September 1860; Sekeletu sent them with a new guide who was to return with fresh medical supplies.

The men purchased canoes in which they ventured forth. At a port below the village of Mpande a large canoe was bought at a good price. However, before the deal was done the seller pleaded plaintively that his bowels yearned for his boat and that he must have a little larger payment to stop their yearning. Such an adroit plea secured higher funds.[25]

Livingstone purposefully preached and took every opportunity to meet chiefs in order to present the gospel of Jesus Christ. One chief, Mowmba, came to Livingstone of his own accord, asking that he and his people may be 'Sundayed' too. The Scot considered preaching the gospel as his primary vocation and was unswervingly faithful. Kirk bore emphatic witness to this fact.

Livingstone kept an eye open to observe the people, their customs and their characteristics. He recorded in his book *The Zambesi and Its Tributaries* a man who

was a great admirer of the ladies. Every pretty girl he saw filled his heart with rapture. 'Oh, what a beauty! never saw her like before; I wonder if she is married?' and earnestly and lovingly did he gaze after the charming one till she had passed out of sight.

---

[24] Zam. & Tribs., p 232.
[25] Campbell, p 273.

He had four wives at home, and hoped to have a number more before long, but he had only one child; this Mormonism does not seem to satisfy; it leads to a state of mind which, if not disease, is truly contemptible.[26]

Another point of interest was that he noticed

the natives of Africa have an amiable desire to please, and often tell what they imagine to be gratifying, rather than the uninteresting naked truth. Let a native from the interior be questioned by a thirsty geographer, whether the mountains round his youthful home are high; from a dim recollection of something of the sort, combined with a desire to please, the answer will be affirmative. And so it will be if the subject of inquiry be gold or unicorns, or men with tails. English sportsmen, though first-rate shots at home, are notorious for the number of their misses on first trying to shoot in Africa. Everything is on such a large scale, and there is such a glare of bright sunlight, that some time is required to enable them to judge of distances. 'Is it wounded?' inquired a gentleman, of his dark attendant, after firing at an antelope. 'Yes! the ball went right into his heart.' These mortal words never proving fatal, he asked a friend, who understood the language, to explain to the man, that he preferred the truth in every case. 'He is my father,' replied the native, 'and I thought he would be displeased if I told him he never hits at all.'[27]

Travelling by canoe they were able to test the navigability of the Central Zambesi. Approaching the Kariba gorge (where the Kariba Dam wall stands today) they were called upon by a man who advised them to hire him to pray to the Kariba god for their safety while they were going down the rapids. This prompted the team to take a further look, and walking along the shore they examined the rapids. Deciding to risk it they continued by canoe. The priest who knew how to pray to the god that rules the rapids followed the retinue

---

[26] Zam. & Tribs., p 307.
[27] *Ibid*, p 309.

with several of his friends and they were quite surprised to see them pass down in safety without the aid of his intercession.[28]

After the Kariba rapids they decided to tow the hippo they had shot earlier and which was now downstream as this would do for their meal. But it attracted more attention from the crocodiles than the villagers. Unafraid of the canoes, the reptiles ravaged the carcass; so much so that they were obliged for safety to cast it adrift.

Thus they passed the Kariba rapids with little difficulty, but very nearly came to grief with those of the Karivua, not far from the confluence of the Loangwa. They survived with only the goods being drenched.

However, Livingstone's obstinacy in persisting to navigate through the Kebrabasa Cataracts nearly resulted in the drowning of Dr Kirk, for his canoe capsized against the ledge of a rock. As the surging, frothing water tried to suck him into the whirlpool he managed to clutch hold of a rock, scramble up on it and save himself from drowning. His steersman also managed to secure a grip on the rock, so saving himself and the canoe. But nearly all its contents, including a chronometer, a barometer, Kirk's notes and drawings of the botany of the upper Zambesi, were lost.

After this they decided to walk the rest of the way back to Tete, which they reached on 23rd November. The journey so far had taken a little over six months.

At Tete they found the two English sailors who were left in charge of the steamer to be in good health, and with excellent record with regard to their conduct. Their garden, however, was a failure. They had left a few sheep for the sailors to slaughter as and when they wished for fresh meat and two dozen fowls.

---

[28] *Ibid*, p 324.

Purchasing more, they soon had doubled the number of the latter and anticipated a good supply of eggs; but they also bought two monkeys and they ate all the eggs. A hippopotamus came up one night and laid waste their vegetable garden; the sheep broke into their cotton patch, when it was in flower, and ate it all, except the stems; then the crocodiles carried off the sheep, and the natives stole the fowls. Nor were they more successful as gunsmiths: a Portuguese trader, having an exalted opinion of the ingenuity of English sailors, showed them a double-barrelled rifle and inquired if they could put on the browning, which had rusted off. 'I think I knows how,' said one, whose father was a blacksmith, 'it's very easy; you have only to put the barrels in the fire.' A great fire of wood was made on shore and the unlucky barrels put over it, to secure the handsome rifle colour. To Jack's utter amazement the barrels came asunder. To get out of the scrape his companion and he stuck the pieces together with resin and sent it to the owner, with the message, 'It was all they could do for it, and they would not charge him anything for the job!' They had also invented an original mode of settling a bargain; having ascertained the market price of provisions, they paid that, but no more. If the traders refused to leave the ship till the price was increased, a chameleon, of which the (superstitious) natives have a mortal dread, was brought out of the cabin; and the moment the natives saw the creature, they at once sprung overboard. The chameleon settled every dispute in a twinkling.'[29]

Livingstone was still set on his course to eradicate the slave-trade. In a letter to his friend, Mr Moore, written from Tete on 28th November 1860, he said:

Thanks to Providence, we have made some progress, and it is likely our operations will yet have a decided effect on slave-trading in Eastern Africa. I am greatly delighted with the prospect of a Church of England mission to Central Africa. That is a good omen for those who are sitting in darkness, and I trust that in process of time great benefits will be conferred on our own overcrowded

---

[29] *Ibid*, p 336.

population at home. There is room enough and to spare in the fair world our Father has prepared for all His progeny. I pray to be made a harbinger of good to many, both white and black.

I like to hear that some abuse me now, and say that I am no Christian. Many good things were said of me which I did not deserve, and I feared to read them. I shall read every word I can on the other side, and that will prove a sedative to what I was forced to hear of an opposite tendency. I pray that He who has lifted me up and guided me thus far, will not desert me now, but make me useful in my day and generation. 'I will never leave thee or forsake thee.' So let it be.[30]

They did not waste time in Tete, and set course for the Kongore as soon as possible, hoping to meet the new vessel. Cautiously they ventured aboard the leaking old lady, the 'Ma-Robert', where Livingstone wrote to Mr Young on 4th December 1860 saying:

We are now on our way down to the sea, in hopes of meeting the new steamer for which you and other friends exerted yourselves so zealously. We are in the old 'Asthmatic', though we gave her up before leaving in May last. Our engineer has been doctoring her bottom with fat and patches, and pronounced it safe to go down the river by dropping slowly. Every day a new leak bursts out, and he is in plastering and scoring, the pump going constantly. I would not have ventured again, but our whaler is as bad—all eaten by the teredo [ship worm]—so I thought it as well to take both, and stick to that which swims longest. You can put your thumb through either of them; they never can move again; I never expected to find either afloat, but the engineer had nothing else to do, and it saves us from buying dear canoes from the Portuguese.

20th December—One day, above Senna, the 'Ma-Robert' stuck on a sandbank and filled, so we had to go ashore and leave her.[31]

[30] D L to W Moore in Blaikie, pp 278–279.
[31] D L to James Young, *ibid*, p 278.

242242

On the morning of the 21st the uncomfortable 'Asthmatic' grounded on a sandbank and filled. She could neither be emptied nor got off. The river rose during the night, and all that was visible of the worn-out craft next day was about six feet of her two masts. Most of the property we had on board was saved; and we spent the Christmas of 1860 encamped on the island of Chimba. Canoes were sent for from Senna; and we reached it on the 27th, to be again hospitably entertained by our friend, Senhor Ferrao.[32]

In these canoes they descended the river to the Kongoni mouth, which they reached on 4th January 1861, and here they were permitted to lodge in the newly-built Portuguese station. Their stores were nearly all depleted; they tried to make imitation tea out of roasted millet. Fortunately, the marshy islands of the Zambesi delta swarmed with game and they kept themselves supplied with fresh meat.

On 31st January 1861 the long-expected steamer, the 'Pioneer', arrived from England and anchored outside the bar, but she was not able to cross until 4th February. Two of Her Majesty's cruisers arrived at the same time bringing Bishop Mackenzie and six missionaries who, inspired by Livingstone's address, were sent out by the Universities' Mission to evangelise the tribes of the Shire and Lake Nyasa.

Sadly slavery was to inflict even deeper wounds on the local inhabitants. The consul's hopes to colonise the area, and thus provide alternative trade to that of humans, would for the moment be crushed, and a further calamity would crumple his endeavours for Christ.

---

[32] Zam. & Tribs., p 338.

SLAVERY.

The horrors of the slave trade

13

The Sickening Sights of Slavery

Included with the supplies was a despatch from the new Foreign Secretary, Lord John Russell, who agreed to extend the expedition's duration. It commended Livingstone's discovery of Lake Nyasa and advised him to moderate his criticism of the Portuguese.

Livingstone was also given orders to explore the Ruvuma, as it might provide an access to the interior, avoiding Portuguese territory. Livingstone's colonisation scheme was considered premature.[1]

Greatly satisfied with the new arrivals, Livingstone introduced himself to the members of the party—not exactly necessary as his faded consular cap had become his trademark.

Bishop Mackenzie was a man in his thirties, well-built and though possessed of a gentle spirit, not averse to hard work. The other senior men represented the Anglicans from High to Low church. The second most senior clergyman, Lovell Procter, was summed up by Livingstone as 'very orderly and sedate and in love', which was exactly what he was, as he had recently left his fiancée in Natal. Parson Rowley, the other clergyman, was by far the most narrow-minded and devout of the new intake to the interior. He was a fanatical writer and never in a hurry to over-exert himself. He was outspoken in his opinion of Livingstone and later published an exaggerated criticism of the consul, causing much confusion.

---

[1] Foreign Office to D L 17/04/1860 NAZ, reference 1139–1153.

Scudamore had a positive influence as a mild, unselfish gentleman. Livingstone liked him, as did he Horace Waller who was to become one of his greatest friends. Both were of the Low church.

In addition to these missionaries the party included a carpenter called Gamble and a Cockney labourer whose title was agriculturalist. A doctor, John Dickenson and another clergyman, Henry Burrup, were expected out shortly.

Livingstone was deeply heartened that these men had come as a result of his Cambridge University address. Later writing to Mr Maclcar Livingstone said, 'The Bishop is A1, and in his readiness to put his hand to anything resembles much my good father-in-law Moffat.'[2]

The mission was the answer to many of Livingstone's prayers; he had high hopes for it and his vision for commerce and Christianity seemed that much closer to fruition.

Mackenzie liked Livingstone. The latter had a way of encouraging inexperienced people. 'How excellent,' the bishop remarked, 'is his way of offering help—not as if he were indispensable but as if he might be of some use. This is the way in which real strength and real knowledge always speaks.'[3] Later, as pressure placed a burden upon the two leaders, their friendship was tested.

A strong bond also grew between the bishop and Kirk, as botany was a common interest they both delighted in.

The bishop was keen to establish his mission station, but Livingstone on receiving his orders was keen to explore the Ruvuma, a river which flowed into the sea 300 miles north of Mocambique. If this was navigable throughout, and extended to Lake Nyasa, it would open up another way into the interior with which the Portuguese could not interfere. The Portuguese regarded Livingstone with suspicion; he was

---

[2] Blaikie, p 283.
[3] Macnair, p 246.

outspoken with regard to their involvement in the slave-trade and they feared he wanted to annex new territories for Britain.

Bishop Mackenzie was upset. The delay involved him in more months of irksome and unprofitable waiting and he was prepared to proceed up-country alone. To this Livingstone objected, as there was no reliable chief to whom they could go and, more important, they had no doctor. Thus he consented to go with Livingstone and arranged to send his missionaries to Johanna, one of the islands of the Comoro group, until they returned.

On 11th March 1861 the 'Pioneer' was ascending the Ruvuma, but eight days later, after they had travelled barely thirty miles, they found that the water was falling at a rate of seven inches per hour. To proceed further would undoubtably mean the boat would run aground until the next rainy season. This they could not afford to happen. The doctor would have to proceed on foot, but the bishop was opposed to the idea, so they returned to Johanna. Once the missionaries and supplies were collected they headed for the Zambesi.

Moving back to Johanna had its problems. The majority of the new crew succumbed to the fever and Livingstone, rather than be delayed, navigated the vessel himself and left Dr Kirk to look after the sick. Livingstone also learned that the bishop had invited his sister and the Revd Burrup's wife to join the mission. This somewhat premature decision prompted Livingstone to be reunited with Mary '. . . and I should never hear the end of it if my better half were not allowed to do the same.'

From Johanna the 'Pioneer' heaved forward under the weight of the cargo. There were fifty-two men aboard, two sheep, tons of coal and other cargo. The ship fared well at sea, but shoals and sand-banks in the river were soon to test the sailors' endurance.

Much to the bishop's dismay Livingstone ordered a large quantity of cargo to be stored at the mouth of the Zambesi. This would be collected later. The ship, though lighter, was still laden and had to be hauled by men over the sandy, shallow Elephant Marsh. There they struggled for six weeks to cross the fifty-mile stretch of the Shire. Endless piles of wood were chopped to stoke the 'Pioneer'; perspiration poured off the workers and as ropes frayed due to the persistent pulling of the 'Pioneer' so did the tempers, particularly those of the junior members; yet there was no turning back.

Livingstone was impressed with the bishop who worked tirelessly, though some of his subordinates sat in the shade of their cabins. Horace Waller was filled with admiration for Livingstone. 'Never shall I forget the untiring patience of the Doctor at this time,' he wrote, 'always cheerful, never tired with the hundred and one questions put to him by those who were bored with the monotonous laying out of anchors and 'guess' warps, walking round capstans and lowering boats'.[4]

A typical day would see the blazing heat give way to tufts of sun-webbed clouds. These would hang delicately in the sky, silently awaiting the crimson splendour of sunset to grace Africa in her scenic beauty. Slowly, sedately, the sunlight would be swallowed in the swell of night's chattering sound. After dinner the men would relax on the quarter deck, smoking and enjoying a drink before going to bed. During these starlit evenings Livingstone was amazed at the speculative 'puerilities' with which the clergymen would vainly sustain their doctrinal arguments. Each would delight, much to Livingstone's disdain, to toss a novel idea into the air or challenge their companions' orthodoxy. Rowley was particularly polemical: it was 'rare fun after Rowley got a little gin into his head', Charles remembered, 'The Bishop had frequently to check him by punching his side.'[5]

Among the religious retinue the old members of the expedition were alarmed to note that there were pilfering

---

[4] Ransford, p 183.
[5] *Ibid.*

parsons who were also prodigious eaters. Procter in particular proved to be 'a great eater and was very fond of jam and jelly . . . He was found one night by the officer of the watch licking the jam pots.' The date store was also dwindling and Kirk set up a rat trap in the date box, though he kindly wrapped the jagged teeth in a cloth. It was set off, but did not hold and the criminal escaped into the night.

They reached Chibisa's village on 7th July 1861 to hear how an aggressive movement, characteristic of tribal life in those days, was progressing. The Ajawas or Yaos were pressing down from the north, working closely with the slavers and laying waste the country. The weaker tribes were in deadly fear. A deputation from a chief near Mount Zomba met the party on landing and invited Mackenzie to settle. His presence would deter barbaric, bloodthirsty deputations disturbing them.

The climb to the top of Mount Zomba was long and tedious. Porters frequently argued with each other over weight distribution which so infuriated the bishop that he was seen prodding the carriers with his crozier (which they believed to be a modern musket) and hauling one of them to his feet by its crook.[6]

Word arrived that a large slave gang was coming in their direction en route for Tete. This confirmed the consul's suspicions. It was a critical situation for if they intervened and freed the slaves the Portuguese might retaliate by destroying the mission party's valuable private property still in Tete. If action was not taken the tribes would see them as condoning this evil practice. Shortly the slave party, a long line of manacled men, women and children, came into view as they trudged along the dusty path. Their proud captors marched, muskets in hand, prodding and whipping the weary slaves.

---

[6] *Ibid*, p 184.

THE SICKENING SIGHTS OF SLAVERY

Livingstone's obvious decision was accelerated when the drivers caught a glimpse of him and their boldness evaporated as they bolted into the bush. Only one remained, he being retained by a Makololo. Livingstone recognised him as a well-known slave with the late commandant at Tete. However, the culprit was not keen on an interview, put up a struggle and scurried off into the scrub. The startled slaves 'knelt down and in their way of expressing thanks, clapped their hands with great energy'.[7] They were thus left in the doctor's hands. Knives were soon busily used, cutting women and children adrift. The men each had their necks in a fork of a stout stick, six or seven feet long, kept in by an iron rod which was riveted at both ends across the throat. The bishop had a saw which was soon in service setting the captives free. Livingstone released eighty-four people, chiefly women and children, but they volunteered to stay, thus the bishop had a ready-made congregation.

One little boy said to Livingstone's men: 'The others tied and starved us, you cut the ropes and tell us to eat; what sort of people are you?—Where did you come from?'[8] Terror in such circles was rife; two women had been shot the day before for attempting to untie the thongs. 'One woman had her infant's brains knocked out, because she could not carry her load and it. And a man was despatched with an axe, because he had broken down with fatigue.'[9] Sights such as these were to have a deep impact upon the Scot. With each sordid scene he became more resolved to eradicate this 'open sore of humanity', however serious the consequences.

As they continued their journey they encountered other slave patrols whose leaders also dispersed with amazing agility. One occasion saw nearly a hundred slaves released;

---

[7] Zam. & Tribs., p 356.
[8] *Ibid*, p 357.
[9] *Ibid*.

on another, six grateful souls savoured the sweet taste
of freedom. Further evidence was obtained regarding the
involvement of the Portuguese at Tete.

On the morning of the 22nd they were informed that the
Ajawa were near and were burning a village a few miles off,
capturing the tribe for sale into slavery. Marching to address
the Ajawa, the consul and his colleagues passed petrified
people running for their lives while the fierce fires engulfed
their food and possessions.

The missionaries, realising the risk of reprimanding a body
of men at war, regrouped for fervent prayer and, on rising
from their knees, they observed a long line of Ajawa warriors
with their captives coming round the hillside. They were seen
by a headman who heard their call for a peaceful interview.
A large contingent of warriors, on hearing the cries, came up
and, concealing themselves behind projecting rocks and long
grass, surrounded the party. Livingstone recorded that

> flushed with recent victory over three villages, and confident of
> an easy triumph over a mere handful of men, they began to shoot
> their poisoned arrows, sending them with great force upwards of
> a hundred yards, and wounding one of our followers through the
> arm. Our retiring slowly up the ascent from the village only made
> them more eager to prevent our escape; and, in belief that this
> retreat was evidence of fear, they closed upon us in bloodthirsty
> fury. Some came within fifty yards, dancing hideously; others
> having quite surrounded us, and availing themselves of the rocks
> and long grass, were intent on cutting us off, while others made
> off with their women and a large body of slaves. Four with armed
> muskets . . . [10]

The bishop had had passive views regarding the use of
firearms. Gradually, however, on seeing the aggression, any
lingering doubt was dispelled. An arrow fell between him and
Livingstone which alarmed the Scot who was not prepared

---

[10] *Ibid*, p 361.

for battle. He did not even have a weapon with him and had to borrow a revolver from the bishop. Livingstone gave the command to return fire. The attacking warriors, on seeing the reply of fire, needed little encouragement to disperse, though before doing so lost six men in the skirmish.

None of Livingstone's men had been injured, though the battle deeply disturbed the Scot. This was the first time he had had to fire a shot, albeit in defence. No longer could he claim to be a man of peace. The Ajawa would not at this particular time be open to the gospel, and violence in the area was on the increase, with slavery gaining popularity.

The site for the mission station had now to be decided. Livingstone chose Magomero, a village in a hollow seventy miles from the River Shire and 3,000 feet up, safe from malaria. The bishop, however, preferred another village closer to the river, but after discussion the decision was made to stay on higher ground.

Livingstone needed to investigate Lake Nyasa and on departing begged the bishop on no account to become embroiled with any of the native tribes again. No matter who was in the right it was wise not to take sides; remaining neutral would reveal their stand as men of peace and over a long term their teachings would take hold. Furthermore, in any dispute neither party is wholly blameless. Thus a moral battle began in the bishop's heart. Setting the captives free was a vital part of Christianity, but by so doing they were interfering with their neighbours' political and social structure.

Soon sickening and terrifying tales of woe were reaching Magomero. Could the bishop begin a mission of peace with barrels blazing? The thought, most incongruous in his own eyes, would look even worse when viewed in Britain. Yet after prayer and debate it was decided that freedom must be sought for the slaves. When the news reached Britain the bishop and Livingstone came under much attack.

In general members of the mission supported the bishop. Charles, on hearing one outburst from Britain, replied, 'If you

were in Africa and saw a host of murderous savages aiming
their heavily loaded muskets and poisoned arrows at you,
more light might enter your mind . . . and if it didn't great
daylight would enter your body through arrow and bullet
holes.'[11]

The bishop's stand in aggressively liberating slaves disturbed Livingstone. He too had a reputation to uphold and
such a course of action would hardly support it. It was indeed
a perplexing problem. In a letter to Whitehall Livingstone
stated: 'A missionary ought in all lawful things to identify
himself with the interests of his people, but it is doubtful
whether this should extend to fighting for them.'[12] Thus,
perhaps selfishly, he exonerated himself from the affair. His
opinion, however, changed and later Livingstone wrote: 'To
my mind the case was one of necessity—of dire necessity, and
no one clergyman or layman would engage in it willingly more
than he would choose to perform the office of the common
hangman.'[13]

In a letter to Horace Waller in February 1863 Livingstone
ridiculed Dr Pusey, one of the strongest protesters against the
militancy of the missionaries. The Scot said of the affair:

> I thought you wrong in attacking the Ajawa till I looked on it as
> defence of your poor orphans. I thought that you had shut
> yourselves up to one tribe, and that the Manganja, but I think
> differently now, and only wish they would send out Dr Pusey
> here. He would learn a little sense—of which I suppose I have
> need myself.[14]

The British intervention in the slave-trade was not looked
upon favourably by the Portuguese. The local authorities made
no protest, for to have done so would have made their

[11] NAZ L I 3/1/1,111 in Ransford, p 189.
[12] *Ibid.*
[13] *Ibid.*
[14] D L to H Waller 12/02/1863 in Campbell, p 287.

complicity too obvious, but influences were set to work against Livingstone in Lisbon and London. He was later charged with exceeding his powers as consul and with using his status to the detriment of Portugal. This charge was totally unfair, but the Royal Family's ties with Portugal complicated matters and schemes were started which brought about, in the end, the recall of the expedition.

The expedition, however, continued up the Shire. The 'Pioneer' was left at Chibasa and on 4th August 1861 Livingstone, his brother and Dr Kirk started out for Nyasa with a four-oared sailing boat. This was carried by porters past the Murchison Cataracts and on 23rd September they sailed into Lake Nyasa.

The lake was examined by earnest eyes. The population was dense and civil, though at the top of the lake the slave-trade had taken its toll. There the people were inveterate liars and the party was even robbed of clothing and supplies. Elsewhere on the west bank Livingstone was appalled at the suffering caused by the slave-trade. Near the great slave emporium of Nkhotakota this 'devilish trade in human flesh' had turned the lakeshore into an abomination. At one place they burned more than a thousand *gorees* (a slave stick with a V-neck) which had been piled up for future use, and Livingstone sighed, 'O, when will Christ's holy gospel enter into this dark region?'[15] He later learned from the British consul at Zanzibar that 19,000 slaves from that region alone had passed annually through that custom house. This was over and above those landed at Portuguese slave ports. In addition to those captured, thousands were killed or had died from their wounds or famine. In Livingstone's estimation only one-fifth of those caught became slaves; in the Nyasa district probably not one-tenth. A small armed steamer would do wonders in arresting this robbery and

15 Ransford, p 190.

murder. An Arab dhow, undoubtably carrying slaves, was seen by the British scurrying across the lake.

This was a depressing time for the Scot and was reflected in his journals. This 'abode of lawlessness and bloodshed' reeked of slaughter and the lake shore was 'literally strewed with human bones and putrid bodies'.[16]

Livingstone's life was threatened on numerous occasions by the aggressive bloodthirsty Mazitu (Angoni) tribes yet, by the grace of God, he survived.

In the course of their investigations Livingstone, while examining the countryside, became separated for four days from the little boat and party which were not at the rendezvous point due to the inclement weather. With a sickening sense of frustration they returned to the south of Lake Nyasa. They never crossed the lake, for fierce sudden squalls threatened to sink the small craft.

The length of the lake was not ascertained, nor was the source of the Ruvuma located. Food was low and in a land where the dead outnumbered the living, supplies were difficult to obtain, particularly since they had been robbed and had nothing with which to trade. Some locals were suspicious of the party and showed extreme caution in their answers or conversely told marvellous tales which they hoped would please. On one such occasion they enquired of an intelligent-looking native, 'How far is it to the end of the lake?' 'The other end of the lake!' he exclaimed, in real or well-feigned astonishment. 'Whoever heard of such a thing? Why, if one started when a mere boy to walk to the other end of the lake, he would be an old grey-headed man before he got there. I never heard of such a thing being attempted.'[17]

On 26th October 1861 they sailed back down the Shire, weak, undernourished and depressed. The stark sounds of

[16] *Ibid*, p 191.
[17] Zam. & Tribs., pp 389–90.

gunfire saluted another torturous Arab manhunt, again deflating the expedition's morale.

The gig was left on top of the cataracts and the crew travelled by foot to the 'Pioneer'. There the bishop met them on 14th November 1861 and plans were made to collect and ferry the bishop's sisters. Livingstone was still annoyed with the bishop for having permitted exaggerated accounts of the battles to pass unchecked into the hands of the press. It was, however, Rowley who was responsible.

Expecting the ladies to arrive when the Shire was low, the 'Pioneer' could not travel very far, so it was agreed that the bishop would meet the steamer on New Year's Day, 1862, at the point where the River Ruo flowed into the Shire 130 miles south-east of Magomero. Livingstone also advised the bishop to open up a route overland whereby the ladies and several tons of supplies could be conveyed to the mission. Though the bishop wanted to travel to the sea to meet his family, the consul cautioned against it owing to the potentially explosive state of the mission station in regard to the surrounding tribes.

The 'Pioneer' left for sea on 15th November 1861; but by then the swelling of the river from early rains had subsided and the 'Pioneer' perched on the Elephant Marsh sand-banks for five weary weeks. During that time, on 17th December, the ship's carpenter died, a victim of the unhealthy region. Dr Kirk did the autopsy and his account indicated the cause to be blackwater fever.[18]

Meanwhile, Procter and Scudamore had been hastened by the bishop to go south and open up a suitable path to the Ruo. The two men had only been travelling for a few days when they were attacked by hostile villagers and narrowly escaped with their lives, while most of their attendants were abducted. They beat a hasty retreat, obtained reinforcements

---

[18] Gelfand, p 179.

and returned to settle the dispute. On their return the villagers gave up their captives and fled. The village was foolishly razed to the ground, rather a pointless move for it still left the route to the Ruo closed.

Hopelessly late, the bishop returned to Magomero, collected Burrup who had recently joined the mission and on 2nd January 1862 made for the River Ruo via the Shire. Unbeknown to the bishop, Livingstone was at the junction, still stranded, although the river was slowly rising. Neither Burrup nor the bishop were in good health; both were suffering from diarrhoea, and the incessant rains did not help matters.

A surgeon, Dickinson, and a 'lay brother' who were following behind Burrup passed the stranded ship and Livingstone thought they would pass a message to the bishop explaining his delay.[19] The message never reached the bishop and Burrup. They continued walking hurriedly through mud and unpleasant conditions to the Shire where they progressed by canoe only to miss Livingstone by a mere five days.

Yet another disaster occurred in the evening of 10th January 1862 when travelling to the Ruo mouth. They arrived at a seemingly convenient spot to rest for the night, but it was so infested with mosquitoes that the remainder of the party suggested they continue to a village further downstream. They repacked the canoe and set off again in the black of night. Unfortunately, at that point the Shire divided into several channels and they could not find the right one in the dark, with the result that they entered a side current and the canoe overturned. They lost everything from food to the vital medical box which Dr Dickinson had carefully packed for them. Unfortunately, Dr Dickinson completely forgot to mention the 'Pioneer's' delay.

The men, soaked to the skin, spent the night on the bank.

---

[19] Zam. & Tribs., chp 20, notably pp 401–402.

At dawn they drank in the sunlight and hastened to the junction, expecting to find the 'Pioneer'. Disheartened on hearing from local tribesmen the news that the 'Pioneer' had not arrived, they decided to wait. They passed the time by learning texts from the New Testament and gained spiritual strength from reciting such challenging and consoling scriptures as, 'Whosoever shall call upon the name of the Lord shall be saved.'

Without quinine the malarial sickness continued to sap their strength, while the bishop, unaware that the incubation period of malaria is only ten days, looked forward to seeing his sister. Livingstone, oblivious of the dilemma, arrived at the mouth of the Zambesi on 11th January 1862, the day before the bishop and Burrup reached the Ruo. There was still time for Livingstone to reach the two men so long as the entourage encountered no problems.

14

Death Darkened Days

The 'Pioneer' bobbed up and down as the gentle waves met with the mighty Zambesi. On board an anxious Livingstone scanned the sea for the ship. Nothing could be seen which would relieve the tension. The 'Gorgon' had been at the mouth, but it had to move on after a forceful gale threatened to engulf it. Livingstone had been too late for the rendezvous by only a few days. No matter how hard he tried he invariably missed target dates, through no fault of his own. The 'Pioneer' had been stranded at Elephant Marsh having waited for passengers from the mission station.

The delay threatened the return journey up north as not only did mosquitoes and fever menace their health while they were waiting, but they would miss the rainy season. Besides, the men were opposed to hauling the heavy hull over endless sand-banks. If the 'Gorgon' arrived any later the river would have subsided, leaving them stranded for a year. Time was of the essence as the Foreign Office had already given them an extension. Furthermore, the new vessel, the 'Lady Nyassa', built from the profits of Livingstone's book *Missionary Travels*, comprised over forty sections. The boat would have to be constructed, sailed up the Shire, dismantled at the cataracts, carried over forty miles and reassembled before finally being launched.

On 31st January 1862 at the river mouth the consul sighted two ships at sea heading for them. The 'Gorgon' signalled, 'I have steamboat in the brig;' to which Livingstone replied,

'Welcome News.' Then 'Wife aboard' was signalled from the ship. 'Accept my best thanks,' concluded what Livingstone called 'the most interesting conversation he had engaged in for many a day'.[1]

But as he heaved a sigh of relief so Bishop Mackenzie sank deeper into a coma. If the new doctor had told them of the 'Pioneer's' delay the men could have moved away from the mosquito-infested area, but it was too late to correct any errors. By now it was impossible for them to leave, the bishop was too weak and he slowly succumbed to the merciless disease of cerebral malaria.[2] The chief would not let him die in his hut, so a sick and suffering Burrup carried him out to the edge of the River Shire where he breathed his last. The chief then forced Burrup to carry the body, with the aid of a Makololo, across the river and to the bank where a solitary funeral took place.

Burrup must have realised that in order for him to survive he would need to seek help urgently, so he and the other Makololo canoed to Chibisa on 2nd February 1862, but after an exhausting three days canoeing upstream they decided to walk. This was extremely taxing for Burrup and he collapsed exhausted; kindly his followers carried him the rest of the way. Sadly, despite attention, he died on 21st February 1862.

On 1st February the 'Pioneer' steamed over the bar towards the 'Gorgon' and the other vessel, the 'Hetty Ellen'. Ignoring the 'Gorgon' Livingstone made straight for the brig, climbed aboard, embraced his wife and went with her below.

A seaman in 'Gorgon' vividly remembered the impression Livingstone made that day.

> There was something powerful about him [he said] that drew men to him, white and black alike . . . His eyes were wonderful—keen and with a twinkle of humour about them. And his thin face was

[1] Blaikie, p 291.
[2] Gelfand, p 188.

deeply tanned. When he spoke to me, or shook hands with me, there came into his eyes an expression that I have seldom seen so marked in any other eyes. His soul shone through them. They showed you what was in the man . . . and withal he was as gentle as a child.[3]

The components of the 'Lady Nyassa' were loaded onto the 'Pioneer' within a week, with as much of the mission stores which could be safely stored aboard. On 8th February the 'Pioneer', listing dangerously to port with one paddle wheel all but submerged and the other hardly touching the water, continued upstream. She persevered over endless sand bars, grounding frequently. Eventually it was decided to stop at Shupanga and assemble the 'Lady Nyassa' there.

Livingstone was not very comfortable organising men and criticisms quickly arose as to his handling of the off-loading of the boat parts and equipment. From his books and press coverage many people in Britain formed opinions of him which were more often than not shattered on reaching Africa. One such gentleman was James Stewart, a representative of the Free Church of Scotland, who was sent to plan another mission station. He befriended Mrs Livingstone on the journey out and was perhaps a little unwise in the handling of their friendship. It was nothing more than idle gossip motioned by Miss Mackenzie but served to cause all parties concerned a degree of frustration. Stewart furthermore expected greater things of Livingstone and Africa, but he arrived at a time when the expedition was entering into its darkest hour and he too was shaken by the sickening sights of slavery.

Mary Livingstone was in excellent form, chatting pleasantly to everyone and enjoying her husband's company. She was rather plump and her jocularity annoyed Kirk who was growing weary, having been on the move constantly since his arrival in Africa. None the less, the Livingstones were

---

[3] Ransford, p 194.

contented and they were adamant that they wanted to make the most of their own company. When Livingstone wrote to tell John Moffat he would send Mary to the highlands if she fell sick with fever, she added, 'Do not believe him,' in the margin and drew a profile sketch of her head with a derisive thumb touching her nose.

Arriving at Shupanga, a place only about fifty miles from the delta, Miss Mackenzie and Mrs Burrup were transferred by Captain Wilson of the 'Gorgon' onto his ship's gig. They proceeded with Dr Kirk to the River Ruo, but there was no one to meet them. Anxious, they went to Chibisa where they were told of the twofold tragedy.

Grief-stricken, the ladies were taken back to Shupanga where the news dealt Livingstone a deep blow. He silently watched Miss Mackenzie and Mrs Burrup being carried aboard and then went down to his dimly-lit cabin, grieving over his friends and the effect their death would have on the expedition. Putting his head into his hands he murmured, 'This will hurt us all.'[4] Writing to the bishop of Cape Town Livingstone said:

> The blow is quite bewildering; the two strongest men so quickly cut down, and one of them, humanly speaking, indispensable to the success of the enterprise. We must bow to the will of Him who doeth all things well; but I cannot help feeling sadly disturbed in view of the effect the news may have at home. I shall not swerve a hairbreadth from my work while life is spared . . .[5]

Thus with amazing fortitude Livingstone solemnly determined to persevere in the course set before him.

The next day, 15th March 1862, Livingstone set off downstream with the bereaved ladies. Unfortunately, they arrived in Kongone only to find out that a few hours earlier

---

[4] *Ibid*, p 200.
[5] Blaikie, p 296.

the 'Gorgon' had been blown out to sea by a gale. It did not return until 2nd April, thus leaving them in the malarial area; yet there was nothing Livingstone could do but wait.

Livingstone was able to reflect upon the situation, which was not encouraging. He was frustrated by the missionaries. Their militancy in firing and burning villages had become an embarrassment to him. Lacking self-constraint he, in poor taste, stated in front of the mourning Miss Mackenzie, 'This sad loss will have one good effect: better men will be sent out and no one hereafter come for a lark or to make a good thing of playing the missionary for a few years and then reaping laurels.'[6]

It was a trying time for everyone. Kirk was furious with Stewart and he wrote angrily in his diary that 'Dr Livingstone does not see how he has been thoroughly humbugged by this fellow'.[7] It was as if the expedition was being attacked from all sides, from the storms at sea, to sand bars and sickness. The latter was a great curse, for out of a complement of sixty sailors from the 'Gorgon' fifty-nine fell sick with fever on the Zambesi. While they were waiting for the ship, dysentery broke out on top of fever, and when the 'Gorgon' did finally arrive not one was sad to leave that region.

On 14th April 1862 the 'Pioneer', packed with more parts for the boat, limped into Shupanga and the engines, severely damaged through poor maintenance by a lazy engineer, needed attention.

Mrs Livingstone had her share of malarial attacks, but it did not seem to hamper her health too drastically. The attacks were short and easily controlled. However, she took ill on 21st April 1862 and this time did not respond to treatment while Kirk and Livingstone cared for her. The former was furious with Stewart for repeating rumours to her. He noticed

---

[6] Ransford, p 201.
[7] *Ibid*, p 200.

this had upset Mary albeit she was totally innocent; she deeply loved her husband and would give her life for that love. On the 25th the symptoms were alarming and vomiting every fifteen minutes prevented any medicine having effect. She was removed from the 'Pioneer' and gently carried to the spacious, single-storey, whitewashed house at Shupanga. The men improvised a bed out of three tea cases and a mattress. Treatment continued to have no effect. Without sleep Livingstone spent hours with her coaxing her to drink fluids. He remained hopeful until she lost the power to swallow. After that his self-control cracked and he started to shed tears as a well of sorrow burst forth. Livingstone watched his wife slowly sink into a coma in the early hours of Sunday 27th April. At 3am he called for Kirk, who came immediately, a sad scene confronting him. The doctors diligently prayed and utilised all their medical knowledge, but to no avail.

Mary became delirious and her breathing laboured. As the day progressed no improvement was seen and, as dusk cast its long lingering shadows, life slowly ebbed from Mary. At six o'clock Livingstone summoned Stewart who saw the Scot 'sitting by the side of a rude bed formed of boxes, but covered with a soft mattress, on which lay his dying wife . . . the man who had faced so many deaths, and braved so many dangers, was now utterly broken down and weeping like a child'.[8]

Stewart's eyes filled with tears. With glistening red eyes Livingstone asked him to pray while he and Kirk knelt. But Mary's breathing became increasingly laboured and irregular. Wearily Livingstone once more broke down and taking his wife into his arms choked: 'My dearie, my dearie you are going to leave me . . . Are you resting on Jesus?' She thoughtfully looked up, and he took it to mean yes. Just after seven he kissed her and she did not respond; 'lying with her mouth a little open she gently shut it and breathed her last'.[9]

---

[8] Blaikie, p 298.
[9] D L to Mrs Neil L 29/04/62 in Jeal, p 258.

Although exhausted, Livingstone spent much of the night going through Mary's belongings. Doubt tended to accompany her faith and the thought of her dying without believing in God agonised him. He found a short prayer among her papers: 'Accept me Lord as I am, and make me such as Thou wouldst have me to be.'[10] In his diary he poured out his heart, saying: 'It is the first heavy stroke I have suffered, and quite takes away my strength. I wept over her who well deserved many tears. I loved her when I married her, and the longer I lived with her I loved her the more. God pity the poor children, who were all tenderly attached to her.'[11]

Grief gripping his heart he wrote to Oswell, his son: 'With many tears running down my cheeks I have to tell you that poor dearly beloved Mama died last night about seven o'clock . . . She loved you dearly and often spoke of you and all the family, especially little Baby . . .'[12]

The next day Mary Livingstone was buried at noon under the shadow of a massive baobab tree; mist and a heavily-laden sky setting the sombre scene.

Over the next few days Kirk noticed a softening of the Scot's heart as his spirit suffered this severe blow.

On 11th May 1862 at Kongone he penned in his journal: 'My dear, dear Mary has been this evening a fortnight in heaven—absent from the body, present with the Lord. 'Today shalt thou be with Me in Paradise.' Angels carried her to Abraham's bosom—to be with Christ is far better . . . For the first time in my life I feel willing to die—D.L.'[13]

Sorrowfully David sought to be with his Saviour and his beloved wife, and a few days later wrote in the privacy of his

---

[10] Unpublished private journal of David Livingstone 1861–63 in National Library of Scotland, *ibid*.
[11] Blaikie, pp 298–299.
[12] D L to Oswell L 29/04/1862 in Jeal, p 259.
[13] Unpublished journals of Livingstone, p 43, in Blaikie, pp 299–300.

diary: 'I have often wished that it might be in some far-off still deep forest, where I may sleep sweetly till the resurrection morn, when the trumpet of God will make all start up into the glorious and active second existence.'[14]

31st May 1862—The loss of my ever dear Mary lies like a heavy weight on my heart. In our intercourse in private there was more than what would be thought by some a decorous amount of merriment and play. I said to her a few days before her fatal illness: 'We old bodies ought now to be more sober, and not to play so much.' 'Oh no,' said she, 'you must always be as playful as you have always been, I would not like you to be as grave as some folks I have seen.' This, when I know her prayer was that she might be spared to be a help and comfort me in my great work, led me to feel what I have always believed to be the true way, to let the head grow wise, but to keep the heart always young and playful . . .[15]

Though Livingstone's manner had softened a little, his previous inflexible determination had hardened into an obsession in the desire to push himself to the limits of human endurance. His indomitable spirit rose and he set his heart to accomplish goals which dangled beneath the dark horizon. Already the outlook was grim: sickness savaged the men, while the 'Pioneer' was restricted to the Zambesi and the Portuguese hostility was increasing. The mission had poor results as they were reaping the whirlwind of the 'bishop's war'. Furthermore, famine ravaged the countryside in the Shire region creating more havoc as the slave-trade flourished.

Leaving work to progress on the 'Lady Nyassa', Livingstone and Kirk went to Tete in order to see the impedimenta of the expedition brought down in canoes. This time they used sails, a new system to the local sailors who marvelled at the ingenuity. No more pulling with oars, or cutting endless trees

[14] *Ibid*, p 300.
[15] Blaikie, pp 300–301.

for firewood. As the boat cut through the waves, the tribesmen sprang to their feet with wild excitement, singing loudly, gesticulating with might and main. Suddenly the singing ceased—the vocalists were sprawling on their backs—the boat was on a sandbank.

Work on the 'Lady Nyassa' slowly progressed, though fever and dysentery hampered the men, and on 23rd June 1862 she was ready for launching. This attracted much interest from people all over the country, most of whom were

> quite certain that, being made of iron she must go to the bottom as soon as she entered the water. Earnest discussions had taken place among them with regard to the propriety of using iron for ship-building. The majority affirmed that it would never float. They said 'If we put a hoe into the water, or the smallest bit of iron, it sinks immediately. How can such a mass of iron float? It must go to the bottom.' The minority answered that this might be true with them, but white man had medicine for everything . . . The unbelievers were astonished and could hardly believe their eyes, when they saw the ship float lightly and gracefully on the river . . . 'Truly,' they said, 'these men have powerful medicine.'[16]

The river was still too low to move the 'Lady Nyassa' to Chibisa, and rather than waste time Livingstone decided to go to Johanna for stores and make another exploration of the Ruvuma. Many saw this as an illogical decision, but after his bereavement he needed to be kept busy. Whenever circumstances in the past had threatened to crush Livingstone he had fought back by forcing himself to go through some physically gruelling exploration. Opening up the Ruvuma would rid him of the responsibility of the Portuguese and he was determined to do so, regardless of the cost.

They went up in two small boats, Charles and David Livingstone in one and Rae and Kirk in the other. (Rae refused to travel in the same boat as Charles.) They progressed slowly,

---

[16] Zam. & Tribs., pp 423–424.

seriously hindered by shoals as well as the tribes, soured by the slave-trade. Kirk, exasperated, wrote in his journal: 'I can come to no other conclusion than Dr Livingstone is out of his mind.'[17]

Livingstone questioned his own vision while relentlessly riding not only himself but also his men. 'Am I to be a martyr to my own cause? ... Every covenant was ratified with sacrifice ... I hope this may be compensated if I die by my death.'[18]

Danger and death were a constant threat to the men and, on one occasion on 19th September 1862, having paid cloth for the right to pass upstream, locals with many muskets set about firing at them. Kirk quickly despatched one man and his coxswain put an end to another. Within moments the troublesome tribe hurriedly withdrew.

Gradually the reality of the ungracious Ruvuma with her craggy rocks which impaired their progress came home to Livingstone. They returned to the 'Pioneer' on 9th October, having been away for one month, then on to the Zambesi via Johanna where they picked up more men and some oxen. Livingstone still missed Mary and in a letter to Sir Thomas Maclear opened his heart, saying:

I suppose that I shall die in these uplands, and somebody will carry out the plan I have longed to put into practice. I have been thinking a great deal since the departure of my beloved one about the regions whither she has gone ... We shall see Him by whose inexpressible love and mercy we get there, and all whom we loved, and all the lovable. I can sympathise with you now more fully than I did before. I work with as much vigour as I can, and mean to do so till the change comes; but the prospect of a home is all dispelled.[19]

[17] Kirk's Journals, p 475, in Jeal, p 261.
[18] *Scottish Historical Revue XXXIX (1960)*, p 121, *ibid.*
[19] D L to Sir Thomas Maclear 27/10/1862 in Blaikie, p 309.

This note revealed some prophetical insight. However, the more withdrawn and uncommunicative he became the more he estranged himself from the expedition. He had further clashes with Kirk, and the once-firm friendship soon dissolved as the 'Pioneer', with 'Lady Nyassa' in tow, headed for the Elephant Marsh in the Shire Valley.

For the next month they pulled and tugged the vessels over stubborn sand-banks which not only lowered their morale, but strained their nerves. Engineer Rae refused his meals on the 'Pioneer'. On 1st February Livingstone's personal log posed the perplexing question: 'How to live a real Christian life amidst all the worry and cares of our condition?' The following day he wrote, 'Came to first sharp bend and failed;' the next day, 'Tried and failed;' on the fifth day, 'Failed;' on the fourteenth, 'Patience, patience, river rising a little.'

They were confronted with the ravages of the notorious marauder, Mariano, the Portuguese slave-agent who together with his lawless gangs left carnage in his wake. A drought then further devastated the land. Women were seen collecting insects, roots, wild fruits and whatever could be eaten in order to live, if possible, till the next crop ripened. Those not sold into slavery escaped with their lives, using palm-leaf aprons to cover themselves as all their clothing and ornaments had been stolen. Dead bodies floated past the vessels daily and the paddles had to be cleared of corpses, caught by the floats during the night. River banks, once so populous, stood silent. Occasionally a fisherman with a look of cringing broken spiritness was spotted laying traps to save himself from starvation.

Whenever they took a walk human skeletons were seen in every direction. 'Many had ended their misery under shady trees—others under projecting crags in the hills—while others lay in their huts, with closed doors, which when opened disclosed the mouldering corpse with the poor rags round the loins.'[20] 'Musical instruments, mats, pillows, mortars for

---

[20] Zam. & Tribs., p 458.

pounding meal, were lying about unused, and becoming the prey of the white ants. With all their little comforts destroyed, the survivors were thrown still further back into barbarism.'[21]

This scene, like so many similar, burned itself into Livingstone's mind. He felt he was in a sense to blame, for he had opened up the river and thus given the brutal plunderers an entry that before they had feared to take.

Livingstone's inner heart longed for peace, and as the spirit of death settled heavily upon the Shire region it too touched his soul. In his diary on 1st March 1863 he wrote: 'I feel very often that I have not long to live and say, "My dear children, I leave you. Be manly Christians, and never do a mean thing. Be honest to men, and to the Almighty one."'[22]

Finally, however, on 10th April 1863, after three months' toil, they reached the cataracts. The 'Lady Nyassa' was taken to pieces and the daunting task of forging a road over thirty-five miles of rapids lay before them. Morale and sickness were at an all-time low. Thornton, whom Livingstone had earlier reinstated on the expedition, had travelled to Tete to fetch supplies for the missionaries. But the journey had over-taxed him and he succumbed to fever and dysentery, dying a few days after his return.

Kirk and Charles tendered their resignation to the consul and under a cloud of bitter disappointment Livingstone accepted. Their departure was delayed, however, as Livingstone suffered a bad bout of fever. Finally, he rallied and the men felt free to leave on 19th May 1863.

The memory of Mary's death still lay heavily on Livingstone's heart. He had wept on the anniversary of her death, but his faith, though hemmed in by discouragement, remained firm. He encouraged the remaining missionaries to make a final attempt to re-establish a mission station on the highlands, and

---

[21] *Ibid*, p 471.
[22] Blaikie, p 312.

on 27th May, Mary Procter, Waller and Adams departed. Their journey was short-lived as sickness forced their return. The missionaries decided to wait for the new bishop, who on his arrival brought about the closure of the missionary enterprise in that region. This was another resounding blow to Livingstone, who saw the closure of the mission as nothing less than a cowardly abandonment of the Christian's calling. In a letter to Horace Waller he argued that 'the great teacher commanded His missionaries to begin 'at Jerusalem' with those who had committed the worst murder the world ever saw'.[23]

The ship bringing the bishop also brought the death knell to the whole of the expedition. News of the recall came on 20th July 1863, the day on which an already discouraged Livingstone had just returned from a thirty-five-mile trudge in search of a replacement for the boat which had been destroyed by fire. The bearer of these tidings was an insensitive man who hailed the men in his strong Surrey dialect as he drew alongside the ship with the words, 'No more pay for you.'[24]

The despatch from the Foreign Office recalled the expedition. The time limit was long overdue; the expenses incurred, including the help of the Navy, were heavy and there had been no gain. Politically, too, Livingstone was an embarrassment, for the Portuguese Government resented him and his rude comments; the British were not too keen on provoking them.

Livingstone could do nothing but submit—he had no quarrel with the cabinet; in fact they had behaved nobly towards him—but the thought of abandoning his God-given vision disturbed him. In a letter written the following day to Mr James Young he made it quite clear he had no intention

---

[23] D L to Horace Waller 13/08/1863 in Campbell, p 289.
[24] Zam. & Tribs., p 540.

of giving up the fight of faith he had been called to—'I shall work some other point yet. In leaving, it is bitter to see some 900 miles of coast abandoned to those who were the first to begin the slave-trade, and seem determined to be the last to abandon it.'[25]

If ever the Scot had an excuse to abandon his cause he had one now, yet this man, in spite of the hardships that had worn out every European under his charge, resolved to fulfil his high calling. In a letter to Mr Waller he said:

I don't know whether I am to go on the shelf or not. If I do, I make Africa the shelf ... There is a Ruler above, and His providence guides all things. He is our Friend, and has plenty of work for all His people to do. Don't fear of being left idle, if willing to work for Him ... To Him shall be given of the gold of Sheba, and daily shall He be praised. I always think it was such a blessing and a privilege to be led into His work instead of into the service of the hard taskmasters—the Devil and sin.'[26]

These words display the inner strength and security this man had in his Saviour. His faith in Christ was the hallmark of his life and it took him through trials that would have maimed many men spiritually; yet Livingstone remained steadfast, immovable and resolved to continue his work for the Lord.

[25] D L to James Young 3/07/1863 in Blaikie, p 313.
[26] *Ibid*, pp 313–314.

15

The Consul's Crisis: Should Christianity Capitulate?

Ironically, the recalling of the expedition had come as a relief to Livingstone. Five years of hard slog, sickness and the sights of slavery had worn everyone down. With virtually no one available to carry the cumbersome parts of the steamer past the rapids they were at a stalemate. They only had one wagon and the river area was riddled with tsetse fly. How long before the oxen would die?

As early as 17th April 1863 the doctor had written: 'If the Government looks on this as I do we may expect to be withdrawn'. The following week he told Waller, 'I should not wonder in the least to be recalled'. By 1st May he had drafted a despatch to Lord Russell describing the desolation in the Shire Valley making their retirement advisable.[1]

The Zambesi expedition had been launched and backed by the government, for public opinion favoured such a venture. The tide had turned by 1863 and those who had left the expedition earlier were quick to highlight the consul's mistakes. 'God's highway' to Central Africa proved impassable; ten clerics had publicly castigated him for having liberated slaves at gun point after Rowley had accused him of hunting 'for slaving parties in every direction',[2] and of instigating Bishop Mackenzie's war. Furthermore, the Royal

---

[1] National Library of Scotland ref 10715, pp 187, 197 in Ransford, p 214.
[2] NAZ, U N 2/1/1, 24–28, *ibid*, p 218.

Navy resented losing several sailors at the mouth of the Zambesi. Politically, Livingstone's coarse criticism of the Portuguese created a diplomatic debacle. Finally, *The Times* on 20th January 1863 also slated the Scot stating: 'We were promised cotton, sugar and indigo . . . and, of course we got none. We were promised trade; and there is no trade, although we have a Consul at 500 pounds a year. We were promised converts, and not one has been made. . . .' Thus the article continued to decry all that Livingstone, his team and the Christians in the area, were trying to do. It was Lord Russell who in keeping with public consensus compiled the letter recalling the expedition.

The instructions called for the 'Pioneer' to be delivered to the mouth of the Zambesi and surrendered to the Navy as soon as possible. The 'Lady Nyassa', being Livingstone's boat, was of no concern to Whitehall.

The consul calculated that it would take some time before the river rose high enough to carry the ship to the coast. He therefore had several months free. Though sick, this was ideal, for Livingstone, indomitable as ever despite the debilitating hardships, decided to examine Lake Nyasa again. He wanted to obtain information regarding the slave routes into the interior.

He took with him a sick ship steward, a few natives, a sailing boat and supplies for the journey. Unfortunately, disaster struck at the top of the rapids. Five Zambesi men tried to show how much more clever they were than the five Makololo who hitherto had the management of it. The boat broke away from them in a comparatively still reach of the river, and rushed away like an arrow over the cataracts. 'The five performers in this catastrophe approached with penitential looks. They had nothing to say, nor had we. They bent down slowly, and touched our feet with both hands. 'ku kuata moendo'—'to catch the foot'—is their way of asking forgiveness. It was so like what we have seen a little child do—try to bring a dish unbidden to its papa, and letting it fall, burst into a cry of distress'.[3] This scene, though a crushing blow, aroused the Christian's compassion and he forgave their foolhardiness in losing the boat and supplies.

A few more supplies were fetched from the 'Pioneer' and they continued on foot. They soon came to a range of mountains running north and south, which Livingstone dedicated to Dr Kirk. A generous gesture, which in the eyes of the recipient should have come earlier, for Kirk had departed without many words of grateful thanks from Livingstone. He had resented this and lost no time in castigating the consul. Livingstone, though a man of few words, never forgot loyalty and in the case of Dr Kirk helped secure him a position later as the Consul of Zanzibar. It was a unique post, which Kirk handled commendably and like Livingstone he sought to suppress slavery.

The sick steward, Thomas Ward, was suffering from anaemia, but trudged along as the doctor believed exercise to be the solution to most ailments. One must sympathise with the poor man who 'strove manfully to keep up but when we halted he was often seen spread out like a dead frog and at last fell behind confessing that his legs were bad'.[4]

Livingstone, rallying from his malady, sought to investigate as much of the country as possible. They started off towards the north west of the lake, coming upon remains of a stockade where only the day before tribal fighting had taken place. Avoiding the danger zone they turned away to the north east, reached the lake and marched along its shores to Kota-Kota Bay (now known as Nkhotakota), then a busy slave emporium where slaves were collected and transported across the lake in a dhow. Livingstone was recognised by the chief person, Juma, whom he had met during his earlier visit, and the welcome they received was courteous and generous. There

---

[3] Zam. & Tribs., pp 478–479.
[4] NAZ LI 2/1/1 D L to J Moore 12/01/1864 in Ransford, p 220.

Livingstone saw a dhow under construction, being made of fine timber. If he had known earlier that such timber was available he would have been able to build a boat and saved the darkened days of despair trying to haul the 'Lady Nyassa' onto the lake. The consul offered to buy the boat, but at no price would Juma sell it. The slave-trade was too profitable.

The Christian also saw that many people had moved to the village for the peace and security the community, though inspired by an evil trade, afforded them. Livingstone immediately had visions of a mission station. The rate, however, at which the people would perish before the crops could be harvested threw a dark cloud over his hopes. Hunger would before long compel them to sell each other.

Sadness surrounded the village of Kota-Kota, where the haunting and harrowing chink of chains could be heard as man sold man for pieces of cloth. The well-worn slave track stretched to Cazembe, another collection point for tribes that had been sold into slavery.

A few days' march brought the consul through Kasungu to the watershed overlooking the swamps in which this man of prayer was later destined to die. Here Livingstone heard of further lakes hitherto unmapped. One named Bemba, another larger one named Moero and another, Lake Tanganyika.[5] Exploration of those areas would again swing fickle public opinion, while Livingstone's cause—that of spreading the gospel by promoting commerce and Christianity with the abolition of slavery—would be revived. Despite the temptation, the Scot submitted to his orders for all support and salaries for the expedition to cease on 31st December 1863. Their supplies had also run out. Travel became difficult and as they were on the slave route they found the people more churlish than usual. When Livingstone complained they replied, 'We have been made wary by those who came to buy

---

[5] Zam. & Tribs., p 531.

slaves'.[6] Thus on 29th September 1863 they turned back towards Lake Nyasa, visiting several villages en route and reached the 'Pioneer' the following November, having accomplished an amazing feat. They had walked, in fifty-five travelling days, an average of at least fifteen miles a day. (Nearly twenty-five kilometres per day.)

This had been a worthwhile trip and it cemented Livingstone's desire to see the slave-trade cease; a cause which not only captivated his heart, but also motivated a section of his life's work.

On the 'Pioneer' they settled down to what would be a wearisome wait for the river to rise. Rae had successfully finished bolting Livingstone's boat together again. The engines too were now in place and she was in fine condition.

The news that Bishop Tozer had resolved to abandon the mission and transfer operations from the continent to Zanzibar came as a crushing blow to Livingstone. Writing to the bishop he implored him to reconsider the matter.

> I hope, dear Bishop, you will not deem me guilty of impertinence in thus writing to you with a sore heart. I see that if you go, the last ray of hope for this wretched, trodden-down people disappears, and I again from the bottom of my heart entreat you to reconsider the matter, and may the All-wise One guide to that decision which will be most for His glory'.[7]

He opened up his heart in a letter to Sir Thomas Maclear, as the bishop's decision to abandon the mission disturbed him more than his own recall. He could hardly write; he was more inclined 'to sit down and cry'.[8] In his eyes, Christianity was capitulating and that was not the divine commission. To retreat even for a while was defeat; if only he were younger

---

[6] *Ibid*, p 520.
[7] Blaikie, p 320.
[8] *Ibid*.

he would go himself and plant the gospel. It would be done one day without fail, though he might not live to see it.

As before, Livingstone found himself blamed for the removal of the mission. The Makololo had behaved badly and they were his people. However, the bishop, Livingstone believed, wanted an easy life—not likely to be found for a long time in this region. The lowlands brought fever, the highlands brought damp days of mist and rain. In an earlier letter to Mary, Livingstone had written that 'Bishop Tozer, a good man enough, lacks courage . . . What a mission it would be if there were no difficulties—nothing but walking about in slippers made by admiring young ladies! Hey! that would not suit me. It would give me the doldrums; but there are many tastes in the world'.[9]

Livingstone's sentiments were also expressed in his book *The Zambesi and Its Tributaries*. Over many pages he argued the cause of missions, pointing out that the ground had been consecrated by the lives of those brave men who first occupied it. Mission stations established to the west coast of Africa had lost over forty missionaries who had succumbed to the climate. 'In fleeing from Morambala to an island in the Indian Ocean, he acted as St Augustine would have done, had he located himself on one of the Channel Islands, when sent to Christianize the natives of Central England. This is, we believe, the first case of Protestant Mission having being abandoned without being driven away'.[10]

Livingstone was not the only person pained by the bishop's decision. When they finally managed to steam down the Shire they stopped near Morambala on 1st February 1864, 'where the Bishop [Tozer] passed a short time before bolting out of the country'.[11] There they saw the tragic sight of many

[9] D L to Mary L 10/08/1863 in Blaikie, p 323.
[10] Zam. & Tribs., p 574.
[11] D L to Agnes L 24/02/1864 in Blaikie, p 326.

widowed women and orphaned children abandoned by the bishop. The Revd Horace Waller was one of the members of the mission and he, like Livingstone, was incensed by the bishop's policy and determined to get the women and children out of the slavers' clutches. When opposed by Tozer, Waller resigned from the Universities' Mission Christian Association and on his own responsibility shepherded the helpless. Waller felt Whitehall's decision deeply and was haunted by the thought of Christian influence in the Shire valley being replaced by the devil's. 'Why,' Waller wrote, 'don't the very rocks groan on those beautiful hills?—the lamp is flickering and soon enough it will be dark enough, aye, even for the Portuguese slave-trade! Oh, how I dread all this . . .'[12] This was surely the time to sow in tears.

The doctor collected the two remaining men from the mission, together with thirteen women, their children and twenty-five orphan boys. Those who were able to cultivate the soil were left and given seeds to plant as the drought was breaking. The plan was to resettle the orphans and the widows under Waller's care in the Cape.

Livingstone, however, had another problem—the 'Lady Nyassa'. Since the government played no part in paying for her she still belonged to him but, as he earlier told his daughter, 'the Portuguese would have liked to get her, to employ her as a slaver—I would rather see her go down to the depths of the Indian Ocean than that'.[13] Already he had thoughts of crossing the Indian Ocean in that little vessel and selling her in Bombay.

When they reached the coast they officially handed the 'Pioneer' to the officers of the ship 'Orestes' and on 14th February 1864 Livingstone transferred all his belongings to the 'Lady Nyassa'. HMS 'Ariel' took the 'Lady Nyassa' on

[12] Ransford, p 218.
[13] D L to Mary L 10/08/1863 in Blaikie, p 322.

tow towards the port of Mocambique. Troubles were far from over, for en route they encountered a hurricane which struck the 'Ariel' with such force that she was twisted right round and the tow rope became entwined with the screw propeller, putting the engines out of action. Then, helpless, she turned her bow in the raging sea and began to bear down upon the 'Lady Nyassa'. The crew could do nothing but hope and pray that she would miss. Livingstone made ready to catch hold of one of the flying ropes, but 'by God's goodness' she passed safely and they breathed again.

Then followed a fearful night, for the frail vessel was tossed to and fro in the raging sea. Livingstone was offered safety on board the 'Ariel', but he remained with the natives as they braved the bitter night. Finally day dawned and the winds receded, allowing the vessels to forge ahead to their destination, thankful for their 'kind and merciful preservation'.

In Mocambique repairs were made to the vessels and Mr Waller with his retinue transferred to the 'Valorous' whereupon they sailed for the Cape on 16th April 1864, leaving Livingstone to sail on to Zanzibar, which he reached on the 24th. At this stage the doctor wanted to try and keep 'Lady Nyassa' for his own use at a later stage, but if she remained in Zanzibar she would almost certainly be used as a slave carrier. He then embarked on his most dangerous venture yet—to sail to Bombay in a vessel that was built for an inland lake, not the wild open sea. Rae saw no sense in this move, particularly as an offer had been made for the boat, and hastily accepted a position at Zanzibar, leaving Livingstone with no engineer. Dr Livingstone would be both the skipper and navigator, even though he had no experience at commanding a ship at sea and his knowledge of navigation, particularly in this area, was largely self-taught. Only three Europeans accompanied him (a stoker, a carpenter and a sailor); two were sick for most of the journey and the third mutinous. There were seven native Zambesians who, until they had volunteered, had never seen the sea, two youths (one of whom became his devoted servant, Chuma) and a meagre fourteen tons of coal.

The ocean itself was perilous, for the breaking of the monsoon occurred at the end of May or beginning of June. The winds and cloud cover would wreck any hopes they had of sailing and navigating.

The little vessel had no adequate deck protection and when struck by a sharp squall would turn broadside to the wind and risk rolling over. The engines could only be used at the end of the journey to combat the winds and current and even then she could only crawl; thus they had to rely upon the sails—and the Lord for the wind.

Livingstone calculated the voyage of 2,500 miles would take him eighteen days. He was, as usual, highly optimistic. They set out on 30th April 1864, but sickness soon struck the men. The natives quickly learned to steer, but the wind which they so badly needed did not blow. On 20th May Livingstone, after recording only sixteen knots in the last twenty four hours, began to despair. He penned in his journal:

> This very unusual weather has a very depressing influence on my mind. I often feel as if I am to die on this voyage, and wish I had sent the accounts to the Government, as also my chart of the Zambesi. I often wish that I may be permitted to do something for the benighted of Africa. I shall have nothing to do at home; by the failure of the Universities' Mission my work seems vain. No fruit likely to come from J. Moffat's mission either. Have I not laboured in vain? Am I to be cut off before I do anything to effect permanent improvement in Africa? I have been unprofitable enough, but may do something yet, in giving information. If spared, God grant that I may be more faithful than I have been, and may He open up the way for me!'[14]

This was an extreme test of his faith. The following day the sea was glassy calm and sharks stalked the ship under the hot

---

[14] *Ibid* p 330.

glaring sun. David was in a quandary. At their very slow pace
it would take them fifteen days to reach Bombay—just one
day before the expected breaking of the monsoon. If he turned
the ship towards Aden the wind, if it did eventually blow,
would be against him. He could but carry on, though
provisions, especially water, were scarce. Even with rationing
they only had enough for ten or twelve days. In his journal
he cried out to God: 'May the Almighty be gracious to us all,
and help us!'[15]

Despite the problems, his journal observations and writing
were as always perfectly detailed. Tension mounted as the
monsoons began to break on 28th May 1864; a dense cloud
descended from the east and north east and a furious gale
blew, tearing sails and the ship again nearly 'rolled quite over'.
The storm 'lasted half an hour then passed with little rain. It
was terrible while it lasted. We had calm after it, and the sky
brightened up. Thank God for His goodness'.[16] Thereafter
the wind picked up, though the boat, due to its design, could
not travel very fast. On 10th June 1864 a furious squall tore
the fore square-sail to ribbons, and the following day they
were greeted with a wet scowling morning, frequent rains,
and thunder in the distance. Cloud cover meant that they
could not navigate, for they needed the sun and stars to guide
them. Livingstone again cried out to God, 'a poor weak
creature. Permit me to lean on an all-powerful arm'.[17]

Livingstone stood firm in his faith in his Father and his own
reckoning. He told the crew that night of 10th June to look
out for land and the next day they peeled the horizon with
anxious eyes, and finally saw to their glee the hills of India.
They were now only 115 miles from Bombay. Finally, on 13th
June 1864 Livingstone, relieved, wrote in his ship's log: 'I

---

[15] *Ibid*, p 331.
[16] *Ibid*, p 332.
[17] *Ibid*, p 333.

mention God's good providence over me, and beg that He may accept my spared life for His service'.[18]

Due to the fog and the small size of the 'Lady Nyassa' her entrance into bustling Bombay harbour was not observed. It was only after the harbour authorities had looked through Livingstone's papers that they realised who he was and from where he had in fact come.

He spent a short while as a guest of Sir Bartle Frere, Governor of Bombay, who became a close friend. The consul paid off his crew and sought accommodation and schooling for the mission youth, harboured the vessel and on 24th June 1864 set off on his way home to Britain; this time in a more conventional manner.

Much had happened these past six years, though sadly the expedition was an admitted failure and an anti-climax to all that Livingstone had hoped for and predicted. However, he had successfully explored the Ruvuma and the Shire region and even located areas where settlement could be made possible. Unfortunately, the government in 1864 was not open to colonial expansion. Missionaries would not come forward without government aid and few were likely to follow in Livingstone's footsteps.

It was a different person returning to Britain this time. On his way to Bombay he had written in his journal: 'By the failure of the Universities' Mission my work seems in vain. Am I to be cut off before I can do anything to effect permanent improvement in Africa? I have been unprofitable enough . . .'[19] This was certainly a low ebb in his life. Few would welcome him in Britain and he had little money, having spent the remainder from his first publication on building the 'Lady Nyassa'. In memory every fine feature of the African country was bathed in gloom, while the woe and wretchedness of the people in slavery sank heavily into his heart.

---

[18] *Ibid*, p 334.
[19] *David Livingstone: His Life and Letters* by G Seaver, p 442, in Jeal, p 272.

His views on the slave-trade became an integral part of his life as he quietly, resolutely determined to see it stopped. But how? Few, if any, would follow him after the failure of the previous expedition. Besides, he felt more comfortable on his own among the natives than having to care for a crew from Europe. He needed somehow to win the public's heart before he could motivate them to stamp out the scourge—almost an impossible task.

All he could do was expose the sin of slavery for what it was. Foremost, there was the internal slave-trade between hostile native tribes. Secondly, there were the slave-traders from the coast, Arabs or half-caste Portuguese, for whom natives were encouraged to collect slaves by all the horrible means of marauding and murder. Finally, there were the parties sent out from Portuguese and Arab coastal towns with cloth, beads, muskets and ammunition to exchange for the profitable service of people in bondage. This accursed slave-trade had frustrated everything. Britain, having passed its laws on slavery, saw itself free of the burden and its present investment in Africa was only an embarrassment. It would take some persuasion to get them even to listen.

Livingstone believed in Africa, and God had placed a love for the African within his heart. In his conversations and publications he defended the cause of Africa. To him the African was someone who was gifted 'with physical strength capable of withstanding the sorest privations, and a light-heartedness which, as a sort of compensation, enables them to make the best of the worst situations'.[20] He defended the Africans against the critics who said that they were insufficiently intelligent to receive the message of grace and forgiveness. In his book *The Zambesi and Its Tributaries*, he was quick to quote Sir James Stephen that

---

[20] Zam. & Tribs., p 597.

the Apostles assume in all men the existence of a 'spiritual discernment', enabling the mind, when unclouded by appetite or passion, to recognise and distinguish the Divine voice, whether uttered from within by the intimations of conscience, or speaking from without in the language of the inspired oracles ... The Gospel, the especial patrimony of the poor and the illiterate, had been the stay of millions.[21]

The man who was criticised for hardly having won a convert to Christianity was prepared to stand for all that he believed in.

When the Portuguese critics challenged him for taking other men's discoveries as his own, his reply was simple: 'Truly our object was not so much discovery, as a desire to lead the nation, which his Excellency's countrymen had so enslaved and degraded, to a state of freedom and civilisation'.[22]

Though he later changed his status from missionary to explorer, his life was still impelled by the old clear motive of alleviating Africa's misery; his most apparent characteristic being a man of sorrows acquainted with grief.

[21] *Ibid*, p 600.
[22] *Ibid*, pp 460–461.

16

Back to Battles in Britain

Livingstone reached London in July 1864. Not one member of his family came to meet him, so he quietly booked in at the Tavistock Hotel. After dinner he called on Sir Roderick and Lady Murchison, who promptly took him to a reception with the Prime Minister, Lord Palmerston.

Thereafter polite society entertained the Scot, though they kept him at a distance. Livingstone was not the only hero to hail from Africa and his costly expedition was seen as a failure; while perpetual attacks on the Portuguese lacked discretion to say the least. None the less, he still graced the tables of many Ladies, Earls, Duchesses and Dukes, as well as the Prime Minister and Lord Mayor of London.

Lord Russell, the British Foreign Secretary, was reticent in his welcome of Livingstone. The doctor found that 'his manner is very cold, as all the Russells are'. To him Livingstone had lost favour with the Portuguese, the Press, the clergymen (the latter for the failure of the Universities' Mission). After all, it was the Portuguese who gave Livingstone permission to enter the Zambesi, yet he had the gall to upset them by bringing to mention the sensitive issue of the slave-trade, while having the audacity to sneak his waifs with Waller past the customs house.

Business in the Foreign Office was brisk, and before long Livingstone was on his way to Scotland, though his home-coming was marred by two major factors. The first was the illness of his mother, who was slowly dying, and the second was that his son Robert had enlisted in the American army.

The lack of fatherly attention that Livingstone's eldest son, Robert, had received was reflected in the rebellious route he followed. Even at an early age he was extremely restless as if, to use his father's phrase, he had got 'a deal of the vagabond nature' from him. Robert was reared with no real fatherly figure to cater for his strong personality and soon he was upsetting more than just Livingstone's spinster sisters who were looking after him. School was irksome and of little interest to young Robert; his heart was too restless. The sense of security he so longed for was lacking and no boarding school or institution would fill it. This was further frustrated by the death of his mother, and finally his father agreed to have him join the expedition so that his future could be discussed.

Sadly, poor communications snarled the young man's reunion with his father, for the trustees had not arranged for his passage to join the expedition. Thus he soon found himself penniless in Natal. There not being much of a future for him in Natal, and having missed the opportunity of a passage with Tozer, he made his way back to Cape Town. There he lodged uncomfortably in the sailor's home where according to the intolerant Kirk, 'he was doing no good and they will be glad to see him shipped off somewhere else',[1] which is what happened to him as he worked his passage in a brig to Boston. It was not long before he was drugged, kidnapped and forcibly enlisted in the American Civil War on the side of those against slavery, the Northern Forces.

Later, in October, Livingstone received from his son a moving letter in which he addressed his father as 'My Dear Sir'. A depth to the young man emerged as he poured out his heart to the father he never really knew. Robert told his father

---

[1] NAZ reference ST/1/1/1 120.

of his present problems and described the battle skirmishes he had been through, explaining: 'I have never hurt anyone knowingly in battle, have always fired high, and in that furious madness which always accompanies a bayonet charge and which seems to possess every soldier, I controlled my passion and took the man who surrendered prisoner.'[2]

He admitted his regret at throwing away his chance of an education and wished that a 'craving to travelling had not led him astray'. He concluded, 'I have changed my name for I am convinced that to bear your name here would lead to further dishonours to it.'[3]

Sadly before he was nineteen Robert Livingstone, known to the Americans as Rupert Vincent, was wounded in battle, captured and died on 5th December 1864. As his father had feared he had been 'made manure of, for those bloody fields'.[4]

Livingstone's sojourn in Scotland was short-lived. His other children, Agnes, Thomas and Oswell, had grown apart from him and it was a totally new experience for Anna Mary to see her father for the first time at the age of five. Agnes, sixteen, had finished formal education and was thus able to travel with her father. He poured out his love and attention on her and later enrolled her at an exclusive French Finishing School.

In Scotland David received a welcome becoming to a man of his stature, though he lived in perpetual fear of having to speak in public, a function he loathed immensely. His warm friend, James Young, received him gladly and their firm friendship was revitalised when Livingstone was introduced to Young's family.

While in Edinburgh Livingstone also paid a professional visit to Professor Syme, one of the most eminent surgeons of his day. His complaint was haemorrhoids and they were serious.

---

[2] Robert Livingstone to D L in Jeal, p 280, and also in NAZ.
[3] *Ibid.*
[4] D L to Dr Kirk 28/07/1864 in Zam. Doc., p 79.

So much so that the surgeon advised an operation. This he unwisely refused and though the operation was at that time risky, he was also scared of the embarrassment the press coverage would cause. A decision which brought him many years of pain and harassment.

To the Scottish people Livingstone was their hero and was hailed as such. On one occasion he travelled in the same carriage as the Turkish Ambassador, Musurus Pasha, and at one of the stations they were cheered by the crowd. 'The cheers are for you,' Livingstone said to the Ambassador, with a smile. 'No,' said the Turk, 'I am only what my master made me; you are what you made yourself.'[5]

Livingstone regularly attended church and listened attentively to the sermons, commenting on them in his journal afterwards, though to a large degree time was not his own.

Although invitations to public functions were not as numerous as before, Livingstone was eagerly asked to speak to the British Association at Bath on his most compelling subject—the slave-trade. The highlight for the members, however, was a debate on a controversial subject—the source of the Nile. Two violently antagonistic rivals, John Speke and Richard Burton, were to address the Association.

Speke judged Lake Victoria to be the true source of the Nile, while Burton insisted it was the Lusize River flowing out of Lake Tanganyika. Livingstone disliked both men, but the controversy increased his curiosity regarding the true source. In the mind of the British, the interior of Africa had now become a web of lakes and waterways, far from the early idea of dreary desert. However, no party in the dispute had sufficient facts to support their claims which only served to show that further expeditions to the area were necessary to dissolve the argument.

Unfortunately, the debate did not take place, and while the

[5] Blaikie, p 343.

audience was assembling Speke, who had gone game hunting, lay dead with a gaping wound in his chest. His gun had accidently discharged itself, killing him, as he climbed a wall. Many people suspected he had preferred suicide to meeting Burton in public debate. However, thirteen years later Speke was proved right.

At that time Livingstone had other plans he wished to pursue. The Portuguese problem of the slave-trade was a more purposeful work and his attack had raised some attention at the British Association meeting. This pointed the way to Livingstone producing a paper substantiating his claims.

Livingstone accepted the invitation of his friend, W F Webb, a former hunting enthusiast whom he had met in Southern Africa, to stay in his country home, Newstead Abbey, while he compiled his conspectus. Agnes accompanied him and the following months were among some of the happiest of his life. In the relaxed surroundings of the somewhat regal residence, Livingstone succumbed to the Webbs' kindness, and the tension and turmoil of the past few months trickled away. He was always ready for a joke and delighted his hosts with his constant attention to their children, particularly Ethel, their youngest. He was often reprimanded by the nanny for handing the youngster forbidden scones and jam. He enjoyed the walks and the games the children played, even to the extent of bumping into the mantelpiece and cutting his forehead during a boisterous game of 'blind man's buff'. This had given him time to reflect with regret on the lack of attention he had given to his own children. 'Oh why did I not play more with my children in the Kolobeng days? Why was I so busy that I had so little time for my bairns? Now I have none to play with,'[6] became the cry of his heart.

'The book was at first to be a little one—a blast of the

---

[6] Macnair, p 282.

trumpet against the monstrous slave-trade'[7] but it ended up being a full-sized saga. *The Zambesi and Its Tributaries* as it was named dealt with everything in the expedition from the problems with the Portuguese to the observations of the river and its tributaries. Dr Livingstone also used his brother's diary, and as a result it was released as having joint authorship.

The Portuguese received a fair castigation from the consul, but in reality they were not the only nation thriving off the slave-trade. The Arabs had concentrated their efforts in the area to the north and west of Lake Nyasa.

Livingstone still felt it was his mission in life to enlighten people on the evils of the slave-trade and to spread the Christian gospel among the heathen. He loved Africa and had not given up hope of finding a suitable passage to the interior via the Ruvuma River. He was also anxious to preach the gospel at the same time, though his boat, the 'Lady Nyassa', was never launched on the lake.

Sir Roderick Murchison of the Royal Geographical Society was not, however, interested in the Ruvuma. A greater mystery needed to be solved and that was the riddle of the Central African lakes. He wrote to the doctor on the subject and Livingstone wrote in his journal on 7th January 1865: 'Answered Sir Roderick about going out. Said I could only feel in the way of duty by working as a missionary.'[8]

He expanded his motive in the letter to Sir Roderick saying, in regard to the natives, that he preferred to do what he could 'by talking, to enlighten them on the slave-trade, and give them some idea of our religion. It may not be much that I can do, but I feel when doing that I am not living in vain.'[9]

In a personal letter to his friend, James Young, he reaffirmed his position saying, 'I would not consent to go simply as a

[7] Blaikie, p 347.
[8] Journal entry 7th January 1865, *ibid*, p 350.
[9] *Ibid*.

geographer, but as a missionary, and do geography by the way, because I feel I am in the way of duty when trying either to enlighten these poor people, or open their land to lawful commerce.'[10]

Thus Livingstone's motive emerged and although he was to be renowned for his exploration it was, in his mind, a means to an end. By accepting a proposal to carry out the work for the Geographical Society, Livingstone would have the support he so desperately needed. In his eyes he was going ahead of the missionaries to prepare the path for them. He hoped they would follow, bringing others who in their turn would provide lawful commerce and so alleviate the misery that maimed so many. That is why Livingstone took the withdrawal of the Universities' Mission so seriously.

The search for the Nile was destined to become one of Livingstone's major goals, though in time biographers would find it hard to judge whether the search for the river's source or the Scot's desire to expose the slave-trade was his dominant motive. He told a friend that 'the Nile sources are valuable only as a means of enabling me to open my mouth with power among men. It is this power which I hope to apply to remedy an enormous evil [the slave-trade]. Men may think I covet fame, but I make it a rule not to read aught written in my praise.'[11] That he hated attention is certainly true. If he had enjoyed the limelight he would have stayed in Britain to promulgate his second publication. He still loathed public speaking and when invited to a banquet at the Royal Academy ate nothing all evening in anticipation of his speech. He was even hesitant to go to his son's school prize-giving lest he was asked to make a speech. The search for fame was not his aim.

Returning to the debate, the source of the Nile was a hotly-contested issue. Speke and Burton, together with the backing

---

[10] D L to Sir James Young 20/01/1865 in Blaikie, p 351.
[11] F Debenham, *The Way to Ilala*, pp 293–294 in Jeal, p 287.

of the Foreign Office and Royal Geographical Society, explored the region around Lake Tanganyika in February 1858. On reaching the lake they parted company. Travelling north, Speke found a vast lake which he named Victoria Nyanza and argued it to be the source of the Nile. Such news only aggravated Burton, who dismissed contemptuously his companion's excited claims.

Other explorers, Samuel White Baker and James Grant, also caused a stir when they located another large lake 150 miles north west of Lake Victoria Nyanza. Baker stated that this lake, named Lake Albert, was the true source. Each lake had its own falls; Speke named one the Rippon Falls, while the other Baker named the Murchison Falls. Neither individual could prove his claim without tracing the water. Thus the search for the true source was on, and it was not until thirteen years had elapsed before Speke's discovery was verified as correct. The water left Lake Victoria Nyanza and then followed through Lake Albert to become the Nile.

Livingstone concluded it was highly unlikely that the Nile, which flowed for over 4,000 miles and much of the way through the largest and driest desert in the world, could be supplied from one outlet, the comparatively small Rippon Falls.

The search for the source, however, became a battle between the blasphemous and the believer as Burton, an intelligent man, attacked all that Livingstone stood for. Burton's explorations in Africa never accomplished much in comparison with those whose shadow fell under Stanley, another explorer. Yet he persistently plagued those who had a heart for Africa, preferring the Arabs, the slave-dealers, to the Africans. He went so far as to suggest that Africans were 'unprogressive and unfit for change',[12] and that religion was the 'mental expression of a race', thus it was pointless trying to evangelise the African.

---

[12] *Ibid*, p 285.

Such careless, callous remarks even prompted Livingstone to write to Tidman offering condolences for the 'lies' and 'aspersions of that beastly fellow Burton against the missionaries on the West Coast'. In Livingstone's eyes Burton 'seems to be a moral idiot. His conduct in Africa was so bad that it cannot be spoken of without disgust—systematically wicked, impure and untruthful.'[13] He was referring to the rumours that Burton had often failed to pay porters and had regularly travelled with a harem of African women to serve his lust. Burton, who liked shocking people, did little to dispel these rumours. Later the doctor wrote to Murchison saying that Burton did not pay his porters—'I don't like to face people who were witnesses of his bestial immorality.'[14]

Burton had also done damage to the African cause, for he argued his case before a House of Commons Select Committee on West African settlements. Their task was to advise the government as to whether or not to devote more money to bolster existing private British enterprises in the area or to withdraw completely. Sadly, they chose the latter course which further fuelled Livingstone's frustration. It was becoming more apparent that if the cause of Christ and honest commerce were to prosper in Africa, bigots like Burton would have to be silenced.

Livingstone had also appeared before the committee, but to no avail; they thought little of his views on missions. Earlier, in January, there had been a glimmer of hope, for while he was still at Newstead Abbey one of the Prime Minister's confidants, a Mr Abraham Hayward QC, came down to see him, carrying an enquiry from Lord Palmerston as to whether 'there was something he could do' for Livingstone. A decoration or pension was probably in Palmerston's mind, though the doctor did not take it to be on such a personal

[13] D L to A Tidman 25/06/1865 LMS Archives, *ibid*, pp 285–286.
[14] D L to R Murchison 27/11/1865 NAZ reference 2148–2155.

level. Thus disregarding himself, the unworldly missionary merely asked that the Cabinet would use its influence to open up the Zambesi and Shire to foreign navigation. Later he was to regret not having asked for a settlement in favour of his children.

On 11th March 1865 Livingstone was summoned to the Foreign Office and a proposal made to him. Few eminent men have been so shabbily treated; he was graciously offered consularship in the vast region that lay between the Portuguese territory and Abyssinia, but would receive no salary nor prospect of pension. This rebuff from Earl Russell cut the Christian to the heart. He had never asked for pension yet offensively they treated him as if he had shown a greed which required repressing.

This appalling treatment and the subsequent spirit of the Select Committee did little to bolster Livingstone's love for the fellowmen within his country and in later years in the loneliness of Africa he would brood over the shameful treatment afforded him. He became determined not to return to Britain until his work had been finished. Yet without their adequate support Livingstone's expedition was destined to be one of doom from the start.

In accepting the assignment from the Royal Geographical Society Livingstone received a miserable grant of £500 for the expedition. This equalled the similar shameful sum from the Foreign Office. It was hardly sufficient to equip the enterprise.

For their part, the Society listed stringent and detailed directions involving a lot of work for such a small sum. Considering the support and prestige the Scot had raised for the Society on his earlier visit, this was a disgrace.

Had it not been for the £1,000 given to him by his magnanimous friend, James Young, Livingstone would have been in dire straits. The grant equalled the combined support from the Society and the government! Young would have given more had Livingstone permitted it. As it was he agreed to honour whatever debt Livingstone might incur while in Africa.

A few weeks before he sailed Livingstone had the added sorrow of his mother dying. He had spent some time with her and the family in Scotland; though on Sunday 18th June he was away speaking in Oxford when she went to be with her Lord. Livingstone hastily returned to Hamilton and was able to 'lay her head in the grave'—a request his mother had made.

Soon it was time to move south again and the doctor and his eldest daughter Agnes bade farewell to the remainder of the family. In London, on 9th August 1865, they parted company with the Webbs at King's Cross Station, when he wrote in his diary, 'The good Lord bless and save them both, and have mercy on their whole household.'[15]

They stayed for a few days in London with the Revd Dr Hamilton, a man of similar Puritan faith; and on the eve of their departure Livingstone preached in Dr Hamilton's church, where he stressed the need to proclaim the love of Christ, which they had been commemorating in partaking of the Holy Communion. 'His prayers made a deep impression; they were like the communings of a child with his father.'[16]

When Livingstone embarked at Folkestone on 13th August 1865 there was no cheering crowd to see him off—only Kirk and his faithful friend Waller.

He spent several days in Paris where he settled Agnes into a refined French school. He was not noted for his brilliant knowledge of French architecture and managed to persuade Agnes that the dome of Les Invalides was Notre Dame.

---

[15] Blaikie, p 356.
[16] *Ibid*, p 357.

Soon it was time to bid Agnes, whom he loved deeply, goodbye. His constant letters showed that she was special to him and she appreciated his work. Life from then on would not be easy; letters would be rarely received and loneliness would be the chief characteristic of his life.

17

The Scot Sees the Sultan

Livingstone was now fifty-two years of age and the toil of travel through Africa had taken its toll. The furlough had restored his strength, though the reserves of energy were no longer there. 'I am very old and grey,' he had told Oswell. 'My face is wrinkled like a gridiron. A barber offered to dye my hair for ten and six! I must be very good-tempered for I did not offer to fight him.'[1]

None the less, his spirit was willing and he was always an optimist, though discouragement was never far from raising its ugly head. The doctor desired company on the journey and would have liked Robert to accompany him, but his son was many miles away. Kirk was another man with whom Livingstone wanted to work, but he had declined on the grounds that the appointment carried no salary and he had his heart set on a young lady. So Livingstone, not wanting to take a novice, opted to travel alone with a caravan of porters.

From Marseilles he wrote to Agnes closing with a prayer: 'May the Almighty qualify you to be a blessing to those around you, wherever your lot is cast. I know that you hate all that is mean and false. May God make you good, and to delight in doing good to others. If you ask He will give abundantly. The Lord bless you!'[2]

---

[1] Macnair, p 292.
[2] Blaikie, p 360.

The Scot then set sail for Bombay as he had promised to collect those who came over on the ship with him from Africa, and in addition provisions had to be acquired.

From the Indian capital he kept in close contact with his family, writing prolific letters. In another note to Agnes he told her of his plans to recruit folk for the expedition, as well as describing the work of the gospel.

> Christianity [he wrote] is gradually diffusing itself, leavening as it were in various ways the whole mass. When a man becomes a professor of Christianity, he is at present cast out, abandoned by all his relations, even by wife and children. This state of things makes some who don't care about Christian progress say that all Christian servants are useless. They are degraded by their own countrymen and despised by others . . .

He cautioned her to 'avoid all nasty French novels. They are very injurious, and effect a lasting injury on the mind and heart.'[3]

This quiet, resourceful Christian continued to collect his provisions and prepare for the journey. He sold the 'Lady Nyassa', having wisely decided against sailing her to Africa during the monsoons. After several advertisements a buyer came forward, but the faithful vessel only fetched £2,300. A great loss considering she cost over £6,000. He invested the money in the shares of an Indian bank. This was an unwise decision, as within a short while the bank collapsed and Livingstone lost all. It would appear the Scot was destined not to become wealthy.

Livingstone was hospitably received in Bombay and he enjoyed the time spent there. He addressed a number of local merchants, many of whom were Scottish. Money was pledged and the consul suggested that the Bombay merchants use the money for setting up a trade establishment in Africa. Unfortunately, the project was later quietly dropped.

---

[3] D L to Agnes L 20/09/1865, *ibid*, p 361.

Africa was still an unknown land and tales of woe sent shivers down the spine of the less arduous. Disquieting tidings of another explorer, Baron van der Decken, were received. Some of his crew had been murdered up the Juba River and when the Baron and another man went to conciliate a local chief, their launch ran aground. The ship was attacked, only five survivors managed to escape and the Baron was also feared dead. Livingstone soberly noted the facts in his journal, adding a quiet prayer: 'My times are in Thy hand, O Lord! Go Thou with me and I am safe. And above all, make me useful in promoting Thy cause of peace and good-will among men.'[4]

Livingstone had a simple faith and the humility to present it. He dressed as a layman and rarely, if ever, referred to himself as the Revd David Livingstone. This gave rise to the belief that he had surrendered the cause of Christ for that of exploration, though upon scrutiny his true motive was seen. While in Africa, regardless of the number of people present, Livingstone held a service every Sunday if his health permitted. God's message of salvation for mankind was never far from his heart and even in letters to his children he constantly reminded them of Christ. Corresponding to Anna Mary, he told her of our Lord's birth, urging her that 'the Saviour must be your friend, and He will be if you ask Him to be. He will forgive and save you, and take you into His family.'[5]

The consul also kept in close contact with those who had befriended him. One such friend was Kirk and he was always on the look-out for a good position for him. In one letter he advised him of a possible opening as the Curator of the Botanical Garden and Museum in India, pointing out that 'the Governor's band plays in the Gardens and the people

---

[4] Journal entry, 29th December 1865, *ibid*, p 363.
[5] D L to Anna Mary L 24/12/1865, *ibid*, p 365.

flock to hear it. As you are a ladykiller, you might be successful in the matrimonial line there.'[6]

However, the young man was in love with a Miss Helen Cook whom he later married. He had accepted other employment as HM Surgeon in Zanzibar, also prompted by Livingstone who encouraged the Governor to offer Kirk the position. This opening was yet another stepping stone in Kirk's commendable career, for he finally became consul for Britain in Zanzibar.

Even as HM Surgeon Kirk fulfilled a vital role in an intimate triple alliance to suppress the slave-trade. In the field Livingstone was the forward agent, Kirk manned the vital middle station, while Horace Waller secured the main base and stirred consciences at home.

The general plan of Livingstone's expedition was to explore the Ruvuma River and discover its relation to Lake Nyasa and Lake Tanganyika, then examine the unknown territory around Lakes Mweru and Bangweulu and finally to locate the sources of the Nile, the latter being the most important.

To this end he required faithful men and reliable equipment, but poor funds severely hampered him. In India he invited Susi, Musa, Amoda, Wakatani and Chumah to join him. (The two Waiyau lads, Wakatani and Chumah, were in a slave party liberated by Livingstone and Bishop Mackenzie in 1861.) He also employed thirteen Sepoys from the marine battalion, specially commended as being well seasoned to hardship. Barring the corporal, they proved to be lazy and incompetent. Nine others also came from India—freed slaves who had been trained at Nassick. They too proved to be a total disaster. From Johanna nine other men completed the contingent—it was a motley crew which caused the consul much hardship, severely testing his Christian charity.

Livingstone, both in Bombay and later in Zanzibar, stocked

[6] D L to Dr Kirk 02/12/1865 in Zam. Doc., p 129.

up with bales of calico and beads (for currency), clothing, medicines, a tent, cooking utensils and a few luxuries like coffee and sugar. He also bought an accordion and carried two Bibles (one of which was small enough to go into his pocket for 'emergency reading'); the one-volume edition of *Smith's Dictionary of the Bible* and a legal book on justice and peace in Scotland. The latter was a sign that he intended to return to Scotland.

Finally they set off from Bombay in the 'Thule', which was an official present from the Bombay Government to the Sultan of Zanzibar. In presenting the ship Livingstone would receive greater prestige, thus persuading the ruler to assist him.

In setting out Livingstone purposed to keep Christ at the forefront of the expedition. On 17th January 1866 he wrote in his journal that he meant to

> make this a Christian Expedition, telling a little about Christ wherever we go. His love in coming down to save men will be our theme ... Good works gain the approbation of the world, and though there is antipathy in the human heart to the gospel of Christ, yet when Christians make their good work shine all admire them. It is when great disparity exists between profession and practice that we secure the scorn of mankind. The Lord help me to act in all cases in this Expedition as a Christian ought!'[7]

In high spirits he wrote to James Young:

> At sea, 300 miles from Zanzibar, 26th January 1866—We have enjoyed fair weather in coming across the weary waste of waters. We started on the 5th. The 'Thule', to be a pleasure yacht, is the most incorrigible roller ever known. The whole 2000 miles has been an everlasting see-saw, shuggy-shoo, and enough to tire the patience of even a chemist, who is the most patient of all animals. I am pretty well gifted in that respect myself, though shouldn't say it, but that Sandy B-! The world will never get on till we have a few of those instrument-makers hung. I was particular in asking

---

[7] Blaikie, p 366.

him to get me Scripture slides coloured, and put in with the magic
lantern, and he has not put in one! The very object for which I
wanted it is thus frustrated, and I did not open it till we were at
sea. O Sandy! Pity Burke and Hare have no successors in Auld
Reekie![8]

And in a letter to Agnes he informed her:

Most of the marine-Sepoys were sick. You would have been a
victim unless you had tried the new remedy of a bag of pounded
ice along the spine, which sounds as hopeful as the old cure for
toothache ... A shark took a bite at the revolving vane of the
patent log today. He left some pieces of the enamel of his teeth
in the brass, and probably has the toothache. You will sympathise
with him ...

When you return home you will be scrutinised to see if you are
spoiled. You have only to act naturally and kindly to all your old
friends to disarm them of their prejudices. I think you will find
the Youngs true friends. Mrs Williamson of Widdicombe Hill near
Bath writes to me that she would like to show you her plans for
the benefit of poor orphans. If you thought of going to Bath it
might be well to get all the insight you could into that and every
other good work. It is well to be able to take a comprehensive
view of all benevolent enterprises, and resolve to do our duty in
life in some way or other, for we cannot live for ourselves alone.
A life of selfishness is one of misery, and it is unlike that of our
blessed Saviour, who pleased not Himself. He followed not His
own will even, but the will of His Father in heaven.[9]

Not only was the doctor conscious of spiritual issues, practical
needs also prompted his attention. One instance was when
he took over from the sick skipper to save the ship from
foundering.[10]

Finally, after twenty-three days, the ship dropped anchor

[8] *Ibid*, pp 366–367.
[9] *Ibid*, p 367.
[10] D L to John Murray 17/03/1866 in Ransford, p 241.

at Zanzibar on 28th January 1866, much to the relief of the seasick Sepoys.

Zanzibar did not hold many fond memories for Livingstone— the stench arising from the beach which was the general depository for the filth of the town was disgusting; so much so he nicknamed it 'Stinkibar'.[11]

He described his meeting with the Sultan in a letter to Agnes, telling her:

> His highness met us at the bottom of the stair, and as he shook hands a brass band, which he got at Bombay, blared forth 'God save the Queen' This was excessively ridiculous, but I maintained sufficient official gravity. After coffee and sherbet we came away, and the wretched band now struck up 'The British Grenadier', as if the fact of my being only 5 feet 8, and Brebner about 2 inches lower, ought not to have suggested 'Wee Willie Winkie' as more appropriate. I was ready to explode, but got out of sight before giving way.[12]

Although the Sultan accepted him cordially, it did not change the Scot's view of the slave-trade. He pointed out to him 'the Nassick lads as those who had been rescued from slavery, educated, and sent back to their own country by the Governor. Surely he must see that some people in the world act from other than selfish motives.'[13] But as usual the love of money superseded morality. The Sultan received £20,000 of his annual revenue from the trade,[14] and all the main firms in Zanzibar derived benefit from the trade in some way or other. Livingstone learned that the French were also influenced in this nefarious traffic, for they lent their flag to slaving dhows.[15]

---

[11] LJ I 1866, p 7.
[12] Blaikie, p 368.
[13] LJ I 1866, p 5.
[14] Jeal, p 298.
[15] LJ I 1866, p 6.

The British too were allowing much of the traffic to pass unhindered on the high seas, while at home the demand for ivory meant more porters—slaves—to carry the goods to the coast. Thus the wicked web became more intricate.

Livingstone visited the slave-market on 2nd March 1866 and found about 300 slaves exposed for sale, the greater part of whom came from Lake Nyasa and the Shire River. 'All who have grown up seem ashamed at being hawked about for sale. The teeth are examined, the cloth lifted to examine the lower limbs, and a stick is thrown for the slave to bring, and thus exhibit his paces. Some are dragged through the crowd by the hand, and the price called out incessantly . . .'[16] These sights left their scar on Livingstone, the scenes frequently appearing before his mind's eye. Africa in 1866 was literally bleeding to death. He also observed:

> The Arabs are said to treat their slaves kindly, and this also may be said of native masters; the reason is, master and slave partake of the general indolence, but the lot of the slave does not improve with the general progress in civilisation. While no great disparity of rank exists, his energies are little tasked, but when society advances, wants multiply; and to supply these the slave's lot grows harder. The distance between master and man increases as the lust of gain is developed, hence we can hope for no improvement in the slave's condition, unless the master returns to or remains in barbarism.[17]

It was for this reason that Livingstone realised no 'European progress' could come to Africa until total abolition had been achieved. Furthermore, the slave must first be released physically in order to receive the good news that would set him free—providing he repented—spiritually.

---

[16] *Ibid*, p 7.
[17] *Ibid*.

Final preparations were made for the expedition. Livingstone bought baggage animals: six camels, three Indian buffaloes and a calf, two mules and four donkeys. He hoped to find an animal that was resistant to the dreaded tsetse fly.

Arrangements were made with an Arab trader, Lydha Damji, to send up regular supplies to Ujiji. Damji assured him this would be done, and his agent there, Thani bin Suelim, would reliably protect the goods. Livingstone was confident that the British Consul would see that the contract was honoured; a crucial matter, for without supplies Livingstone would lose his men and have no bargaining power for goods nor food for his team.

Livingstone was already taking a major risk. His small crew of men was pitiful against the usual number of at least 130 that usually accompanied Burton and Speke. Livingstone, largely owing to meagre funds, had only thirty-six men, a tiny number and in spite of plans to increase to sixty still woefully inadequate.

Finally, HMS 'Penguin' arrived to ferry Livingstone and his expedition to the mainland, a dhow containing the strange animals in tow.

As they set out on 19th March 1866 Livingstone wrote in his journal: 'I trust that the Most High may prosper me in this work, granting me influence in the eyes of the heathen, and helping me to make my intercourse beneficial to them.'

The Ruvuma mouth being blocked by a sand bar they were dropped at the port of Mikinday, twenty-five miles north of the Ruvuma.

When Livingstone waved goodbye to his English companions, little did he realise that he would only see one white man again. Nor as he turned to face the huge African continent was he to know that before him lay the major test of his life. He was about to embark upon one of the greatest epics of endurance that modern man has withstood. For many years hunger and lack of medical supplies would haunt him, as would the harrowing chink of chains and the persecuted people's painful cries.

18

Tormenting Times—Travelling to Tanganyika

Livingstone, now fifty-three, began this journey with a tremendous tactical error, resulting in torment and utter tragedy.

Both Livingstone and Sir Roderick Murchison mistakenly believed that a river flowed out of the northern end of Lake Tanganyika to join Lake Albert, and that the river which flowed into Lake Tanganyika would be the source of the Nile. Livingstone failed to take the advice of Sir Roderick and check there was a connecting river between the two lakes. He presumed that one existed and 'much more time would be required for this than by my plan of going at once to the headwaters'.[1]

When he eventually found out that the lakes were not connected, after trekking many hundreds of miles, his health was pitifully poor and his judgement impaired.

None the less, he was very optimistic. His theory also gave him a chance to ascertain finally whether or not the Ruvuma flowed into Lake Nyasa. He would not give up without having completed the task he had set himself years earlier. Disappointments, however, marred his progress. He had hoped to hire porters to carry equipment into the interior, but they were not forthcoming for fear of being captured and sold into slavery. This meant Livingstone had to leave behind stores

---

[1] D L to R Murchison 27/11/65 NAZ in Jeal, p 300.

which he could ill afford to lose. The first few weeks of travel were fraught with frustration. The thick jungle along the coast had to be penetrated and a huge path capable of letting the camels through had to be hacked out of virgin bush. The smothering atmosphere soon sapped the porters' strength. A thornbush also caused much discomfort as Livingstone noted: 'This species seems to be eager for mischief; its tangled limbs hang out ready to inflict injury on all passers-by'.[2]

The Sepoys 'were a waste of rations'. They left the animals loaded in the hot sun without water, beating and even stabbing them in an endeavour to coax them to move under the extra burden of their personal baggage which the deceitful men refused to carry when Livingstone's back was turned. In villages they would eat, gorging their faces until they retched. They would pursue the same habit while on the march, forcing down food which they had stolen.

Initially on the expedition Livingstone was euphoric for 'the mere animal pleasure of travelling in a wild unexplored country is very great . . . and a day's exertion always makes the evening repose thoroughly enjoyable'.[3] But his excitement was shortlived and within six weeks of starting he was writing: 'If I remain behind to keep the Sepoys on the move, it deprives me of all the pleasure of travelling . . . Sepoys are a mistake'.[4]

The Nassick porters were abominable in their treatment of the animals, while the Johanna men were inveterate thieves.

Livingstone's mastery of these people was not as good as that of the Makololo, possibly because the Makololo were more disciplined and had greater respect for him. Furthermore, the members of his new team had tasted the easy life of civilisation. Suffering night and day journeying across a continent was hardly value for life.

---

[2] LJ I 1866, p 20.
[3] *Ibid*, p 13.
[4] *Ibid*, pp 35–36.

None the less, Livingstone persevered, enjoying the company of a plucky little poodle dog, Chitane, which had a superiority complex, particularly when encountering other dogs, when it would bark profusely. Not being able 'to distinguish at which end his head or tail lay'[5] they would bolt off in all directions.

Livingstone regularly held services, especially on Sundays, and he often noted the spiritual state of the tribes he encountered. Regarding the language barrier, he regretted that 'I cannot speak to them that good of His name which I ought'.[6]

Food was scarce and as they advanced the horrors of the slave-trade presented themselves. Women were found dead, tied to trees, or lying in the path shot and stabbed. Their fault had been their inability to keep up with the caravan, so their owners, in order to prevent them from becoming the property of anyone else, put an end to their lives. Livingstone encountered some men who were bound with slave-sticks or 'abandoned by their master from want of food; they were too weak to be able to speak or say where they had come from; some were quite young'.[7]

Instead of his heart hardening upon seeing such sights Livingstone's softened. He tried to speak to the tribes who sold weaker folk into slavery, but was invariably told that they would stop if other tribes whom they viewed as more sinister would do likewise.

The Sepoys continued their shocking habits, horrifying Livingstone who more than once tried to reason with them, but to no avail. 'They killed one camel with the butt ends of their muskets, beating it till it died', Livingstone wrote in his diary. 'I thought of going down and disarming them all, and taking five or six of the willing ones, but it is more trouble

[5] *Ibid*, p 33.
[6] *Ibid*, p 29.
[7] *Ibid*, p 62.

than profit'.[8] The Nassick boys were less truculent, but no more satisfactory. They were bone idle and rid themselves, on various pretexts and at every opportunity, of their loads. One went so far as to strip the tinfoil wrapping from a package of tea to lighten the load. Needless to say he gradually threw away three quarters of the precious leaf.

The problems persisted, the men becoming more intolerable by the day. They even dawdled days behind the main party and 'retaining their brutal feelings to the last they killed the donkey which I lent to the havildar to carry his things, by striking it on the head'.[9] They then slaughtered a buffalo, which was carrying a load and after devouring it told Livingstone that it met its fate at the jaws of a tiger. 'Did you see the stripes of the tiger?' asked Livingstone. 'All declared that they saw the stripes distinctly'.[10] This gave him an idea of their truthfulness as there are no tigers in all Africa.

Despite the difficulties Livingstone retained his dignity and took each disappointment in his stride. Though fairly healthy he became concerned, for food was scarce and he wrote to his son, Thomas, telling him that his 'finest cloths only brought miserable morsels of the common grain. I trudged it the whole way, and having no animal food save what turtle-doves and guinea fowls we occasionally shot, I became like one of Pharaoh's lean kine'.[11]

Evidence of such hardship came to light, together with an endearing testimony of Livingstone, when in 1877 Bishop Chuancey Maples met at Newala on the upper end of the Ruvuma Valley an old man who, with much ceremony, presented to him a coat, mouldy, partially eaten, but of

---

[8] *Ibid*, p 43.
[9] *Ibid*, p 75.
[10] *Ibid*.
[11] D L to Thomas L 28/08/1866 in Blaikie, p 373.

decidedly English material. That had been given him, he said, ten years before by

> a white man who treated black men as brothers and whose memory would be cherished along the Rovuma after we were all dead. A short man with a bushy moustache and a keen piercing eye whose words were always gentle and whose manners were always kind, whom as a leader it was a privilege to follow, and who knew the way to the heart of all men'.[12]

The trek continued and finally the Ruvuma source was located, though many miles still lay between it and Lake Nyasa. Livingstone was now satisfied this river could not provide an entry into the interior. Leaving behind the famine-stricken, depopulated country with its burned grass, stunted trees and shrubs, they entered green, undulating hills.

Finally, on 8th August 1866, they reached the glistening lake which Livingstone likened to an old familiar home he had never expected to see again. He thanked God, bathed again in the delicious water and felt quite exhilarated.[13]

The villagers were quite content in their huddles of small round huts of clay and wattle with only a low doorway for the egress of its inmates, both human and animal, as well as smoke from the common fire. They warmly received Livingstone, and one headman, Mokalaose, told the doctor of his misfortune in losing one wife who had run away. Livingstone asked him how many he had; he told him twenty in all. Livingstone told him that he thought he had nineteen too many, to which he received the reply: 'But who would cook for strangers if I had but one?'[14]

In order to save time and much energy Livingstone tried unsuccessfully to obtain a lift in the Arab slave dhows. His reputation had preceded him, however, and the slavers only

---

[12] Macnair, p 302.
[13] LJ I 1866, pp 90–91.
[14] *Ibid*, p 92.

saw him as a spy who was out eventually to stop their career. How right they were. Livingstone and his entourage had to walk.

He showed incredible perception and wisdom in his observation of the slave-trade. He had compiled two despatches to the Foreign Secretary, setting out his reasons as to why the British restriction treaties, which legalised slavery within specified limits, could never work. He calmly asked them why the Foreign Office and Admiralty countenanced vast expenditure in attempting to stop the slave-trade and yet had so little effect. He believed that all exporting of slaves should be stopped. This would cause the slave-trade to die slowly and peacefully. The British Government, however, adopted a plan of controlling it and therefore kept Zanzibar open. They believed, wrongly, that if Zanzibar were closed to slave traffic other less controllable areas would spring up on the mainland. Livingstone disagreed and his theory proved to be correct. He also suggested that they build depots for freeing slaves along the coast. This would rapidly release the British ships back into service after they had captured an Arab dhow.

Prior to setting off Livingstone worked on his journal, calculated lunars and altitudes and wrote letters home. To Thomas he confided his heart saying:

> I sometimes remember you with some anxiety, as not knowing what opening may be made for you in life . . . Whatever you feel yourself best fitted for, 'Commit thy way to the Lord, trust also in Him, and He will bring it to pass'. One ought to endeavour to devote the peculiarities of his nature to his Redeemer's service, whatever these may be'.[15]

Trudging around the southern shore of the lake, Livingstone came across skulls and bones, testifying to times of drought and slavery. At the point where the Shire leaves Nyasa,

---

[15] D L to Thomas L 28/08/1866 in Blaikie, p 373.

memories welled up inside him. Livingstone quietly wrote in his diary:

> Far down on the right bank of the Zambesi lies the dust of her whose death changed all my future prospects; and now, instead of a check being given to the slave-trade by lawful commerce on the Lake, slave-dhows prosper!
>
> An Arab slave-party fled on hearing of us yesterday. It is impossible not to regret the loss of good Bishop Mackenzie, who sleeps far down the Shire and with him all hope of the Gospel being introduced into Central Africa. The silly abandonment of all the advantages of the Shire route by the Bishop's successor I shall ever bitterly deplore, but all will come right some day, though I may not live to participate in the joy, or even see the commencement of better times'.[16]

Had he been able to look into the future he would have seen the realisation of his prayers, but for now he clung on by faith. He was almost a broken-spirited man, his many visions too vast to be grasped by his contemporaries. Gradually as time progressed he surrendered his life wholeheartedly to the sovereign will of God, spending more time in prayer and study of the Bible. His aim was twofold—teaching some of the great truths of Christianity, and rousing consciences to the atrocious guilt of the slave-trade. The search for the Nile was to provide a platform from which he could denounce this evil.

In conducting services Livingstone found it easier to convey the fact of communing with God—an unseen being—by kneeling and praying with eyes closed. He remonstrated with slavers whenever he came across them and even mentioned 'our relationship to our Father, the guilt of selling any of His children, the consequences. . . .'[17] He mentioned the Bible, future state of mankind and the need for prayer.

On 20th September 1866, Wakatani—Bishop Mackenzie's

---

[16] LJ I 1866, pp 100–101.
[17] Blaikie, p 374.

favourite lackey whom he managed to set free from slavery—
found he had relatives in the area and that his father who
had sold him into slavery was now dead. The loss of a helper
to Livingstone's tiny entourage was certainly felt, but the Scot
urged him to rejoin his family, gave him some cloth, a flint
gun, some paper to write to Horace Waller and commended
him to the care of Chief Mponda until he reached his family.

Continuing up the mountainous peninsular of Cape Maclear
they came to Marenga. Here the chief, dressed in splendour in
red silk shawl and attended by his court harem, received them
in state. Though the welcome was warm, distressing news
followed. The Johanna men heard rumours of the Angoni
Zulus, whose attitude for destruction did little to strengthen
the lazy backbones of the Johanna men. The eyes of their
leader, Musa, stood out in terror. The Johannas refused to
go any further and used this excuse to head for home.

The deserters were to cause further alarm, for upon
returning to Zanzibar they concocted a tremendous story so
as to ensure they would be paid. On 6th December they
reported Livingstone was dead. They had fallen behind on
the march and so escaped the plight which befell Livingstone
who was nearly decapitated along with the Nassick men by
a band of Mazitu. So skilfully was the story woven that Dr
Kirk finally accepted it after interrogating the men. On 7th
March 1867 England was to hear of the so-called 'tragedy'.

However, Horace Waller and 'Gunner' Young, an able
seaman who had grown to admire Livingstone while serving
on the 'Pioneer', knew Musa to be an inveterate liar. They
not only challenged the tale, but offered to lead the expedition
to Lake Nyasa to verify the report. Sir Roderick Murchison
arranged sponsorship for the scheme and the sailors left for
the Cape on 11th June 1867 with three other companions
plus sections of the steel boat the 'Search' which was modelled
on the 'Lady Nyassa'. They quickly assembled the boat on
the mouth of the Zambesi and travelled up river; stopping to
tend the graves of Mrs Livingstone, Scudamore, Mackenzie,

Dickinson and Thornton. They had no difficulty in recruiting 250 porters to carry the parts past the cataracts, thus confirming the practicality of Livingstone's earlier scheme. On interviewing various tribesmen they found Musa's story to be false and so returned with news that the doctor was still very much alive. Young was back in England by 21st January 1868 and interest in the intrepid explorer was again revived. Further news had also been received confirming he was alive and this gave the Scot an image of being invulnerable. Sadly this romantic flavour covered the real facts, for Livingstone was indeed suffering.

After the desertion of the Johanna men there were but eleven men left in Livingstone's party. Retreat was not on his mind, so forward they trudged.

Livingstone was encouraged when in October he again met an old chief, Kimsusa, who joyously received him and ordered a fatted ram be killed for a feast in his honour. Livingstone was quick to note: 'He speaks more rationally about the Deity than some have done, and adds, that it was by following the advice which I gave him last time I saw him, and not selling his people, that his village is now three times its former size'.[18]

Turning westward they continued across the Loangwa River, then gradually northward. On 24th October 1866 they met villagers who, terror-stricken, were running for their lives from the marauding Mazitu. They heeded the villagers' advice and narrowly escaped death.

Despite the difficulties, Livingstone's diary revealed him as a man with deep inner peace; he accepted each day as it came and occasionally wrote beautiful descriptions. On 29th October he recorded that 'the morning was lovely, the whole country bathed in bright sunlight, and not a breath of air disturbed the smoke as it slowly curled up from the heaps of

---

[18] LJ I 1866, pp 117–118.

burning weeds, which the native agriculturist wisely destroys'.[19] The first rains fell that afternoon, so the porters rushed to commit their seeds to the soil and so delayed the party yet another day.

Moving in a north-westerly direction was difficult, for they came across tribes living in apprehension of the Mazitu. They were understandably very suspicious and grew only enough grain for themselves. Too much, they feared, would attract the attention of the Mazitu. Very little food could be bought with material and what maize they obtained was coarse and reactivated the stomach ailments Livingstone had previously suffered. They also had to depend upon what he shot, and at such times the handicap of his damaged arm became more noticeable. Often they returned from hunting exhausted and without food.

On Christmas Day Livingstone's goats were stolen. The little milk they provided was greatly missed: 'The loss affected me more than I could have imagined'.[20] Hunger haunted him as his stomach cried out for food; unlike his staff he could eat little maize for this caused further dysentery. There seemed little solution to his dilemma. By the New Year they had neither sugar nor salt and the continuous rain threatened to destroy their meagre stores of cloth and gunpowder.

On 31st December he wrote:

We now end 1866. It has not been so fruitful or useful as I intended. Will try to do better in 1867, and be better—more gentle and loving; and may the Almighty, to whom I commit my way, bring my desires to pass, and prosper me! Let all the sins of '66 be blotted out for Jesus' sake.

1st January 1867—May He who was full of grace and truth impress His character on mine. Grace—eagerness to show favour; truth—truthfulness, sincerity, honour—for His mercy's sake'.[21]

[19] *Ibid, p 141.*
[20] *Ibid,* p 164.
[21] *Ibid,* pp 168–169.

Though hunger, rain and damp continually tormented Livingstone, a major calamity befell him on 6th January. They were clambering down the steep slopes of a ravine and the path was so slippery that two of the porters fell; one of these men was carrying the precious chronometers, without which no accurate longitudes could be taken. With gracious understatement he wrote: 'This was a misfortune, as it altered the rates, as was seen by the first comparison of them together in the evening'.[22] Owing to the cloudy conditions, accurate readings could not be recorded, therefore Livingstone was not to know that the chronometer was badly out of alignment and that due to this they would in error be twenty miles to the east. This disaster occurred some eighteen months later and played a major part in frustrating Livingstone's travels and was indeed a cause in precipitating his death.

For the moment, however, hunger was their greatest concern. On 9th January, what maize Livingstone had for himself was depleted. Simon, one of Livingstone's porters, graciously gave him his and the following day he did likewise. Livingstone appreciated such generosity for Simon was going without food himself. Livingstone's health was rapidly failing. He had lost so much weight that he had to take his belt up three holes. Finally, later the next day, drenched to the bone, they reached the village. 'Some men had killed an elephant and came to sell the dried meat: it was high and so were their prices; but we were obliged to give our best from this craving hunger'.[23]

On Sunday 12th January 1867 Livingstone opted against his principles to continue marching so as to reach the area where more food was available. Moving on the day of rest troubled his conscience, although they had prayers before starting. Livingstone recorded that he came across a very

---

[22] *Ibid*, p 170.
[23] *Ibid*, p 172.

pretty little puff adder that lay in the path.[24] A cheerful observation, for that is one of Africa's deadliest snakes.

Sadly, three days later while traversing the Chimbwe River, the men were so preoccupied with crossing the mile-wide, leech-infested river, that they neglected to look out for little Chitane, and the poodle drowned. Livingstone sorely missed his little companion. Other disappointments were to follow. On 20th January 1867 two of his bearers absconded with his medicine chest and other stores. The forest was so dense and high there was no chance of getting a second glimpse of the fugitives. He wrote:

> I felt as if I had now received the sentence of death, like poor Bishop Mackenzie . . . this loss I felt most keenly. Everything of this kind happens by the permission of the One who watches over us with most tender care; and this may turn out for the best by taking away a source of suspicion among more superstitious, charm-dreading people further north.

As he battled with forgiveness, Livingstone honestly, graciously, wrote:

> It is difficult to say from the heart, 'Thy will be done'; but I shall try. These Waiyau had few advantages: sold into slavery in early life, they were in the worst possible school for learning to be honest and honourable, they behaved well for a long time; but, having had hard and scanty fare in Lobisa, wet and misery in passing through dripping forests, hungry nights and fatiguing days, their patience must have been worn out . . . they gave way to the temptation . . . true; yet this loss of the medicine-box gnaws at the heart terribly'.[25]

In keeping with his New Year prayer, Livingstone became a man of meekness, exercising 'peace, patience, kindness . . .

---

[24] *Ibid*, p 173.
[25] *Ibid*, pp 177–178.

gentleness, self-control'.[26] These qualities were not evident in the Livingstone who created a stir in Kolobeng and riled sensitive spirits on the Zambesi. A cognisance of his own failings is evident. Even Oswell in later reading Livingstone's journal wrote to Agnes saying: 'The dear old fellow, how quiet and gentle he has grown in these last Journals. Though his unflinching courage and determination remain where they ever were, his gentleness seems to become more and more diffused through all he did'.[27] He gradually became a more severe censor of his own conduct and spiritual state, while waiving the misconduct of others; 'his expressions of indignation against other people's unrighteous behaviour were habitually tempered by reminders of his own frailty and imperfection'.[28]

Livingstone desperately needed his medicine to combat dysentery, malaria and other diseases. To continue without it was certainly suicidal. But he had walked over 800 miles from Mikindani in nine months and to turn back now could prove fatal. For all he knew, he may just have been within reach of the watershed draining to the north.

Fighting hunger and faintness they crossed over the Chambeshi River and thanked God for what they could obtain, albeit only a meagre amount of maere (a staple food) and ground nuts. Livingstone dreamed of 'the roast beef of bygone days. The saliva runs from the mouth in these dreams, and the pillow is wet with it in the mornings'.[29]

Depleted apart from a concentrated will, he continued his recordings searching for a river which flowed north— possibly from Lake Bangweolo into Lake Tanganyika.

---

[26] Galatians 5:22b–23a.
[27] Macnair, p 310.
[28] Campbell, p 344.
[29] LJ I 1867, p 181.

Three days march from the Chambeshi brought Livingstone into contact with Chief Chitapangwa who detained him for three harassing weeks. Livingstone consented and spent what time he could discussing the Book of books with him, as well as compiling letters for despatch to the coast with a party of Swahili whom he met.

The mail did reach Zanzibar, but only a year later. Tragically Seward's successor, Churchill, thought Livingstone would have left Ujiji and so ignored the request for much-needed supplies.

Departing from Chitapangwa, Livingstone was frustrated, for the chief demanded blankets, but he had none to spare. 'It is hard to be kept waiting here, but all may be for the best: it has always turned out so, and I trust in Him on whom I can cast all my cares. The Lord look on this and help me . . . I feel quite alone'.[30] Fortunately, food was abundant and strength was gained, though in marching in the rain Livingstone's health deteriorated. He suffered greatly from fever; 'every step I take jars in the chest, and I am very weak; I can scarcely keep up the march, though formerly I was always first . . . I have a constant singing in the ears, and can scarcely hear the loud tick of the chronometers'.[31]

On 1st April 1867 he set eyes upon Tanganyika and was captivated by the lake which peacefully lay in the huge cup-shaped cavity, surrounded by lush green trees, beautiful cascading waterfalls and picturesque palm-oil trees. This rich reservoir was home to an abundance of animals from the enormous elephant to the little field mouse. Livingstone was 'deeply thankful at having got so far', though he was excessively weak—'cannot walk without tottering, and have

---

[30] *Ibid*, p 190.
[31] *Ibid*, pp 200–201.

a constant singing in the head', but he faithfully wrote, 'The Highest will lead me further'.[32]

Fever flared without restraint. He found himself floundering outside his hut and, unable to get in, tried to lift himself up from his back by laying hold of two posts at the entrance. Nearly upright he lost his grip and fell back heavily, hitting his head on a box. Devoted Chumah and Susi, witnessing the wretched state he was in, hung a blanket at the entrance of the hut, that no stranger might see his helplessness.[33]

Still determined, Livingstone aimed to travel north west up the lake, but was deterred by reports of Mazitu raids. Feverish but persistent, they trudged as far as the River Liemba, but again were advised to turn back as Arab slavers had upset certain villages, who now wanted revenge. Returning to Chitapangwa's village they met many Arabs who, upon reading Livingstone's letter from the Sultan, extended him help and gifts.

Frustrated by the faction-fighting in the region Livingstone decided to travel west, map Lake Mweru and follow the watershed. He needed to ascertain this watershed to be that of the Congo or of the Nile. Again he was stalled as fierce fighting blocked the path, so he waited, studying his Bible dictionary, holding Sunday services and speaking out against the slave-trade which he, without support, was so helpless to stop.

By 2nd August 1867 still no word was given regarding the safety of travel. An earthquake had shattered the peace on 6th July and stopped the chronometer. He reset it after the tremor, but a further error crept in, and from then on his longitudes erred in the opposite direction, being fifty miles out to the west. Now Livingstone would have an additional seventy miles of space on his map than was in fact there, thus making the maps more inaccurate.[34]

---

[32] *Ibid*, p 204.
[33] *Ibid*, p 205.
[34] Jeal, p 312.

Finally peace was struck between the Arabs and their adversaries and Livingstone, realising his vulnerability, opted to journey with the Arabs travelling in that direction. Livingstone was obviously aware of the ambiguity of his position, but there was little he could do; if he starved he would not be able to report on the slave-trade and his data was his only hope of having the system stopped. Furthermore, by travelling with them he would also be able to attain a wealth of information from suspicious tribes engaged in this nefarious traffic.

Tippu Tip (or Tipo Tipo as he wrote in his journal) was the Arab leader of the party; he had no objection to Livingstone accompanying him, though progress over the hundred miles was slow, as he constantly stopped to trade in ivory and humans. It was over a month before Livingstone stood on the shore of Lake Bangweulu. He soon ascertained that this small lake was linked to Lake Mweru by the Luapula River. The same river flowed out of Lake Moero. If it joined Lake Tanganyika it would ultimately be the source of the Nile, or likewise even if it flowed into Lake Albert.

By the end of 1867 Livingstone was aware that he would have to travel south to Lake Bangweolo to ascertain it to be the most southerly source of the Lualaba. Secondly, he would have to follow the Lualaba north from Lake Bangweulu until he could confirm it was indeed the Nile. On paper it was a simple task, but he was in poor health. His nine loyal followers were also tired, and moreover supplies were very scarce.

This prompted Livingstone to make an additional journey 250 miles to Ujiji on the eastern shore of Lake Tanganyika, collect stores and return. He travelled with Tippu Tip, who assured him that after a journey to Casembe's village twenty miles south they could travel together to Ujiji.

So on 21st November 1867 Livingstone met this remarkable chief whose gate was ornamented with about sixty human skulls. An executioner was seen; he had a broad Lunda sword on his arm and a curious scissor-like instrument at his neck for cropping ears. As 'many of Casembe's people appear with the ears cropped and hands lopped off',[35] it was obvious such tools were more than ornaments.

Here Livingstone also met Mohammed bin Saleh who had been held prisoner by Casembe for over ten years. Under the Scot's influence he was released and, fortunately for Livingstone, Mohammed was eager to travel to Ujiji. Sadly Mohammed, many months later, repaid Livingstone's benevolence in a malicious manner. Livingstone also met another Arab trader, Mohammed Bogharib, who presented Livingstone and his loyal retinue 'a meal of vermicelli, oil and honey, also cassava meal cooked, so as to resemble a sweet meat'.[36] Livingstone had had no sugar or honey since he left Lake Nyasa in September 1866.

Eager to reach Ujiji, Livingstone departed with Mohammed bin Saleh on 22nd December 1867. Once again they were on the march. His New Year prayer ended with a simple request: 'If I am to die this year prepare me for it'.[37] Gradually as time progressed Livingstone became more heavenly-minded. Before retiring each night he spent some time in prayer and even sang a bedtime hymn; only intense fever prevented him communing with his Creator. These hymns he also taught to his faithful followers. Wakatani, who had left the Scot nine years earlier and had forgotton most of his English, was recognised one night by the seaman, Young, to be singing a hymn. This Wakatani said was a four-line bedtime hymn Livingstone had taught him.[38]

---

[35] LJ I 1867, p 248.
[36] *Ibid*, p 248.
[37] *Ibid*, p 268.
[38] Coupland, p 65.

In travelling Livingstone imparted his knowledge of the gospel of Christ, diffusing the understanding of Christianity, sowing seeds which would eventually bear fruit.

Mohammed, once away from Casembe, started trading and travelled very slowly, oblivious to Livingstone's needs. Frustrated, Livingstone decided on 12th April 1868 to explore the Bangweulu region. The next day he assembled his remaining retinue and three tired men mutinied, including Chumah and Susi, leaving only Abraham, Simon, Gardner and Mabruki to accompany him. Mohammed had succeeded in turning some of Livingstone's men against him by 'selling the favours of his concubines to them, thus reducing them to a kind of bondage'.

Livingstone compassionately admitted in his journal: 'I did not blame them very severely in my own mind for absconding: they were tired of tramping, and so verily am I ... Consciousness of my own defects makes me lenient'.[39]

In returning towards Bangweulu Livingstone sent a request to Mohammed Bogharib to ask Casembe for a guide, which was finally granted and they recommenced their trek, often coming across slave gangs. The suffering of those in bondage severely distressed the Scot who was helpless to intervene. On seeing a grave he wrote: 'This is the sort of grave I should prefer: to lie in the still, still forest, and no hand ever disturb my bones ..., but I have nothing to do but wait till He who is over all decided where I have to lay me down and die. Poor Mary lies in Shupanga brae'.[40]

On 18th July 1868 Livingstone casually noted the siting of Lake Bangweulu. A Babisa traveller asked him why he had come so far and Livingstone replied that 'we were all children of one Father', and he was 'anxious that we should

---

[39] LJ I 1868, p 287.
[40] *Ibid*, p 308.

know each other better . . .' and he told of how he had been thwarted by slave-traders and their abettors.

Livingstone came across many large marshy areas consisting of slightly depressed valleys, barren of trees and bushes with grass a foot high. They were saturated with water, and blood-sucking aquatic leeches caused much pain as they latched onto their victims.

His men refused to travel around the lake, so Livingstone was unable truly to recognise its true shape. Further, owing to his defective chronometers, he envisaged Bangweulu as being four times its real size; thus when he returned later he was hopelessly lost.

On 30th July they retraced their route to join the Arabs, Livingstone now elated with the belief that these bogs were probably the head sources of the Nile (and even possibly the sources of the Zambesi). A noble theory, but sadly not correct, for Livingstone was to perish in the pursuit of one objective, while God simultaneously used this very man's perseverance and self-sacrifice in the attainment of another.

The deserters, including Chumah and Susi, professing penitence were waiting for Livingstone who re-engaged them commenting, 'I had my own faults'.

The country between Lakes Mweru and Tanganyika was still very unsettled, with anarchy reigning. There was no alternative but to accompany a slave party, which was ironic, for incongruously assiduous attention was being paid to Livingstone by the very men who barbarically treated the slaves. Furthermore, to add insult to injury, they were 'procrastination incarnate', taking weeks to travel a few miles.

Before they were halfway to the lake, Livingstone was incapacitated by the gravest illness that had yet attacked him. During the height of the rains on 1st January 1869 Livingstone, discouraged, wrote, 'I have been wet times without number, but the wetting of yesterday was once too often: I felt very ill, but fearing that the Lofuko might flood,

I resolved to cross it. Cold up to the waist, which made me worse, but I went on for two and an half hours'.[41] Within a few days he was down with pneumonia of the right lung. Fever plagued him and Livingstone saw himself 'lying dead on the way to Ujiji'.[42] Indeed he would have died had not Mohammed Bogharib intervened. He ordered Livingstone be carried, for he was too weak even to sit up. All he could do was hope that he could hold out until he reached Ujiji. Pain racked his thin frame, while the scorching sun blistered any part of the skin exposed. He tried to shelter his face with a bunch of leaves, but was too weak even to hold them. One evening they stopped to rest in a hut infested with Putsi flies. These insects laid their eggs in his damp clothing, which then hatched into maggots under the skin of his legs. These later caused further excruciating pain as the growing little maggots wriggled about under his skin.

Finally they reached the shore; canoes were obtained and weary slaves seconded to row the party across. Livingstone's heart leapt as his hopes were realised; letters would be awaiting him, as well as medicines, food, new clothing and other special supplies.

On 14th March 1869 they arrived in Ujiji. On being shown his supplies Livingstone's heart sank. Battered and emaciated he was to receive yet another shattering blow.

[41] LJ II 1869, p 2.
[42] *Ibid.*

Susi carrying Livingstone across a swollen river

19

Massacre in Manyuema

The doctor was more than disappointed. There was no news, nutritious food, medicines or stores. Almost everything had been stolen or left behind in Unyanyembe (also known as Tabora).

Staying over four months in Ujiji and making do with what short supplies he had, Livingstone slowly convalesced. He wrote forty-two letters, but only one was to reach the coast; the rest were destroyed by slaves influenced by the rogue who had robbed Livingstone. Recuperating in the 'den of the worst kind of slave-traders . . . the vilest of the vile'[1] was not easy.

He had sent messages to Kirk in Zanzibar and hoped that supplies would be on their way. Rather than return himself, he preferred to regain strength for the expedition he was planning.

Plants in Lake Tanganyika drifted north, which supported Burton's theory that the lake drained into Lake Albert. There was also the Lualaba which could either drain into the Nile or Congo. If it flowed into the former, the great Nile source puzzle would be solved—with the exciting prospect of finding the remains of the ancient city of Meroe at the confluence as an added bonus.

Without calico Livingstone could not hire a canoe to explore the head of Tanganyika, and fighting in that region also

---

[1] LJ II 1869, p 11.

restricted his plans, so he concluded providence was leading him to Manyuema. From a distance this green-gladed tropical paradise of towering trees and sparkling streams entertained the eye. Exploring this region would be another matter, as grass as sharp as a flourish of swords, thick thorns and dense forests frustrated the traveller.

A large caravan of Arab and Swahili traders in search of slaves and ivory set off with Livingstone on 12th July 1869. The doctor disagreed with their deeds, but comforted himself maintaining his presence restrained them. They landed less than twenty miles north of a small river—the Lukugs—which flowed out of Lake Tanganyika. If Livingstone had seen the direction in which it moved, he would have realised that the river at the top of Tanganyika flowed into, and not out of, the lake, thus being in no way connected to the Nile.

The locals were very suspicious of Livingstone; the Arabs having destroyed any fibre of faith they may have had in humanity. When villagers tried to obtain a decent price for their wares they were often murdered and their villages fired. Though Bogharib, with whom Livingstone travelled, was more restrained, the going was tough. Suspiciously, one tribesman questioned Livingstone, 'If you have food at home, why come so far and spend your beads to buy it here?'[2]

These were trying times for Livingstone, who found himself studied by all and sundry. He wrote, 'I can bear the women, but ugly males are uninteresting.'[3] On enquiry Livingstone told them that he prayed to 'the Great Father, 'Mulungu' and He hears us all; they thought this to be natural'.[4]

The Muslim Arabs too were introduced to Livingstone's faith. When Mohammed killed a kid as a sacrifice, they prayed to Hadrajee before eating it. Livingstone, devouring the food,

[2] *Ibid*, p 34.
[3] *Ibid*.
[4] *Ibid*, p 29.

pointed out that he liked 'the cookery, but not the prayer'.[5] This they accepted.

Often Livingstone would eat in the open to avoid eating in dark huts. Crowds would gather to watch as he drew a line on the ground, told them to keep out of the circle and then proceeded to eat with a knife, fork and spoon. Amazed they would exclaim, 'See!—they don't touch their food!—what oddities to be sure.'[6]

But he was frail, and in a letter to Agnes Livingstone he wrote: 'I shall not hide from you that I am made by it very old and shaky, my cheeks fallen in, space round the eyes ditto; mouth almost toothless—a few teeth that remain, out of their line, so that a smile is that of a he-hippopotamus, a dreadful old fogie.'[7]

Delays were now inevitable, but he determined to make the most of the months he had to wait before Mohammed Bogharib would move on. He studied the Scriptures and gained strength and inspiration from the Psalms, Proverbs and Pentateuch. His well-thumbed Bible saw much service, particularly at Psalms 23, 40–43, 45, 90, 95–112, whereby he identified himself with the writer, his namesake.

He was treated with respect by the tribes who must have wondered about this emaciated old man who wandered about for no understandable purpose, regardless of the rain and cold; asked questions and even put speech on to paper, prayed a great deal to a God whose name was new to them, gently spoke about forgiveness and did no one any harm.

On Boxing Day, after a delay of several months, a renewed attempt was made to travel in torrential rain to the Lualaba. On New Year's Day 1870 he wrote, 'May the Almighty help

[5] *Ibid*, p 20.
[6] Blaikie, p 406.
[7] D L to Agnes L, *ibid*, p 405.

me to finish the work in hand, and retire through the Basango before the year is out.'[8]

Within a short while he came down with suspected cholera. Progress was slow and on arrival at one village they were refused permission to sleep under cover, but a woman with leprous hands gave him her hut, a nice clean one. 'Of her own accord she prepared dumplings of green maize, pounded and boiled . . .' and seeing that he did not eat for fear of the leprosy, she kindly pressed him: 'Eat, you are weak only from hunger; this will strengthen you.'[9] He ate it all.

Walking continued in the relentless rain. On 3rd February, exhausted and soaked, Livingstone sat for a while. He noticed that a 'little tree-frog, about half an inch long, leaped on to a grassy leaf, and began a tune as loud as that of many birds, and very sweet; it was surprising to hear so much music out of so small a musician'.[10] Soon he was on the march again, encountering bloodthirsty Arabs. One party even admitted killing forty Manyuema and burning nine villages—all because a man tried to steal a single string of beads. Wisely Livingstone warned them, 'Don't shed human blood, my friends; it has guilt not to be wiped off by water.'[11]

Progress, however, was abominably slow with being delayed much at villages. When the call came on 26th June 1870 to set out again his men, aside from his faithful friends Susi, Chumah and Gardner, refused. This trek was nearing the end of the expedition, but they were forced to turn back within a month of setting out. Huge sores and tropical ulcers developed from the cuts on Livingstone's feet. If not treated, these would painfully, rapidly spread the infected organisms to eat their way through muscles, tendons, nerves and even

[8] LJ II 1870, p 38.
[9] *Ibid*, p 41.
[10] *Ibid*, p 42.
[11] *Ibid*, p 46.

blood vessels.[12] Slaves who suffered from these inevitably died an excruciating death. Thus Livingstone limped back into Bambarre, where he was to remain bedridden. Pondering his plight he was fearful that his present condition might prevent him finishing his task. He wrote: 'Patience is all I can exercise: these irritable ulcers hedge me in now, as did my attendants in June, but all will be for the best, for it is in Providence and not in me.'[13]

Crushed malachite applied with a feather was all he had to fight the infection. It worked, and after eighty days, on 10th October 1870, he emerged from his hut, albeit the last twenty days having also succumbed to fever.

These months gave Livingstone more time to think and to reassess his actions. To Thomas, his son, he expressed his assurance that 'by different agencies the Great Ruler is bringing all things into a focus. Jesus is gathering all things to Himself, and He is daily becoming more and more the centre of the world's hopes and of the world's fears.'[14]

Livingstone longed to be back in Britain with his family, although he did not even have a home to go to. He asked Horace Waller to secure lodgings for him, as well as a set of artificial teeth.

He was weary of the Manyuema people. He discovered they had cannibalistic propensities and this depressed him, particularly since one of his deserters, James, was killed and eaten. Livingstone also learned that they would cook and eat the bodies of their enemies to give them courage and that 'a quarrel with a wife often ends in the husband killing her and eating her heart mixed up in a huge mess of goat's flesh'.

Livingstone's heart was sore and his soul vexed over the frightful deeds that he saw so flagrantly displayed. Man's

---

[12] Ransford, p 262.
[13] LJ II 1870, p 50.
[14] Blaikie, p 394.

inhumanity to man. He grieved before God, 'sowing his seeds weeping'; yet the more he persevered and the longer he lived the greater the debauchery of mankind he witnessed. So far was he from bringing back his sheaves rejoicing, he had not yet seen the full travail of his soul. In opening up Africa it would seem he had thereby also opened it up to seditious slave-traders. The Universities' Mission near the Shire was shattered, together with the 'Ma-Robert' and all hopes of developing the interior. Furthermore, the memory of Mary and other souls who gave their lives hung heavily on his heart.

Livingstone was giving himself as a freewill-offering, a living sacrifice. While in Manyuema he read the Bible through four times.[15] Riveted to the well-worn book, he pondered its riches. In prayer he poured out his heart to his Saviour: 'The Lord be my guide and helper. I feel the want of medicine strongly.'[16]

He pondered his calling, combining faith, fact and theory in an attempt to understand God's dealings in his life. As Livingstone read the Scriptures, he grasped a glimmer of hope which would give his work the dignity which no geographical search could provide. He longed to discover whether the 'legendary tales about Moses coming up into Inner Ethiopia with Merr his foster-mother, and founding a city which he called in her honour 'Meroe' may have a substratum of fact'.[17] With his usual optimism he recalled Arab descriptions of a handsome white race living in the Manyuema county who were surely the descendants of the lost tribes of Israel. The ivory doors and pillars which the slaves said they had seen in Manyuema could only represent the work influenced by inherited images of King Solomon's palace. The Arabs with their cherished fantasy of Moses passing through this part of Africa gave further credence to these hopes—if he could only

[15] LJ II 1871, p 154.
[16] *Ibid*, 1870, p 70.
[17] *Ibid*, p 59.

locate the confluence of these rivers, the Nile and Lualaba, his theory, though flimsy, stood a chance.[18] He wrote:

> I dream of discovering some monumental relics of Meroe, and if anything confirmatory of sacred history does remain, I pray to be guided thereunto. If the sacred chronology would thereby be confirmed, I would not grudge the toil and hardships, hunger and pain, I have endured—the irritable ulcers would only be discipline.[19]

Amazingly Livingstone lay so close to discovering the truth, yet he was bound by circumstances. His riverine theory fitted the facts at his disposal and although fundamentally mistaken in many respects, Livingstone's assumptions regarding the Central African watershed were correct. He, in piecing together the reports from Arabs, correctly concluded that three main interconnecting 'lines of drainage' dispersed from the region; namely, the Zambesi and Kafue to the south, and the Congo and Nile to the north. The thought that the Lualaba was a tributary of the Congo and not the Nile often troubled Livingstone, though he shrugged it off and held to his hopes of it leading to the Nile, whereby the source of the Lualaba would be the fountain of this great mystery. This in essence was the error.

If Livingstone's theory was wrong, his heart's motive was certainly correct. Revealing the Nile's sources would provide him with new fame. This he could use to generate public opinion against the slave-trade which, in turn, would force the government to act. 'The Nile sources are valuable to me,' he told his elder brother John, 'only as a means of enabling me to open my mouth with power among men.'[20]

On 25th October 1870 he wrote in his diary:

---

[18] The ruins of Meroe had in fact been unearthed far away to the north beyond Khartoum and had been examined by Bruce in 1772.

[19] *Ibid*, p 60.

[20] Ransford, p 267.

In this journey I have endeavoured to follow with unswerving fidelity the line of duty. My course has been an even one, turning neither to the right hand nor to the left, though my route has been tortuous enough. All the hardship, hunger and toil were met with full conviction that I was right in persevering to make a complete work of the exploration of the sources of the Nile. Mine has been a calm, hopeful endeavour to do the work that has been given me to do, whether I succeed or whether I fail. The prospects of death in pursuing what I knew to be right did not make me veer to one side or the other.[21]

Fired with a fresh enthusiasm Livingstone wanted to recommence his exploration, but decided to delay as he hoped to receive fresh stores being sent to him via Ujiji. Restless, he penned: 'I groan and am in bitterness at the delay, but thus it is: I pray for help to do what is right, but sorely I am perplexed, and grieved and mourn: I cannot give up making a complete work of the exploration.'[22]

The relatives of a boy captured at Monanyembe brought three goats to redeem him: he is sick and emaciated; one goat was rejected. The boy shed tears when he saw his goat was rejected ... 'So I returned, and considered all the oppressions that are done under the sun: and behold the tears of such as were oppressed, and they had no comforter; and on the side of their oppressors there was power; but they had no comforter.' Ecclesiastes IV: I. The relations were told either to bring the goat, or let the boy die; this was hard-hearted.[23]

Livingstone noted that many of the recently captured people, despite having food and little or no forced labour, wasted away within a few weeks.

They ascribed their only pain to the heart, and placed the hand correctly on the spot ... One fine boy of about twelve years was

[21] LJ II 1870, p 72.
[22] Ibid, p 78.
[23] Ibid, p 79.

carried, and when about to expire, was kindly laid down on the side of the path, and a hole dug to deposit the body in. He, too, said he had nothing the matter with him, except the pain in his heart.[24]

His New Year prayer was: 'O Father! help me to finish this work to thy honour.'[25] The end of January 1871 heralded the approach of the stores caravan and on 4th February ten of the long-expected porters arrived. The joy in seeing them was premature, as the despicable porters soon divulged their characters.

Kirk had despatched them from Zanzibar. A three-month journey had taken fourteen months, as they continually stopped to sell off the goods consigned to Livingstone, while living luxuriously off the proceeds. Upon reaching Ujiji the leader, a Mohammedan Swahili named Shereef, despatched ten porters to locate Livingstone, bringing with them the poorest quality calico, meagre amounts of tea, coffee and quinine. On meeting Livingstone they demanded higher wages and refused to carry his goods any further until, frustrated at this mutiny and blackmail, Livingstone put his foot down and threatened to shoot the two leaders if they persisted.

Frustrated, Livingstone wrote to Agnes: 'The men sent by Dr Kirk are Mohammedans, that is, unmitigated liars.'[26]

Finally, Livingstone and his party, now numbering thirteen, marched out of Bambarre heading north west towards Lualaba. Within seven weeks Livingstone reached its broad banks and set up his base at Nyangwe. Here he heard uncomfortable reports of the river bending north west, but he wanted to investigate it for himself. This was easier said than done, for his porters had persuaded the Arabs and locals not to support him. For four months no canoe could be

---

[24] *Ibid*, p 93.
[25] *Ibid*, p 95.
[26] D L to Agnes L in Blaikie, p 406.

obtained and his Banian porters were also overheard plotting to lead him into a Manyuema trap. Driven to the depths of discouragement he wrote: 'It is excessively trying, and so many difficulties have been put in my way I doubt whether the Divine favour and will is on my side.'[27]

For a time they ventured forth on foot, but the marauding Manyuema made life difficult and he was forced to bide his time in Nyangwe. There the locals were friendly, if not co-operative, and fondly referred to him as Douad. When Stanley visited there five years later, one grey-haired man 'told him that Douad had saved him from being robbed many a time by the Arabs, and he was so gentle and patient and told us such pleasant stories about the wonderful land of the white people. Hm' the aged white man was a good man, indeed.'[28]

However, some folks' liking for him was rather extreme and on 11th March 1871 he 'had a long, fierce oration . . . in which I was told again and again that I should be killed and eaten—the people wanted a "white one" to eat'![29]

Livingstone liked his visits to the market where many would 'come eagerly, and retire with careworn faces'.[30] There they would sell dried cassava, chickens, goats, earthen pots, palm-oil, relishes, salt and pepper.

> It is a scene of the finest natural acting imaginable. The eagerness with which all sorts of assertions are made—all creation is called on to attest the truth of what they allege—and then the intense surprise and withering scorn cast on those who despise their goods . . . Little girls run about selling cups of water for a few small fishes to the half-exhausted wordy combatants.[31]

---

[27] LJ II 1871, p 110.
[28] Ransford, p 271.
[29] LJ II 1871, p 107.
[30] *Ibid*, p 115.
[31] *Ibid*, p 126.

On 15th July 1871, Livingstone wandered down to the market for his usual brief visit. It was a hot sultry day and the 1,500 people busied themselves with their bargains. Livingstone noticed three Arabs had guns, but said nothing, presuming they had brought them in ignorance. Turning to leave he saw one of them haggling about a fowl in their usual spirited manner. Thinking little of it he continued walking for another thirty yards when he heard the discharge of two guns in the middle of the crowd. The slaughter had begun. 'Crowds dashed off from the place, and threw down their wares in confusion, and ran. At the same time as the three opened fire on the mass of people near the upper end of the market-place volleys were discharged from the party down near the creek on the panic-stricken women, who dashed at the canoes.'[32] Utter pandemonium broke out and over fifty canoes were swamped without even leaving the shore. Many screaming, injured people tried helplessly to swim out to an island; 'the heads above water showed the long line of those that would inevitably perish'.[33] Some would sink quietly beneath the volley of gunfire 'whilst other poor creatures threw their arms high, as if appealing to the great Father above, and sank'.[34]

Hundreds upon hundreds died in an insensible blood bath. Livingstone saved as many as he could using the British Consulate flag as a shield. (He raised the flag, which gave British protection to those who stood beneath it.) Enraged, he wanted to shoot the murderers, but the Arab chief prevented him as he would have been helplessly outnumbered. The massacre continued from village to village as Muslims on the rampage asserted their authority, razing countless houses to the ground, killing those they could. Over twenty-seven villages were destroyed and loud wails carried across

---

[32] *Ibid*, p 133.
[33] *Ibid*, pp 133–134.
[34] *Ibid*, p 133.

the bloody water. Devastated, Livingstone recorded the events. He cried out: 'Oh, let Thy Kingdom come! . . . it gave me the impression of being in Hell.'[35] He 'proposed to Dugumbe [the chief Arab] to catch the murderers, and hang them up in the market-place'.[36] To this Dugumbe would not consent, for the massacre had been a deliberate campaign to frighten the Manyuema into Arab demands. The Arabs tried to pacify by offering Livingstone a share of whatever they had, but he refused—though he did accept gunpowder.

Shattered, the Scot retreated to his house where he cared for the injured. Two days later he was laid up 'with the depression the bloodshed made—it filled me with unspeakable horror . . . I cannot stay here in agony'.[37] To Livingstone the murderous assault was like Gehenna and what he imagined burning in the bottomless pit to be like.

Livingstone knew he could never depend on Arabs again—his sense of outrage and disgust was too strong. However, without their assistance he could not explore that region and as he had too much integrity to ignore the evil, he resolved to return to Ujiji. Two years of work and waiting were cast aside in vain.

It is ironic how he was always prevented from realising his ambition, be it putting a boat on Lake Nyasa or searching for the source of the Nile. Yet he never grumbled against God.

Although poised, as he believed, on the brink of success he saw no other option as a Christian but to leave the accursed city. If he stayed, locals would have seen him as siding with the slavers.

To Livingstone, the long toil and torment had been to no avail. Sickened, he compiled an account of the massacre for the British Government, though he was not to know what

---

[35] *Ibid*, p 135.
[36] *Ibid*.
[37] *Ibid*, p 139.

affect his report would have. It so enraged the British people that it was one of the main issues in ending the evil slave-trade.

The three-month journey back to Ujiji was a nightmare— tight shoes were all Livingstone had to walk in and moreover he was now bleeding profusely from ruptured haemorrhoids. Intense heat and humidity sapped his strength, as sorely discouraged he stumbled back 'ill and almost every step in pain'.[38]

At one village they were stoned by suspicious tribes, who tried to kill those who went for water. In passing through a dark, dense forest they were ambushed. 'A large spear from my right lunged past and almost grazed my back, and stuck firmly into the soil ... As they are expert with the spear I don't know how it missed, except that he was too sure of his aim and the good hand of God was upon me.'[39]

Livingstone survived, but sadly two of his men were killed in the skirmish. The enemy were foiled, but went ahead and burned a gigantic tree. This was felled as Livingstone walked into the clearing; he heard the crack and looked up to see it come straight for him. He ran back, narrowly missing death by a yard. Three attempts on his life in one day! Livingstone later wrote: 'I became weary with the constant strain of danger, and—as I suppose happens with soldiers on a field of battle—not courageous, but perfectly indifferent whether I were killed or not.'[40]

Months later they crossed Tanganyika and entered Ujiji on 23rd October 1871, eager to see the rest of the stores sent up by Kirk.

That evening Livingstone found Susi and Chumah weeping bitterly. 'All our things are sold,' they told him. The Muslim, Shereef, had divined in the Koran that Livingstone was dead,

---

[38] *Ibid*, p 145.
[39] *Ibid*, p 146.
[40] *Ibid*, p 147.

so everything was sold. This devastating act left Livingstone with only a very small quantity of calico and he would have to sell his watch, gun and instruments to buy enough food for himself and his loyal porters for one month. He would then be reduced to a pauper. He thought of travelling, alone if necessary, to find Samuel Baker who he learned was leading an expedition up the Nile. He would never again seek the aid of Her Britannic Majesty's Consul in Zanzibar.

He wrote in his diary: 'I felt in my destitution as if I were the man who went down from Jerusalem to Jerico, and fell among thieves; but I could not hope for Priest, Levite, or good Samaritan to come by on either side.'[41] In one of his darkest hours, little did Livingstone realise that his Father in heaven would not see the righteous begging bread. A miracle would shortly materialise.

[41] *Ibid*, p 155.

Henry Morton Stanley and Kalulu

20

Union in Ujiji

Unbeknown to Livingstone, a white man was enquiring about him several days journey from Ujiji. 'He is old. He has white hair on his face, and is sick,'[1] was the reply.

Excited, the young American stirred his huge caravan on towards the blue mountains that stood sedately in the distance.

They surged forward, steadily gaining ground until finally the lake was visible. Elated, the young explorer could hardly contain himself. It was a glorious day, the sky seemed to smile upon the earth as the emerald green, tufted banks of the lake and rivers languished peacefully.

Outside the village of Ujiji the large entourage of over 190 people stopped. Although the attention of the tranquil settlement had been attracted, a command was given for flags to be unfurled. This was followed by a sonorous fanfare and a volley of fifty guns firing in unison, shattering what peace remained.

Suddenly the place was seething with people as all manner of African and Arab pressed forward to see the spectacle. Flags and streamers created a colourful sight as the crowd pressed in around the egotistical white man and his pagazi. 'Good morning Sir!'. Startled upon hearing English spoken in the middle of Africa, the American turned around sharply to see a young man with the 'blackest of faces, but animated and joyous'.

---

[1] Stanley, p 384.

'Who the mischief are you?' he asked.
'I am Susi, the servant of Dr Livingstone,' said he, smiling, and showing a gleaming row of teeth.
'What! Is Dr Livingstone here?'
'Yes, sir.'
'In this village?'
'Yes, sir.'
'Are you sure?'
'Sure, sure, sir. Why, I leave him just now.'
'Good morning, sir,' said another voice.
'Hallo', said I, 'is this another one?'
'Yes, sir.'
'Well, what is your name?'
'My name is Chumah, sir.'
'What! Are you Chumah, the friend of Wakatani?'
'Yes, sir.'
'And is the Doctor well?'
'Not very well, sir.'
'Where has he been so long?'
'In Manyuema.'
'Now, you Susi, run, and tell the Doctor I am coming.'
Off he darted like a mad man.[2]

Susi told the doctor of the arrival of this very important man. Livingstone then enquired what the man's name was. Amazed at himself for not finding that out, Susi hurried back to enquire.

Livingstone's faithful cook Halimah winced when the first guns announced the arrival of another white man. She flew about in a state of excitement, then into despair at the scantiness of the larder as Livingstone should lay on a feast. She was astounded at the flashy young man's paraphernalia. 'Talk about Arabs!', she exclaimed. 'Who are they that they should be compared to white man? Arabs indeed!'[3]

Soon Livingstone was seen by the newcomer—standing in

[2] *Ibid*, pp 409–410.
[3] *Ibid*, p 418.

front of his house. The young man could hardly control himself; he wasn't sure if he should bite his hand or turn a somersault. With his heart racing he tried not to let his face betray his emotions lest it should lessen his dignity.

Livingstone for his part saw the huge American flag followed by a retinue of people carrying sufficient stores to sustain a traveller for years. Tin baths, tents, saddles, a folding boat, and an impressive array of gigantic kettles. Whoever the leader of the party might be, Livingstone mused, he was 'no poor Lazarus like me'. Then out of the crowd stepped the white man himself; a huge native preceded him carrying the Stars and Stripes. The stranger was immaculately dressed in a freshly pressed flannel suit; his boots glistened and his helmet dazzled white. This amazing man, while surrounded by onlookers, contemplated his next move in order that it would appear dignified. As he advanced towards Livingstone he noticed 'he was pale, looked wearied, had a grey beard, wore a bluish cap with a faded gold band round it, had on a red-sleeved waistcoat, and a pair of grey tweed trousers'.[4]

Livingstone stepped towards the stranger, who in turn formally raised his helmet and, in spite of a voice that trembled with excitement, with all propriety said: 'Doctor Livingstone, I presume?'

'Yes.' Smiling kindly and lifting his cap slightly Livingstone felt tears coming into his eyes.

Henry Morton Stanley introduced himself. This entrepreneurial young man was the intrepid reporter from the *New York Herald* whom Mr James Gordon Bennett, the proprietor of the newspaper, had wisely despatched to find Livingstone, regardless of the cost. This would be the scoop of the century.

Oblivious of the crowd, the men exchanged a few more words and turned towards the Tembe. Livingstone pointed to the mud platform under the broad overhanging grass roof

---

[4] *Ibid*, p 411.

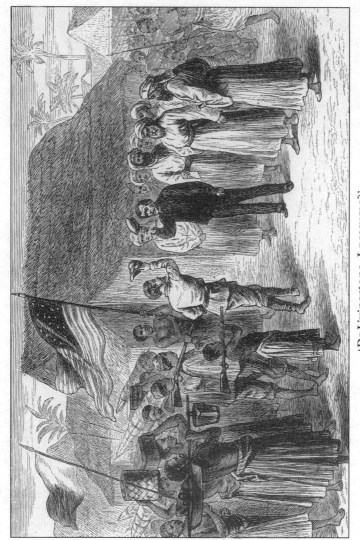

'Dr Livingstone, I presume?'

and beckoned his guest to take his only humble seat: a straw mat with a goatskin over it, nailed to the mud wall.

Seated, they began talking and Livingstone was handed letters—the first he had had in five long years. 'The Doctor kept the letter-bag on his knee, then, presently, opened it, looked at the letters contained there, and read one or two of his children's letters, his face in the meanwhile lighting up.'[5]

He asked his guest to tell him the news, but Stanley replied, 'No, Doctor, read your letters first, which I am sure you must be impatient to read.'

'Ah,' said he, 'I have waited years for letters, and I have been taught patience. I can surely afford to wait a few hours longer.'[6]

And so the exuberant traveller recounted the news, while Halimah, ecstatic that her culinary skills were appreciated, dashed to and from the kitchen area.

Livingstone had come to seem immortal in the eyes of the British public, whose interest in him revived when they thought him dead. Other explorers either entered the dark continent and emerged a short while later, or succumbed to its dangers and died. Livingstone had plodded on single-handed year in year out, no one knowing where he was or what he was doing.

Stanley was born in Wales, the illegitimate son of a cottager, John Rowlands. Deserted by his mother in infancy, he was reared by two uncles until the age of five and then despatched to a workhouse. There he suffered constant brutalities and humiliations perpetrated by James Francis, the master, who was later found to be insane and sent to an asylum. Stanley's traumatic childhood even included him seeing the bruised and battered remains of his best friend who had been murdered by Francis. Stanley was driven until eventually, aged fifteen,

---

[5] *Ibid*, p 414.
[6] *Ibid*.

he reacted and beat Francis unconscious. He had no option but to flee.

Rejected by his relatives, he signed on as a cabin boy on a ship bound for New Orleans. He met a kind and wealthy man who adopted him and gave him his name of Henry Morton Stanley.

Young Stanley, however, was too troublesome and was soon sent off to work. Finally he enlisted in the Confederate army, was wounded in battle and imprisoned. He agreed to join the Federal Artillery in exchange for his freedom, but was later discharged on grounds of ill health.

He enlisted as a ship's writer covering the war at sea off the southern coast, progressing from there to a career in journalism. The *New York Herald* provided the room for Stanley's many talents to grow. He managed to land many stories, outdoing the other papers. Adventure, war and anything with a challenge attracted him.

Stanley's discovery of Livingstone was to have an incredible impact on the outside world. The lonely explorer who lingered in Africa would become a legend.

The journey to find him, however, was understandably difficult. In Zanzibar the journalist was told by Kirk that Livingstone would probably be extremely angry to be 'found'. He said that 'if Burton, or Grant, or Baker, or any of those fellows were going after him, and he heard of their coming, Livingstone would put a hundred miles of swamp in a very short time between himself and them'.[7]

Stanley, every bit the journalist, did not divulge that he was off in search of Livingstone, though Kirk was not fooled. The interest in the explorer was renewed, while the government had even voted, in May 1870, for funds of £1,000 for Livingstone. Further, the government appealed to the Royal Geographical Society to organise a relief expedition, which

---

[7] *Ibid*, p 15.

sailed for Zanzibar on 7th February 1872, four months after
Stanley had been with Livingstone.

The timing of the meeting was indeed nothing short of
miraculous. Stanley was commissioned to find Livingstone in
October 1869, yet he only reached Livingstone nearly two
years later, and three weeks after Livingstone had returned
from his wanderings in the wilderness on the other side of
the lake. Any earlier and Stanley may not have found him.
The reporter was quick to admit: 'I began to recognise the
hand of an overruling and kindly Providence.'[8]

Although quite different in character, the two men had a
lot in common. Both had had a hard upbringing, were
stubborn, fearless, intolerant of other men's weaknesses and,
when drawn to a goal, as tenacious as a terrier.

Each man had a pleasurable effect on the other. Stanley
was the Good Samaritan to Livingstone, who told him often:
'You have given me new life.' Stanley, acting as a son to
Livingstone, craved for a father. Livingstone was a man whom
he admired and whose wisdom and gentleness he revered.
Stanley's respect for Livingstone was complete. The latter, by
his presence alone, often prevented Stanley from shooting at
marauders. On one occasion they were fired at and a mere
look from Livingstone was enough to dissuade Stanley from
returning fire. However, Stanley's harsh upbringing ensured
that he was quick to use the whip on any problem porter,
male or female. His harshness affected two white companions
who accompanied him earlier on the trip and they begged to
be left behind, where they later perished miserably.

A firm friendship flourished between the two men. Instead
of finding Livingstone as Kirk suggested, having a 'splenetic,
misanthropic temper',[9] being garrulous, demented and one
that takes no notes or observations, Stanley found him the

[8] *Ibid*, p 425.
[9] *Ibid*, p 429.

opposite. 'In him there is no guile,'[10]; he wrote later. 'The Doctor has a fund of quiet humour, which he exhibits at all times whenever he is among friends.'[11]

> His gentleness never forsakes him; his hopefulness never deserts him ... He thinks 'all will come out right at last'; he has such faith in the goodness of Providence ...[12]

> His religion is not of the theoretical kind, but is a constant, earnest, sincere practise. It is neither demonstrative nor loud, but manifests itself in a quiet, practical way, and is always at work ... In him, religion exhibits its loveliest features; it governs his conduct not only towards his servants, but towards the natives, the bigoted Mohammedans, and all who come in contact with him. Without it, Livingstone, with his ardent temperament, his enthusiasm, his high spirit and courage, must have become uncompanionable, and a hard master. Religion has tamed him, and made him a Christian gentleman.[13]

Livingstone, however, was not without his faults. He battled with forgiveness as he recalled the skirmishes he had had during the Zambesi expedition. He continued to resent Baines, Bedingfield and Tozer, as well as others who had hurt him. Also the feeble support from the government and the Geographical Society understandably wounded him. He saw the insincerity of others towards him and his cause as conspiracy, collectively combined to frustrate his hopes. His suspicious nature towards these men and institutions was not helped by Stanley who was quick to tell him of Kirk's statements.

The doctor judged actions as well as words. Each time Livingstone was sent stores they were despatched with

---

[10] *Ibid*, p 428.
[11] *Ibid*, p 430.
[12] *Ibid*, p 432.
[13] *Ibid*, p 434.

abominable rogues. Thus he received, years later, only a portion of them at great cost to himself. Understandably this upsct him.

Livingstone wanted to finish the task allotted him on his own rather than go cap in hand back to Britain. The doctor's mind was set upon making yet another attempt to find the sources of the Nile. Then—not beholden to any man—he could stand up and denounce the slave-trade. It would either be death or success.

The source of the Nile still had to be identified, so the two travellers set off to explore the top of Lake Tanganyika. Livingstone was to call this trip the 'picnic', as they relaxed on Stanley's persian carpet and sipped tea from his silver service. They discovered that the Lusize River flowed into Lake Tanganyika and not out of it and therefore it was not connected to Lake Albert and the Nile. Unperturbed, the gentlemen and their staff rowed back, enjoying the journey.

Susi, in particular, had no hesitation in consuming vast quantities of pombe—the local brew. One night, intoxicated, he climbed into Livingstone's bed. The Scot, half asleep, thought nothing of the intruder until he lost all his blankets to the slumbering sloth. 'The Doctor, with that gentleness characteristic of him, instead of taking a rod, had contented himself with slapping Susi on the back saying, "Get up, Susi, will you? You are in my bed. How dare you, sir, get drunk in this way, after I have told you so often not to?"'[14]

By Christmas they were back in Ujiji. The day was spent with little interest. Stanley had endeavoured to instil into the cook, Ferajji, 'some cunning secrets of the culinary art',[15] but needless to say both the roast and custard were ruined.

Livingstone's health was much stronger thanks to the

[14] *Ibid*, p 498.
[15] *Ibid*, p 565.

care of Stanley, who even cooked dainty morsels of food in order to tempt the doctor to eat. Livingstone told Agnes, 'The tears often started into my eyes on every fresh proof of kindness.'[16] Stanley's generosity was very gracious, for he divided all that he had—from bath tubs, tents and food, to clothing, writing materials and cutlery—into two heaps; one for himself, the other for the doctor.

Livingstone for his part had no objection to Stanley making money out of finding and interviewing him. He stated: 'He is heartily welcome, for it is a great deal more than I could ever make out of myself.'[17]

Livingstone also used Stanley as a mouthpiece to make his cause—slavery—known. He argued: 'I have no prejudice against their colour; indeed, anyone who lives among them forgets that they are black and feels they are just fellow-men.'[18]

He told Stanley of the many incidents which he had encountered on his expeditions from the Chambezi River to Chief Casembe who was perplexed when Livingstone told him of his desire to explore the area's lakes and rivers. Casembe questioned, 'What can you want to go there for? The water is close here. There is plenty of large water in this neighbourhood.'[19]

All too soon it was time for Stanley to make plans to return, and it was decided that they travel together to Unyanyembe (Tabora) where Livingstone's goods were still detained.

They travelled south by boat as far as possible before turning inland, thus avoiding the war. Through virgin bush they trampled; Livingstone laboured immensely, his feet

[16] Blaikie, p 426.
[17] Footnote, Coupland, p 213.
[18] *Ibid*, p 171.
[19] Stanley, p 445.

extremely painful with bleeding blisters brought on by the tight shoes. Stanley led the way using the compass rather than a guide for direction. In fact the poor guide was very disconcerted when he discovered that the tiny compass, 'the pearly monitor', knew the way better than he did and he declared 'as his solemn opinion that it could not lie'.

On 18th February 1872, drenched from persistent rain, they arrived in Unyanyembe. Livingstone was overjoyed to see some of his stores still remained, despite thieves and white ants. Two pairs of boots sent by Horace Waller were a sight to behold.

Stanley again tried to persuade Livingstone to accompany him to England, but the doctor, much as he yearned to, would not hear of it. His work was not complete.

The time came for Stanley to leave, taking with him an accumulation of letters, Livingstone's journal, his maps and screeds of observations. On 14th March 1872 the men had a sad breakfast together. Stanley wrote: 'I could not eat my heart was too full; neither did my companion seem to have an appetite.'[20]

Livingstone determined to walk with Stanley a little way to see him 'off on the road'. It was a time of tearing the bond which had grown so strong. They walked side by side. Stanley took 'long looks at Livingstone, to impress his features thoroughly on my memory'.[21] When they parted Stanley, could barely keep back his tears, and when Chumah and Susi ran up to him to kiss his hands, it was too much for him: 'I betrayed myself. . . .'[22]

---

[20] *Ibid*, p 624.
[21] *Ibid*, p 625.
[22] *Ibid*, p 627.

Livingstone being carried into the hut where he died

21

March to Martyrdom

Unyanyembe (Tabora) became a lonely place without Stanley, and Livingstone tried desperately to busy himself with the planned expedition. Ever an optimist, he calculated to be home within a year after marching and mapping the southern shore of Lake Tanganyika, travelling further south, crossing the Chambeshi and skirting the bottom of Lake Bangweulu to ensure there were no major tributaries flowing into it and then heading west to the ancient fountains which he believed to be the source of the Nile. After an inspection of the area he would gradually head back home.

Five days after Stanley left, Livingstone turned fifty-nine, a ripe old age to be running around exploring Africa. He wrote in his diary on 19th March 1872: 'My Jesus, my king, my life, my all; I again dedicate my whole self to Thee. Accept me, and grant, O gracious Father, that ere this year is gone I may finish my task. In Jesus' name I ask it. Amen. So let it be.'[1]

Stanley trekked back to Zanzibar—a perpetual struggle against hostile natives, flooded paths, slush, mire and insects, which he described as the ten plagues of Egypt. On reaching Bagamoio on 6th May 1872 he was surprised to see members of the Royal Geographical Society on a search expedition about to look for Livingstone. On learning that Stanley had preceded them, and not wanting to face the trek to

---

[1] LJ II 1872, p 174.

Livingstone, they hastily decided to return home. On this expedition was twenty-one-year-old Oswell, Livingstone's son, who sadly opted to return, having had an interview with Kirk. Stanley urged him to lead the Pagazi he intended to recruit and to send them, with supplies, back to his father.

When Livingstone learned of his son's decision he was deeply hurt, then angered. In a letter, Oswell told his father that he believed the government intended awarding him a considerable grant of money and a pension, so he wanted to take his father back to England in order that he and the family might benefit from it. Also, perhaps, persuade him to write another bestseller before he died. Oswell's letter also reprimanded Livingstone for neglecting his family.[2]

Livingstone lamented over the letter, writing to Agnes saying her brother should have had 'the sense to come with me and gain a little credit that may enable him to hold up his head among men and not merely be Dr Livingstone's son'.[3]

He felt more alone now that he sensed his family, excepting Agnes with whom he had a close relationship, were against him. Trying to see providence in Oswell's decision, Livingstone wrote in a little notebook: 'To die alone will give me an influence which I pray may be turned for good in the abolition of this nasty slave-trade.'[4]

Livingstone had now come to a point in his life where he was prepared more than ever to lay down his life as a voice against the slave-trade. The geographical task was far less significant than his heart's desire to see Africa and her people set free. He wrote to a friend: 'What I have seen of this horrid system, makes me feel that its suppression would be of infinitely more importance than all the fountains (sources)

---

[2] Ransford, p 289.
[3] D L to Agnes L 01/07/1872 British Museum additional manuscript 50184 in Jeal, p 354.
[4] National Library of Scotland 10728, p 14 in Ransford, p 290.

together.'[5] Even the natives were wary of Livingstone's true
purposes of exploration. He told Sir Thomas Maclear:

> They consider the sources of the Nile to be a sham; the true object
> of my being sent is to see their odious system of slaving, and if
> indeed my disclosures should lead to the suppression of the East
> Coast slave-trade, I would esteem that as a far greater feat than
> the discovery of all the sources together. It is awful, but I cannot
> speak of the slaving for fear of appearing guilty of exaggerating.
> It is not trading; it is murdering for captives to be made into
> slaves.[6]

The sickening sights of the massacre in Nyangwe still haunted
him and often he would wake up from a nightmare sweating.
The burden on his heart became very great. Livingstone was
to become like his Saviour, a man of sorrows, acquainted
with grief, and he interceded desperately for its cessation.
Writing to the *New York Herald* he tried to 'enlist American
zeal to stop the East Coast slave-trade',[7] concluding, 'All I
can add in my loneliness is, may Heaven's rich blessing come
down on everyone, American, English, or Turk, who will help
to heal the open sore of the world.'[8]

Livingstone saw himself as having a divine mandate which
gave him the strength to persevere and persist against amazing
odds. His ruling disposition was that nothing must be allowed
to stand in the way of his goal and if anything threatened to
do so, he was apt to show irritation. Kirk, referring to
Livingstone's refusal to give up when exploring the Ruvuma,
said of him, 'His determination seems to amount to infatuation.'[9]

Though many viewed this as one of Livingstone's weaknesses, it was ironically one of his strongest features. Where

[5] D L to Dr Wilson 24/01/1872, National Library of Scotland, in Jeal, p 355.
[6] D L to Sir Thomas Maclear in Blaikie, p 426.
[7] LJ II 1872, p 181.
[8] *Ibid*, p 182.
[9] 13th September 1862, *Kirk's Journals* in Ransford, p 206.

many thousands of men would have given up Livingstone was prepared to press on. He had a profound conviction that he had been divinely chosen for the specific calling he was engaged in. Some saw this as madness, whereas more enlightened individuals regarded it to be a fine faith in his Creator, with absolute lack of fear. He would not give an extra thought to going into the most perilous positions, quite confident that God would protect him. Indeed he was looked after; any other man would probably have left a trail of bitterness and bloodshed, not merely a testimony of simple faith.

Amid the spiritual darkness it was hard for him to believe that Africa could ever be won, and Livingstone had to strengthen his faith daily. On 13th May 1872 he wrote:

> He will keep His word—the gracious One, full of grace and truth—no doubt of it. He said, 'Him that cometh unto me, I will in no wise cast out' and 'Whatsoever ye shall ask in my name, I will give it.' He will keep His word: then I can come and humbly present my petition, and it will be all right. Doubt is here inadmissible, surely.[10]

Waiting for his supplies to arrive was a weary affair and much time was given to reflection. His one other major concern was the source of the Nile. Quite openly, on 21st May 1872, he wrote, 'I am oppressed with the apprehension that after all it may turn out that I have been following the Congo; and who would risk being put into a cannibal pot . . .'[11]

Perplexed, doubtful thoughts traversed his mind as Livingstone calculated the course that the river he was pinning all his hopes on was connected to the Nile. 'I am even now,' he wrote, 'not at all 'cock-sure' that I have been following down what may after all be the Congo.'[12]

---

[10] LJ II 1872, p 186.
[11] *Ibid*, p 188.
[12] *Ibid*, p 203.

As with the Ruvuma, there would be no turning back until he had proved its course.

Wearily, they continued waiting while stores were checked and packed and the tent from Stanley was tarred and prepared. Much patience was needed.

Livingstone at one stage even fancied himself as a matchmaker. A fine-looking, hard-working and unattached woman joined the expedition. He proposed that she should marry one of his three worthies—Chumah, Gardner or Mabruki—'but she smiled at the idea. Chumah was evidently too lazy ever to get a wife; the other two were contemptible in appearance, and she has a good presence and is buxom. Chumah promised reform: he had been lazy, he admitted, because he had no wife.'[13]

Livingstone reiterated the need for the gospel to be taught: 'I would say to missionaries, Come on, brethren. To the real heathen, you have no idea how brave you are till you try.'[14]

'No great difficulty would be encountered in establishing a Christian Mission a hundred miles or so from the East coast.'[15] He then described how in training local people they too would create further missions. He saw the fruitlessness of so much of the church. 'A great deal of power is thus lost in the Church. Fastings and vigils, without a special object in view, are time run to waste.'[16] Missionaries would provide the goal and direct church activities, and in so doing be a great benefit to others.

The Pagazi was finally on its way to Livingstone. Stanley had found and equipped fifty-seven fine men. Medicines, muskets, ammunition, food, cloth, a chronometer and even two donkeys were generously given. Sadly, Oswell and Kirk

[13] *Ibid*, p 201.
[14] *Ibid*, p 190.
[15] *Ibid*, p 209.
[16] *Ibid*, p 211.

would not even assist in seeing the caravan off and the American consulate finally took that responsibility.

Mid-August saw its arrival. Livingstone was ecstatic: 'Bless the Lord, O my Soul, and all that is within me bless His Holy name.'[17] The supplies came together with a warm letter from Stanley: 'My dear Doctor, very few amongst men have I found I so much got to love as yourself.'[18] In similar view Livingstone wrote to Agnes: 'That good brave fellow has acted as a son to me.'[19]

After giving them a few days' rest, Livingstone rallied together his team of just over sixty men. They would shortly be off on what many felt was a pointless permutation of military-like meander. Conversely, it was a journey that astounded the world.

On 25th August 1872 they moved out, saying goodbye to the Arabs and friendly people who had gathered to wish them well. Unfortunately, a box of powdered milk was left behind which would have been a major source of food when Livingstone fell into ill health. They did have ten cows, but they strayed into a belt of tsetse and died. The sun relentlessly sapped their strength and slowed down their pace, even the most rugged porters' feet being scorched by the soil. In October Livingstone wrote, 'Inwardly I feel tired too,'[20] but he would not allow that to mar his mandate. Even the problem of his haemorrhoids bleeding did not deter him from persevering.

Warring tribes and Arab aggression caused further problems as, suspiciously, village after village hid their food and would not barter, for fear of being overpowered.

[17] *Ibid.* p 229.
[18] H M Stanley to D L 27/5/1872, National Library of Scotland in Jeal, p 358.
[19] D L to Agnes L 23/08/1872, British Museum additional manuscript 50184, *ibid.*
[20] LJ II 1872, p 238.

The intense heat of October and November heralded the rainy season and the full fury of the rains transformed the country. Streams burst their banks, low-lying plains became a multitude of marshes which bred millions of mosquitoes and leeches. Cloud cover prevented proper observations being made. The rain dampened their morale, but the leader would not turn back. Sick men were cared for and carried if necessary.

They came across a little girl who had been abandoned by her mother in the pouring rain, and was benumbed by cold. Livingstone saw to it that she was picked up and carried; and he gave her to one of the childless women accompanying the expedition.

Hungry and more often than not wet, they plodded on towards Lake Bangweulu. Amazingly not one of the party rebelled or even complained; it was as if a bond had brought them together.

They reached Lake Bangweulu, where Livingstone made a major decision which caused unimaginable suffering. The guide told Livingstone that they were near the western shore of the lake. Livingstone often had to contend with poor guides, so he relied on what facts he had. When he did manage to get a position, he related it to his old observations which were forty miles out, as unbeknown to him he was using the faulty chronometer. He therefore reckoned he was far east of the position the guide claimed to have brought them to. Thus he opted to head south east—the long way round.

Familiar landmarks were hidden by the rain and further reckoning was nearly impossible, so they persisted in forging their way around through wide streams and marshes, trying to hire canoes where possible, Livingstone's health failed and he started losing more blood through the haemorrhoids, which severely weakened him. Soon he joined the ranks of those who had to be carried in the pouring rain. Susi struggled with Livingstone on his shoulders. Once, when crossing a stream, the water even came up to Susi's mouth, but the faithful servant and friend did not complain.

On 14th February 1873 Livingstone wrote: 'If the good
Lord gives me favour, and permits me to finish my work, I
shall thank and bless Him, though it has cost me untold toil,
pain, and travel; this trip has made my hair all grey.'[21] Every
Sunday they would hold a service and Livingstone would
preach a short message in Swahili. Though he was never
blessed as an orator he used his other gifts to the full. He
observed

> that men think that greatness consists in lofty indifference to all
> trivial things. The Grand Lama, sitting in immovable contempla-
> tion of nothing, is a good example of what a human mind would
> regard as majesty; but the Gospels reveal Jesus, the manifestation
> of the blessed God over all as minute in His care of all. He exercises
> a vigilance more constant, complete, and comprehensive every
> hour and every minute, over each of His people than their utmost
> self-love could ever attain. His tender love is more exquisite than
> a mother's heart can feel.[22]

> What is the atonement of Christ? It is Himself: it is the
> inherent and everlasting mercy of God made apparent to
> human eyes and ears. The everlasting love was disclosed by
> our Lord's life and death. It showed that God forgives,
> because He loves to forgive. He works by smiles if possible,
> if not by frowns; pain is only a means of enforcing love.[23]

Livingstone too endured pain. He so loved the African that
he was prepared to suffer incredible hardships. His interest
in life was not just amassing information about rivers and
natural history, but also bringing to bear upon the heathen
the fraternal spirit of the gospel of Christ: 'The spirit of
Missions is the Spirit of our Master: the very genius of His
religion. A diffusive philanthropy is Christianity itself. It
requires perpetual propagation to attest its genuineness.'[24]

---

[21] *Ibid*, 1873, p 276.
[22] *Ibid*, 1872, pp 228–229.
[23] *Ibid*, p 228.
[24] *Ibid*, p 246.

Livingstone's goals were to open the door for missionary expansion to take place and the cessation of the slave-trade. He wrote to his brother in Canada saying:

> If the good Lord permits me to put a stop to the enormous evils of the inland slave-trade, I shall not grudge my hunger and toils. I shall bless His name with all my heart. The Nile sources are valuable to me only as a means of enabling me to open my mouth with power among men. It is this power I hope to apply to remedy an enormous evil, and join my poor little helping hand in the enormous revolution that in His all-embracing Providence He has been carrying on for ages, and is now actually helping forward. Men may think I covet fame, but I make it a rule never to read aught written in my praise.[25]

The progress of the sodden crew was slow, and suspicious tribesmen also tried their patience. Almost in desperation Livingstone penned this on his sixtieth birthday: 'Can I hope for ultimate success? So many obstacles have arisen. Let not Satan prevail over me, Oh! my good Lord Jesus.'[26]

One headman promised to hire Livingstone canoes, but continually hedged and procrastinated although a deal had been struck. The men were getting desperate and Livingstone noticed that his meekness was seen as a weakness. Frustrated, he pulled out his pistol and calmly discharged one bullet through the roof of the grass hut. The remaining canoes were quickly promised and promptly produced.

They paddled out trying desperately to reach dry land as the merciless rain persisted. The tent was torn and was of no use; the situation was getting desperate. On 25th March 1873 he wrote, determinedly, 'Nothing earthly will make me give up my work in despair. I encourage myself in the Lord my God, and go forward.'[27] From 31st March to 10th April

---

[25] D L to Charles L in Blaikie, p 444.
[26] LJ II 1873, p 287.
[27] *Ibid*, p 289.

Livingstone had been bleeding profusely: 'An artery gives off a copious stream, and takes away my strength. Oh, how I long to be permitted by the Over Power to finish my work.'[28]

Susi, Chumah and the rest of the crew were worried seeing the change in the doctor's condition. On land they noted that he walked wearily, lead-legged, almost fainting, and frequent stops were essential. Finally they persuaded Livingstone to allow himself to be carried.

Despite his ailing condition he continued to make observations—the vegetation, the terrain, the characteristics of the Fish Eagle's cry. He even recorded the rainfall.

Although they were out of the marshes and on dry land the rain persisted, and streams had to be crossed. Livingstone rode on the one surviving donkey—the beast of burden whose finest hour was when it carried Christ into Jerusalem a week before his death.

In a classic understatement Livingstone wrote: 'I am excessively weak . . . It is not all pleasure this exploration.'[29]

He held a service that Sunday, though he was hardly able to stand. The next day he tried to ride the donkey, but had only gone a short distance when he fell to the ground, utterly exhausted. Susi immediately undid Livingstone's belt and pistol and picked up his cap, while Chumah ran to stop the men ahead. When he came back Livingstone asked to be carried, as he had no more strength left in his legs.

The next day they made him a kitanda—a bed made of wooden branches covered with grass which hung under a long pole held between two strong men. They carried him over saturated grasslands to the next village where Chief Kalufanjofu extended the doctor his utmost help. Livingstone was still determined to go forward, and this meant they had to cross

---

[28] *Ibid*, p 294.
[29] *Ibid*, p 297.

a river. Unable even to walk to the door they had to break the side off the grass hut to take him out without pain. They carried him in the kitanda and placed his 'bed' in the bottom of the strongest canoe and tried to lift him into it, but he could not bear the pain of a hand being pressed on his back. Beckoning to Chumah, he asked him in a faint voice to stoop down so that he could clasp his hands around his neck and be lifted that way into the canoe.

Slowly they crossed the river and Susi rushed ahead to Chief Chitambo's village where he superintended the building of another house. Livingstone lay on the canoe, pain racking his body and hardly able to lift his head. He asked for water to quench his thirst; Susi had thoughtfully sent some fresh water back.

When they reached the village he was laid under a tree while they finished constructing his hut. Many locals gathered silently around him in the drizzling rain; they had great respect for this man.

Inside his hut a bed was built above the floor with sticks and grass. Bales and boxes were brought inside and one was placed next to the bed to be used as a crude table. Livingstone was lifted up onto the bed and a young lad, Majwara, slept just within the hut to attend to Livingstone's needs if he called.

At nightfall the men silently took to their huts while others mounted watch around the fire.

Susi tended to Livingstone, remembering to wind his watch, and brought him boiling water and calomel which he placed next to the lonely flickering candle.

It must have been about 4 am when Susi heard Majwara's step once more. 'Come to Bwana, I am afraid; I don't know if he is alive.' Susi quickly called Chumah, Chowpere, Matthew and Muanyasere. The six men went immediately to the hut.

Passing inside they looked towards the bed. Dr Livingstone was not lying on it, but appeared to be engaged in prayer, and they instinctively drew backwards for the instant. Pointing to him, Majwara said, 'When I lay down he was just as he is now, and

it is because I find that he does not move that I fear he is dead.'
They asked the lad how long he had slept. Majwara said he could
not tell, but he was sure that it was some considerable time: the
men drew nearer.

A candle stuck by its own wax to the top of the box shed a
light sufficient for them to see his form. Dr Livingstone was
kneeling by the side of his bed, his body stretched forward, his
head buried in his hands upon the pillow. For a minute they
watched him: he did not stir, there was no sign of breathing; then
one of them, Matthew, advanced softly to him and placed his
hands to his cheeks. It was sufficient; life had been extinct some
time, and the body was almost cold: Livingstone was dead.

His sad-hearted servants raised him tenderly up, and laid him
full length on the bed, then, carefully covering him, they went out
into the damp night air to consult together.[30]

Like so many of the world's spiritual pioneers, and
especially his divine Master Jesus Christ, Livingstone had
given his life to the outworking of his conviction. The hour
of passing was dark, the forces of evil apparently triumphant,
but a victory, unbeknown to Livingstone and his faithful
followers, had been won.

The men loved Livingstone. He had given his life for them
and their fellow Africans. They too would shortly make a
decision whereby they could risk losing their lives for him.

---

[30]*Ibid*, p 308. This was written by Horace Waller on evidence supplied by
Susi and Chumah.

22
Lessons in Love

Before daylight the men in each hut were quietly told what had happened, and that they were to assemble. As light was breaking Susi and Chumah said they wished everybody to be present while the boxes were opened. Jacob Wainwright (who could write) was given the task of opening Livingstone's personal chests. He wrote: 'In the chest was found about a shilling and a half, and in other chest his hat, 1 watch and 2 small boxes of measuring instrument, and in each box there was one compass, 3 other kind of measuring instrument. 4 other kind of measuring instrument. And in other chest 3 drachmas and half half scrople'. (sic)[1]

Those items, aside from his Bible, diary and a few other items of clothing, were about all that Livingstone possessed.

The men knew the superstitious traits of the local tribes concerning the dead, for if a traveller died in a village there were serious consequences for those who brought him. Notably heavy fines. After some consultation they amazingly agreed that the body should be borne to the coast and not removed to a safe location and just buried.

A plan was made and Chief Chitambo was visited. He was asked to give permission for them to build accommodation away from the village. This was consented to.

Unfortunately, later on that day two of the party went into

---

[1] LJ II 1873, p 312.

the village and told some people the news. This ultimately brought Chief Chitambo to the village to ask why he hadn't been informed. Thankfully, instead of being angry, he had a compassionate heart and told the men not to fear. On hearing this they divulged their plan—to take the body all the way to Zanzibar. The chief said it was an impossible task. Tribesmen did not like people dying in the villages, let alone being carried through. Furthermore, it would mean a journey of over 1,500 miles over unbearable terrain and through touchy tribes.

None the less, they were resolute in their decision. The villagers adorned themselves in mourning attire and assembled to pay their last respects to Livingstone.

Livingstone died on 1st May 1873 at the age of sixty, and the next day a small service was held. Farijala, a member of the expedition, had been a doctor's assistant in Zanzibar and therefore knew a little about post-mortem procedures. (This itself was no coincidence.)

The heart, along with the other organs, was removed discreetly and placed in a small flour tin. This was decently and reverently buried under a Mpundu tree.[2] Jacob then read the burial service to everyone.

The reality of the scene touched many and they 'cried a good deal'.[3] Through the toil and strife of battling against hostile elements, tribes and terrain, a link had been forged between Livingstone and his followers. The journey back to the coast was the crowning proof of the love he inspired.

The body was preserved with salt and brandy. It was dried in a special enclosure constructed for that purpose, and finally wrapped in a shirt Agnes had sent her father. It was then covered in calico, the legs being bent at the knees to shorten the package so as to remove all suspicion when passing through hostile territory. The corpse was then wrapped in

[2] Ransford, p 306.
[3] *Ibid.*

bark, a crude coffin, which in turn was covered with sailcloth, sewn securely to a pole and then tarred.

Before parting from Chief Chitambo, they gave him a present of a large tin biscuit box and some newspapers to serve as evidence that a white man had been to his village, and an inscription was carved into the tree above the grave.

The procession of the body to the coast would mark the longest in history if completed and was not without its dangers. Through forests, swamps, rivers and ravines they forged their way back to Lake Tanganyika and then on to Unyanyembe (Tabora). Sickness plagued many members of the cortege, which as a result was halted for over a month. Ten men died during the march and many more were close to losing their lives when they had to fight their way out of a hostile village.

Generally many villages took them to be a trading party. Arabs near Nsama'a guessed their secret and strangely, respecting all that Livingstone stood for, turned out to fire a salute in his honour.[4] As the cortege trekked back to Zanzibar they were not aware of the amazing turn of events which had occurred in Britain since Stanley's visit.

*   *   *   *

Stanley's arrival in Britain a year prior to Livingstone's death had created a storm. The British were embarrassed that a loud-mouthed American journalist had beaten them in their search for Livingstone. Initially they scorned Stanley, but the facts worried many people; the slave-trade may have been stopped in Britain, but it was continuing in Africa, particularly on the east coast. The Queen's speech drew the attention of Parliament to the slave-trade, while Livingstone's description of the massacre in Manyuema horrified many. A Royal

---

[4] *Ibid*, p 308.

Commission, and then a Select Committee of the House of Commons, prepared the way for further action. Sir Bartle Frere was sent to Zanzibar for the purpose of negotiating a treaty with the Sultan. Finally, only a month after Livingstone's death in 1873, an agreement was reached between Dr Kirk, the British Consul and the Sultan. The cunning Sultan found a loophole in the treaty. In the agreement, sending slaves over the sea was taboo, but nothing was mentioned concerning the passage of slaves overland, so it was stepped up, increasing the suffering of the poor souls. The British shortly discovered this and the slave-trade overland was stopped. This in effect dealt the death blow to the horrendous traffic in humans. Livingstone's prayers had been answered. Sadly he was not alive to see it.

The British press had taken up Livingstone's cause and attacked the British Government for having abandoned Livingstone, thus requiring Stanley and then the expedition (which had included Livingstone's son) to search for him. The Foreign Office was castigated for meanness and indifference to the fate of one of Britain's greatest men. In over seven years Livingstone had only been sent an additional £1,000 by the Government, on top of its original mean £500. In comparison, Stanley's sponsored expedition cost £4,000. The government argued it had also given £1,200 to the search party sent out in 1867; but the fact remained: Livingstone had been badly treated.

With Stanley and the press focusing so much attention on the solitary Scot, public opinion soon rose to the question of Livingstone's latest whereabouts. Two expeditions were despatched to search for him: one from the west coast up to the Congo, and the other to the east coast.

Little did anyone know that his remains were being affectionately carried back across Africa by those who had the highest regard for him, the extent of which we shall possibly never know. In Unyanyembe (Tabora) the cortege met a group of Englishmen who were leading out the

Livingstone relief party from the east coast. It was one of two financed by Livingstone's friend Mr Young. Young was deeply concerned for Livingstone's safety, knowing how he was hated by the slavers, and the new chain of events regarding the cessation of the slave-trade would surely bring the Scot's life into jeopardy.

Lieutenant Cameron, who led the expedition from the east coast, used all his influence in order to persuade the loyal entourage merely to bury the body there, leaving Livingstone in Africa. He warned them of the dangers in the country that lay further on. But they were adamant. 'No! No! very big man, cannot bury here,'[5] was their answer.

Cameron, though an officer, was no better than a common thief, for he ordered the men to give over Livingstone's instruments. These were never returned.

Further on near Kasekera they met tribesmen from Unyanyembe (Tabora) who were opposed to the body being transported through their territory, so they secretly removed the bark surrounding the corpse and buried the bark in a hut in a thicket and then wrapped the remains in a cloth to resemble an ordinary travelling bale. Information that they were to bury Livingstone in Unyanyembe was spread around for all to hear. They then packed a 'mock coffin' and six men from the cortege, complete with a paper folder to imitate a letter in a cleft stick, ostentatiously carried the corpse for burial out of the public's eye. They secretly disposed of the 'coffin' and covertly rejoined the rest of the crew, whereupon they marched on.

After travelling a further ten months they reached the coast and arrived in Bagamoio, which means 'lay down the burden of your heart'. This they did literally and surrendered Livingstone to the British Consul from Zanzibar.

Like their master they too were shabbily treated. At great

[5] Macnair, p 358.

personal risk they had brought the body of a man, whom they supposed to be famous in his own country, to the coast and were merely thanked and sent away with their wages. For Chumah, Susi and Gardner it was a shocking end to eight years' service.

Jacob Wainwright accompanied the body back to Britain. He was sponsored by the mission school who had taught him to write. Susi and Chumah were later brought over to Britain by Sir James Young to assist in the final editing of Livingstone's last journals.

Livingstone would not have been surprised that his followers did not receive any reward whatsoever from the government; it would have been another incident to add to his long list of disappointments.

Aside from a few articles which accompanied the body back to Britain the remainder were auctioned off for £3. Yet a further blunder made by the British Consulate.

News of Livingstone's death preceded him and preparations were in hand to give him a State funeral. It is ironic that a man who saw so much failure in his life should have had such mighty influence upon the lives of so many, particularly on his death.

The darkest moments in his life wrought the greatest victories. The massacre in Manyuema prevented him searching for the possible link to the Nile. If he had regarded the search for the great river to be of more importance than the need to stop the slave-trade then Livingstone might well have turned a blind eye to the tragedy. Instead it broke him; all he could do was tell the world, which he did, and it racked the conscience of the nation to become the biggest victory for his cause. He never knew this. Dispirited and lonely in heart, he died an heroic death in the middle of Africa. His sacrifice inspired many to 'count their lives but nothing for the cause of Christ'.

He was classified a failed evangelist in terms of souls won for Christ. Some biographers today even say that he converted only one soul. This is erroneous. Wakatani, the porter whom Livingstone reunited with his family near Lake Nyasa, was later witnessed by able-seaman Young singing a bedtime hymn and praying; evidence that he was a Christian.

Many of Livingstone's porters went on to work in mission stations. In 1991 the author received this testimony on Matthew Wellington from his great-great-granddaugher, herself a committed Christian living in Kenya.

Matthew Wellington lived to be 85 or 105 years. He was baptized and later sent to India for studies. He learned a physician's work, sewing, cooking, carpentry, laundry and building.

At the age of 30 years, a young man, he started travelling with David Livingstone. They were about sixty people.

This Matthew was used to saying: 'Fear God and work diligently.' Since he knew the work of a physician, he was able to operate on the body of David Livingstone. After the death of David Livingstone, he married in Zanzibar to a Christian girl.

I believe he is a man who had surrundered his life to Jesus. Every Sunday, he would sit by his house under a mango tree reading the Bible to all people passing by that road. That Mango tree is there to this day. He loved to read from the book of Isaiah 1:18—'come now and let us reason together, saith the Lord'.

In short, I believe he was born again and God may have prolonged his life. He died a very old man.

Livingstone's life influenced the beginning of many missions after his death. Livingstone's valedictory message was: 'It is [to be] hoped that on the African continent our deeds may in our children's day bear fruit worthy to be held in everlasting remembrance'.[6]

Lesser men may carp at his legacy. The greatness of any man is seen in his uniqueness. Livingstone was such a man. He lacked the grace to suffer fools gladly unless, of course,

---

[6] NAZ reference LI1/1/1, p 2009, in Ransford, p 311.

they happened to be weak, ignorant or unsophisticated; then his patience and benevolence were limitless.

Livingstone was more severe on himself than other people and was a rigorous censor of his own conduct and spiritual state. He had disciplined himself by the consistent exercise of a working faith in Christ so that grace grew out of his nature.

He always regretted not spending more time with his wife and their children. Mary's death saw him overwhelmed with sorrow; indeed his life took on greater sobriety since that sad day in Shupanga.

A further testimony of his greatness is remembered today. A missionary, Miss Shaw, recalled how a very old man described the time he first saw Livingstone (and possibly the last man on the Luapula River to have seen him). As a little boy he had seen the white man rounding the bend in a little dug-out canoe. 'The people scattered, climbed trees, the roofs of their houses. "He had fallen from the sky," they said. "He had clothing on his feet," the old man said excitedly. "I was a boy, I went near, I touched, but the headman pulled me back." "You'll be bewitched by his medicine," they said.'

The old man sat in long silence as he remembered his encounter with Livingstone. At last he said, as if to himself talking about Livingstone: 'He laughed, there was love in his eyes, he was not fierce'. Turning to Miss Shaw, with misty eyes he spoke through the silence. 'He made a path through our land, and you his followers have come, God's Light-bringers; and more come today'.[7]

Livingstone struggled and sowed in tears. There were rocks on what he believed to be God's highway, the Zambesi River, preventing his dream being realised. But still he did not give up. By the hand of God he provided another path which would grow into a highway as the gospel germinated. Africa would soon no longer be called the 'Dark Continent'.

---

[7] Journal letter of Miss Shaw, June 1928 in Campbell, pp 348–349.

Jesus Christ changed Simon's name to Peter, the rock on which he would build the church and the gates of Hades would not prevail against it. The young Scots lad, David, was one such 'spiritual descendant'. His life was testimony to the grace of God; he was a living stone.

As the boat docked in Southampton and the body was brought to London where it was positively identified and placed in a casket for the State funeral, many people pondered life. Livingstone is the only pauper to be buried in Westminster Abbey with full State honours.

At the service Canon Conway preached a sermon in which he said that 'the last resting place into which they lowered the remains of Dr Livingstone, was also his first'.

The epitaph included his prayer: 'All I can say in my solitude[8] is, may Heaven's rich blessing come down on every one—American, English, Turk—who will help to heal this open sore of the world.' And: 'Other sheep I have which are not of this fold, them also I must bring, and they shall hear my voice' (John 10:16).

Florence Nightingale said of him:

There are few enough, but a few statesmen. There are few enough, but a few great in medicine, or in art, or in poetry. There are few great travellers. But Dr Livingstone stood alone as the great Missionary Traveller, the bringer-in of civilization; or rather the pioneer of civilization—he that cometh before—to races lying in darkness. I always think of him as what John the Baptist, had he been living in the nineteenth century, would have been'.[9]

Livingstone's life so convicted James Stewart, the man who caused much bitterness and anxiety when he published articles on the Zambesi expedition, that he repented and went back to Africa to work on a mission station.

---

[8] Livingstone used the word 'loneliness'.
[9] Blaikie, p 458.

Livingstone gave his life trying to save the lost sheep. This same spirit that motivated him lives on; the Spirit of the Lord and Saviour controlling all things. Though Livingstone sowed in tears we, in yielding to Christ, may reap with joy.

BROUGHT BY FAITHFUL HANDS
OVER LAND AND SEA
HERE RESTS

DAVID LIVINGSTONE

MISSIONARY
TRAVELLER
PHILANTHROPIST
BORN MARCH 19. 1813.
AT BLANTYRE, LANARKSHIRE,
DIED MAY I. 1873.
AT CHITAMBO'S VILLAGE, ULALA:

FOR 30 YEARS HIS LIFE WAS SPENT
IN AN UNWEARIED EFFORT
TO EVANGELISE THE NATIVE RACES,
TO EXPLORE THE UNDISCOVERED SECRETS,
TO ABOLISH THE DESOLATING SLAVE TRADE.

OF CENTRAL AFRICA,

WHERE WITH HIS LAST WORDS HE WROTE,
"ALL I CAN ADD IN MY SOLITUDE, IS,
MAY HEAVEN'S RICH BLESSING COME DOWN
ON EVERY ONE, AMERICAN, ENGLISH, OR TURK,
WHO WILL HELP TO HEAL
THIS OPEN SORE OF THE WORLD."

"OTHER SHEEP I HAVE, WHICH ARE NOT OF THIS FOLD: THEM ALSO I MUST BRING, AND THEY SHALL HEAR MY VOICE."

"TANTUS AMOR VERI, NIHIL EST QUOD NOSCERE MALIM, QUAM FLUVII CAUSAS PER SÆCULA TANTA LATENTES."

Inscription on Livingstone's tomb

23
Epilogue

Livingstone's adventures seemed to be fruitless . . . at the time. His journal on Sunday June 19th 1853, eighteen years before his death, revealed no expectation of a spiritual harvest during his lifetime, but showed confident faith for the future. He wrote

> Another century must present a totally different aspect from the present . . . Future missionaries will be rewarded by conversions for every sermon. We are their pioneers and helpers. Let them not forget the watchmen of the night, we who worked when all was gloom and no evidence of success in the way of conversion cheered our path. They will doubtless have more light than we, but we served our Master earnestly and proclaimed the same Gospel as they will do.[1]

In fact few souls were won for the kingdom of God, despite tears of agony. Christ said,

> Behold I say to you, lift up your eyes, and look on the fields, that they are white for harvest. Already he who reaps is receiving wages, and is gathering fruit for life eternal; that he who sows and he who reaps may rejoice together. For in this case the saying is true, 'one sows and another reaps'. I sent you to reap that for which you have not laboured; others have laboured, and you have entered into their labours.[2]

---

[1] Sunday 19 June 1853 P J page 168
[2] John 4:36–38 NASB.

Africa had been for centuries the 'dark continent' until Livingstone beat a path through its impenetrable gloom, followed by many another intrepid worker. True, Africa became the grave of many of these that loved its peoples, but Livingstone's prophecy was to be fulfilled. Indeed even his vision to see mission stations established around Lake Nyasa was later accomplished.

Dr Edward Steere of the Universities' Mission to Central Africa succeeded Bishop Tozer (who closed down the mission after Bishop Mackenzie's death) and continued the work in Zanzibar. He trained up local Africans to evangelise and established a Gospel literature printing press.

In 1876 Steere led two missionaries and a large party of converts in a ten day walk inland towards Lake Nyasa. They established a settlement among the Masasi tribe. One of their first visitors was a man who had been set free by Bishop Mackenzie and Livingstone. He bought them a fowl—the best gift he had to offer.

Dr Steere returned to Zanzibar and sent John Swedi, an African, together with a missonary from England, Rev Porter, to help.

The Mission grew, but on 15th September 1882 four hundred Angoni warriors attacked the village, initially killing one man. Their aim was to kill the 'white man' and take his heart for a charm. Johnson and Maples were away, Porter was alone.

The missionary stood his ground and refused his men permission to arm themselves. A tense scene followed. The church was plundered and Rev Porter surrounded. The Angoni Chief, amazed that there was no resistance, listened to the missionary preach. The Chief's heart softened and he ordered all the items be restored to the church. Miraculously the marauders left the mission virtually intact, though for twelve days the Angoni warriors burnt and pillaged the neighbouring villages capturing, terrifying and killing many people.

With dauntless courage Rev Porter went repeatedly to the

Angoni's camp and bought as many of the prisioners with calico as the Chief would permit. These men he then set free.

When the Chief finally left the area he presented Porter with a blunt spear as a sign that the Angoni promised to never again attack a mission station. They kept their word.

With the death of Bishop Steere the vision to preach the gospel on the shores of Lake Nyasa was taken up by William Johnson who worked with such zeal that the Masasi nicknamed him 'the man who never sits down'.

Johnson had a lonely existence establishing another station nearer the lake, battling against famine and disease. In 1881 Rev Charles Janson joined him, though sadly not for long. They explored the region and finally reached the shores of Lake Nyasa, but Charles Janson succumbed to fever and died.

His death prompted Johnson to return to England where he rallied support for the missions. Men and women, as well as a launch for the lake were needed. The response was heart-warming. A boat—the *Charles Janson*—was built in Britain, taken apart and in three hundred and eighty packages transported to the lake. Godly men and women followed, gospel fires were once more lit among the hills surrounding Lake Nyasa and further inland. In time the harvest would be reaped.

Today, springing to life in the hearts of multitudes is a simple faith in Christ which is ousting the ancestral worship and its cultish mysticism. This continent of cultural and racial barriers is discovering the Christ who breaks them down and builds up a new order around himself.

Africa was already showing fruit at the beginning of this twentieth century with maybe two million people acknowledging Christ, but as the century closes that figure has been multiplied by one hundred, though often Christian profession is only nominal. The coming of the Pentecostal-charismatic movement has had the greatest impact, with a stream of

Spirit-baptised men and women devoting themselves to Africa and, serving God in a hundred capacities. It is not possible to name all these men and women, some of whom have actually laid down their lives for Christ, but perhaps we can mention a few.

Among Pentecostal pioneers there were such notables as W F P Burton and James Salter, joined by men like Teddy Hodgson, who was martyred during the Congo revolution while carrying medical supplies for his African converts. They founded the (then) Congo Evangelistic Mission and saw a thousand churches planted. One lone missionary took the gospel to Ghana fifty years ago and began a work that has expanded to over four thousand churches by 1991. And so it goes on, a tale of triumphs—often unheralded and unsung—of people who shine as stars in the skies in the eyes of God.

My own personal experience has given me first-hand knowledge of one of the most remarkable lovers of Africa, whose work has exceeded anything of its kind ever seen before as he has explored new ways of reaching out to the four hundred and fifty million people of his chosen territory. I refer to the German evangelist Reinhard Bonnke. Livingstone and Bonnke seem to have special bonds. The heart of a missionary is a mystery to those who in materialistic blindness are oblivious of the call of the needy and the love of Christ. In attempting to give readers an insight into the ancient passion, spirit and psychology of such servants of God, I can do no better than to outline the story of this one modern recruit in the noble army of God, one hundred and twenty five years apart from Livingstone, yet hand in hand with him.

I lift my curtain on that epic to reveal a mother with six children fleeing from a burning city. It is 1945. Mrs Bonnke had dragged her frightened brood from their beds in the middle of the night as aircraft targeted bombs on the three hundred and fifty thousand people of Konigsberg, capital of East Prussia. The Russian armies were closing in on the doom of Hitler's Germany. Taking what belongings they could carry the family ventured out into the streets. Sirens wailed, and blazing shops and homes were engulfed in an inferno of destruction. One of those children was Reinhard, five years old.

At the main road Mrs Bonnke desperately waved her arms in an effort to obtain a lift with one of the military trucks which trundled past. Finally one stopped and, despite the driver's protest that there was only room for three, the family of six squeezed in.

When the truck could transport them no further Mrs Bonnke and the children struggled on foot for several days, tired and hungry, until they managed to get another lift. Their escape route was across the frozen Haff Sea—a treacherous route, as the ice was starting to thaw. With difficulty they made the hazardous crossing and headed for the port of Danzig (Gdansk today) where they hoped to catch a refugee boat to Denmark. Behind them the frozen sea was bombed and many lost their lives in the icy waters.

The Bonnkes managed to embark on a coal ship which, packed with refugees, stole across the Baltic sea towards Denmark. On several occasions they survived attacks by aircraft, but only to have the hull holed by a mine. Pumps struggled to keep the boat afloat, prayers were offered, and somehow they were able to keep going until the coast came into view.

Mrs Bonnke and her children lived as refugees in Denmark for three and a half years. Her husband was a prisoner of war, and it was not until 1948 that the family were reunited in Gluckstadt.

Although both his parents were Christians, Reinhard at the age of nine had other thoughts, one of which money—and money was a novelty. As refugees they had not seen any currency, and now that this amazing commodity was available Reinhard took to helping himself from his mother's purse and nipping out to the sweet shop.

One day she caught him and Reinhard expected to receive

a thrashing. Instead his mother, who regularly disciplined her children, looked at him in horror. She put her arm around Reinhard and with tears in her eyes said, 'Do you know where you are going, Reinhard? You are on your way to hell.'

A tremendous conviction of sin swept over him as he saw his lost soul heading for eternity in hell. There and then he cried out to God for forgiveness and, led by his mother in prayer, gave his life to Jesus Christ.

From then on, young as he was, life took on a new meaning and Reinhard fell in love with his new-found Saviour while his father, now a pastor, eagerly guided his enthusiastic son. Almost at once his great vision came. Youthful games paled in significance as young Reinhard realised that the Lord had a great work for him—he would be a missionary. He practised preaching in boyish style. The trees in the forest became members of his make-believe congregation as Reinhard, with a young friend, preached to them.

The prayer meeting was also a place of great excitement to him and the youngster eagerly tried to attend them all. Cautions were given by his now concerned parents who were worried by his over-zealousness.

During one small meeting in the little village of Suderau, an old faithful member, Mrs Olga Jess, stood up. She declared that she had seen a vision of a young boy breaking bread (ministering the emblems of Holy Communion) before thousands of black people. She then turned to Reinhard, who stood next to his father, and announced: 'This is the boy I saw in the vision.'

This incident further encouraged Reinhard, who was being mocked by family and friends. They called him the 'little missionary'. Undeterred, he was all the more determined to accomplish what he believed to be a God-given goal.

Not satisfied with his state before God Reinhard urged his parents to allow him to be baptised. This suggestion they did not accept too warmly. They felt Reinhard was getting rather carried away with his enthusiasm. Besides, he was too young to take such a bold display of faith. Finally, however, they relented and Reinhard was baptised.

But still he wanted more. Frustration gripped his heart and mind. He read the book of Acts in the Bible where a conversation Jesus Christ held with his disciples is recorded. The Lord declared to them that after his ascension they would be 'baptised with the Holy Spirit' . . . 'You shall receive power when the Holy Spirit has come upon you; and you shall be My witnesses . . .'[3] This was fulfilled on the day of Pentecost. The disciples were 'filled with the Holy Spirit and began to speak with other tongues, as the Spirit was giving them utterance'[4]—a phenomenon that has stirred and excited the hearts of many saints throughout the centuries.

In recent years, as if in fulfilment of another Biblical prophecy (Joel 2:28), 'In latter days I shall pour out my Spirit upon all mankind . . .', many Christians have experienced for themselves this wonderful outpouring.

Reinhard's mother had prayed for years that she might receive this blessing, but to no avail. Until one night, sitting up in her bed during a time of prayer, she felt a mighty presence of the Lord in the room. The peace that passes all understanding swept over her heart as God by his Holy Spirit answered her prayers and baptised her in the Holy Spirit.

The next day, while everyone was seated at the breakfast table, she told the children of her wonderful experience, similar to that spoken of in the Bible. Reinhard's heart leapt with excitement. 'Did you speak in another language?' he asked.

'Yes'.

'Was there fire on the top of your head?' the young lad eagerly questioned.

---

[3] Acts 1:8 NASB.
[4] Acts 2:4 NASB.

'No', came the damping reply. Reinhard resumed his breakfast.

This experience filled his mother with an even greater sense of joy and peace. Reinhard longed for that blessing and he was not disappointed. A year later, in their small church, at the age of eleven, he was baptised in the Holy Spirit.

This boosted his faith and fuelled his enthusiasm to accomplish great deeds for God. Encouraged by his father, Reinhard devoured Christian literature; reading stories of great Christian men from Hudson Taylor to Charles Wesley. One book in particular had a mighty impact on his life: 'A Passion for Souls' by Oswald Smith. He read it through several times as the passion to win lost souls gripped his heart. The seeds that were to make Reinhard Bonnke an evangelist were firmly implanted in his soul and spirit. But before he could venture out into the world to fulfil his commission, he had to go through Bible college. He set his heart on attending an evangelical missionary college in Swansea, Wales, much to the disappointment of his German friends. As he spoke no English the college refused him entry, but this decision was reversed on the advice of Rev Morris, a friend of the family, who knew the Principal of the college. It was agreed that Reinhard would be given a chance.

He packed his belongings and headed for Wales. Reinhard soon learned English, and the solid evangelical teachings were further to cement his faith in God. The teachers did not draw a salary—they 'trusted God' to provide their income. It seemed rather a risky course, yet Reinhard Bonnke was amazed to see their prayers being answered, although no one ever begged. They simply believed God would provide and he did. Gradually Reinhard also lived by this principle—if he saw a need and felt the prompting of the Lord to give then he gave, knowing that when he himself had a need God would provide for him.

In 1961, at the age of twenty-one, Reinhard had completed the course and he returned to Germany. On his journey home he had a day to spare in London so he wandered the streets of the city.

While walking he noticed a name on a panel—'George Jeffreys'. He was one of the greatest British evangelists since Charles Wesley. Jeffreys was converted in the 1904–1906 Welsh revival. His ministry from 1912 saw many healed both spiritually and physically and he also founded the Elim Church movement. Inquisitively the young Bonnke walked up the steps and knocked on the door. The housekeeper opened the door, but would not allow Bonnke to enter the house. From another room a deep musical Welsh voice called 'Let him come in'.

Excitedly Reinhard met the elderly evangelist and they talked about the work of God. Suddenly this frail man of seventy-two years fell on his knees, pulling Reinhard down with him. He placed his hands upon Reinhard's head and prayed for him, and an amazing sense of the presence of God filled the room. Peace tinged with power and excitement flooded into Reinhard's heart. Waves of blessing flooded over him—it was as if he were being anointed from on high.

This was no ordinary meeting, and it had a profound effect upon Reinhard Bonnke. Several weeks later George Jeffreys died and 'passed on to glory'. Could it have been the transferring of a great mantle from one evangelist to another?

Up to 1964 Reinhard based himself at his father's church where he was kept busy fulfilling preaching engagements throughout Europe. When he preached, people previously hardened to the gospel gave their lives to God. More invitations followed from pastors eager to employ the services of this tall, well-built young man who had the gifting of an evangelist.

Bonnke wanted to go to Africa but needed experience, so he decided to start and to pastor his own church. He moved to Flensburg, where he knew no one, and with a friend pitched a tent and for six weeks held crusade meetings. At night Reinhard curled up and slept in his little Volkswagon Beetle car. During the crusade fifty people gave their hearts to God and received further counselling from Reinhard. The church was started and continued to grow.

It was during this time at a youth meeting that he met Anni, the young German lady who was to become his wife. She was a practical person whose love for the mission field further attracted her suitor. They were married on 20th November 1964 in Flensburg, and two years later they were blessed with the birth of their first son, Freddy. By then the call to Africa had become a reality. Plans were underway to travel to South Africa as missionaries. Another pastor would look after the church in Flensburg and the Bonnkes would travel out by ship.

At the end of May 1967 the Bonnke family arrived at the port of Durban in South Africa. Freddy was then only seven months old and Anni, being four months pregnant, had suffered considerably throughout the voyage.

Reinhard Bonnke was now twenty-seven years old (interestingly, the same age as Livingstone when he arrived in Africa) and the challenge of being an evangelist in Africa lay before him. They had come to an unsettled continent plagued with problems, yet with the belief that nothing was too difficult for God. God had already placed a burden to win souls for the kingdom of heaven in Reinhard and Anni's hearts.

Then followed a frustrating twelve months as Reinhard had to submit to the standard missionary church constitution whereby he was required to study under local pastors for a year before being sent out. Gabi, their first daughter, was born in Ermelo, a town in the Transvaal, and within a short while the Bonnkes moved to Ladybrand, near the border of Lesotho, a region which had a large population of rural Africans.

Reinhard visited Maseru, a town in Lesotho, and it was here that he felt the tremendous call of God to move and work among the poor, unsophisticated people.

In 1969 Susi, their third child, was born. Reinhard received permission to establish a work for God in Maseru. No time was lost and in May they moved home.

Reinhard, with his rough, deep German voice, took his accordion and sang choruses and hymns on the street corner as the people gathered to listen to the white man. He went on to hold gospel meetings—often four a day—his heart eager to introduce the African people to their Saviour.

Church services were sparsely attended. If fifty people came he thought 'revival had broken out'. Anni Bonnke held meetings for the ladies, teaching them knitting as well as basic Bible principles. Gradually the work grew, but the pace was too slow for Reinhard whose desire was to reach Africa for Christ, not merely Maseru.

He started a small basic Bible correspondence course, offering diplomas to the students who completed it. That brought in a huge response and the enlistment grew to several hundred and then to thousands.

Bicycles were bought, and young pastors with a thirst to win souls for God were put into service taking the gospel into villages in the surrounding areas. Even horses were used to enable the evangelists to reach formerly inaccessible areas. Yet still Bonnke was far from satisfied.

One afternoon while visiting some pastors outside Maseru, Reinhard drank some water which had not been boiled. That night at home he fell violently ill, and what appeared to be a bout of dysentery escalated into a frightening fever. He lay in bed exhausted, slipping into fits of delirium. At his bedside Anni prayed, together with fellow African pastors. The message went out across Lesotho 'The Moruti is sick. Pray for him.'

On the third day Bonnke experienced a strange vision. His eyes were open and he saw a black blanket floating downwards to cover him. Instinctively he knew what the blanket meant—death. Suddenly it was is as if he could see through the blanket and on the other side there was the face of the Lord Jesus. Despite his delirious condition a soothing comfort swept over him and he became aware of someone praying for him. He recognised the voice as that of Mrs Eliese Kohler, a dear member of his father's church in Germany. She was nowhere near Lesotho, yet he was aware of her praying, agonising in soul, crying, pleading with God.

The vision of the blanket faded, and almost immediately the fever subsided, though it was several weeks before he was strong enough to write about his experience to his father. His father's reply confirmed that the vision Reinhard saw was not a mere illusion. Mrs Kohler had, on the same day as Reinhard saw the vision, spent hours in prayer interceding for his very life; wrestling with God in prayer until she became sure that Reinhard was safe.

This had a major impact on Reinhard Bonnke. He now appreciated the mighty power of prayer. Later, as his desire to see Africa won for Jesus Christ grew, he would employ those whose function in the team would be to wrestle 'against the world forces of this darkness, against the spiritual forces of wickedness in the heavenly places.'[5]

A real turning point in his ministry came when he invited a visiting evangelist to preach in Maseru. This man with an anointed ministry would, he felt sure, almost certainly shake the people out of their lethargy. He would pray for the sick, and the combination of righteous prayers and their faith would see many healings take place.

The evangelist was to preach on Saturday and Sunday. The church was packed to capacity. Reinhard believed the breakthrough he so desperately wanted was near. The superstitious minds of those who trusted in witchcraft would see what the Lord Jesus Christ could do.

The evangelist preached a short message and then asked Pastor Bonnke to close the meeting. Flabbergasted that he had not prayed for the sick Reinhard spoke to him and then agreed, on condition that the visitor prayed on Sunday.

Next day Reinhard hurried around to see the evangelist and

---

[5] Ephesians 6:12 NASB.

to his horror saw him about to get into a waiting car. Reinhard challenged him. The church was full to capacity, the man couldn't leave. Calmly the reply came: the evangelist believed he had heard God, by his Spirit, telling him to go.

Reinhard checked himself. This was different. He waved goodbye and climbed back into his own car. He was upset and cried out to God: 'I am not a big name preacher, I am just a missionary, one of your little men, but now I will preach at this meeting and you will do the miracles.'

Reinhard stopped his car outside the church and stepped out. He called the African pastors together and explained the story. 'God will do the miracles', he stated boldly yet with some trepidation in his heart.

When Reinhard began to preach he did so with all the boldness he could muster. Suddenly he became aware of the presence of God in the room in a powerful degree. His interpreter broke down in the middle of the message, sinking to the floor with tears pouring down his face—the presence and power of God was almost tangible. As Reinhard waited for the interpreter to regain his composure an incredible thought flashed across his mind. It was as if God was saying 'My words in your mouth are just as powerful as my words in my mouth.' Suddenly Reinhard Bonnke realised the responsibility God was giving him to proclaim the word of God and pray for the sick.

Blind people came forward; they were prayed for by Pastor Bonnke and the other Pastors. Suddenly one person exclaimed, 'I can see! I can see!' A miracle had taken place. The crowd, stunned at this amazing display of God's power, stood in awe. Applause broke out—not for Reinhard Bonnke or his team, but God.

The meeting lasted several hours, and when it was over Reinhard Bonnke went quietly to a corner of the church and prayed a prayer of thanks.

But still he was not satisfied. Miracles were wonderful but they could not guarantee eternal life in heaven; only the forgiveness of Christ sweeping over the soul of a sinner could do that.

The Bible correspondence school was still in operation with an enrolment now of approximately fifty thousand students. Financially this put great demands on Reinhard Bonnke's faith; he was not one to beg for money, but believed that God, who knew his needs, would prompt people to give.

The monthly office rent was only thirty dollars but one month he was unable to raise the cash, although he prayed all day for the money to come. In the evening, disheartened, he walked home, pondering over the problem, ignoring the bustling crowds of people and wrestling with God in silent prayer. Suddenly, in the middle of the dirt road, the power and presence of the Lord came upon him. He 'heard' a voice in his heart—'Do you want me to give you one million dollars?'

If God wanted to give Reinhard Bonnke one million dollars surely he could bombard the whole world with the Gospel! Then another thought struck him, and with tears running from his eyes he cried, 'No, Lord, don't give me one million dollars. I want more than that. God give me one million souls. One million souls less in hell and one million more in heaven—that shall be the purpose of my life.' Then the Holy Spirit quietly spoke into Reinhard Bonnke's heart words that he had never heard before: 'You will plunder hell and populate heaven for Calvary's sake.' That day a new determination gripped him.

With this renewed surge of determination Reinhard decided to expand his horizons. By the end of 1974 the Bonnkes had settled on the outskirts of Johannesburg. The sprawling suburb of Soweto was home to hundreds of thousands of poor African folk. They desperately needed to hear the good news of Jesus Christ. With the move came the launching of another dream—Christ for all Nations. Reinhard Bonnke by the grace of God would form a team to reach multitudes for Jesus Christ.

In 1975 a 'bicycle strategy,' was devised. One hundred bicycles fitted with large box carriers on the front went from house to house in Soweto. Gospel literature was distributed and the cyclists gave their testimony as to how they met Jesus and how they prayed for the sick. This venture took a lot of prayer. A businessman offered to give Reinhard Bonnke the money for the bicycles and they were ordered. Then the shock came; the businessman was broke and had withdrawn his offer. Reinhard Bonnke could not cancel the contract—he had to trust God. Slowly the money came in and miraculously, by the time the last bicycle was received, funds were there to pay for it.

As gospel work continued in Soweto and Reinhard Bonnke spent more time preaching in local churches, another challenge faced him—Botswana, a nation to the north-west of South Africa with a large population. Initially he went to buy some air time on the local radio station but as the Botswana Pastors were keen to have a gospel crusade, Reinhard Bonnke jumped at the opportunity, confident they should hire a stadium. The Pastors, however, considered he would have a struggle to fill even the City Hall. As a compromise the City Hall was booked for a few nights with the final three nights of crusade meetings being held at the stadium.

At the first meeting the hall was virtually empty, yet several deaf and blind people were miraculously healed during the preaching. Curiosity gripped many and the next evening the hall was filled to capacity.

More people were miraculously healed, attracting more crowds wanting to witness for themselves the power of Jesus Christ.

From the start Bonnke had to be careful not to emphasise healing above the preaching of the gospel. The Christ for all Nations team primarily preached salvation to men and women in slavery to sin.

Reinhard Bonnke was quick to point out the need for caution regarding the seeking of the miraculous for the sake of seeing spectacles:

'God is a consuming fire. He is all love, a furnace burning for his creatures. Whenever we carry the gospel, it must be because we care. We are not to heal for the sake of seeing a wonder. God is not in show business. He didn't come to earth to make a name for himself. If he did, his audience only made a nail for him . . . Our own motives must be his. The love of God shed in our hearts by the Holy Spirit makes it possible. He loves us to love others.'[6]

At one gospel meeting an elderly woman, her ebony face wrinkled and worn by the harshness of her life, stood in line for prayer. She had no sight – her eyeballs were missing. After prayer tears filled the sockets and trickled down her dusty face. 'I see, I see, I see,' she whispered quietly. Reinhard Bonnke turned and asked her what she could see: 'I cannot see you. But I see a white cross and I see Jesus there.'

The gospel meetings continued, gaining momentum and size throughout southern Africa. As pastors saw the benefit of inviting a visiting evangelist into their area so they united, crossing denominational barriers. Pre-crusade planning became a vital key so that those who gave their lives to Christ could be placed into churches. Counsellors were taught procedures in how to 'follow up' after meetings so that all new Christians would continue to grow in Christ.

1976 saw the completion of the Soweto outreach—the final crusade was held in Swaziland with the Swaziland royal family attending the meetings.

Working alongside Pastor Bonnke were many faithful believers. One evanglist, Pastor Ngidi, took time away from his home in the Natal region to preach with Bonnke. Then another man joined the team, Michael Kolisang, a former zealous supporter of a local political party in Lesotho. He had been interested in this white man who had played a piano accordion, sang religious songs and preached an enthusiastic gospel message at the local bus-stop in Maseru.

---

[6] Bonnke page 125.

Michael Kolisang shrugged off his political ambitions as a deeper fire burned within his heart. Reinhard Bonnke likewise steered clear of the political arena and if questioned would reply, 'We are part of the solution, not the problem.'

The challenge of introducing the love of Jesus Christ to men who found themselves sinking in a sea of hatred, both racial and tribal, became ever more apparent.

Christ for all Nations had acquired a small tent, but the tent rapidly became totally inadequate. A much larger one for ten thousand people was considered; the only drawback being the cost. After pondering the matter in prayer Reinhard Bonnke received a further word from the Lord: 'Don't plan with that which is in your own pockets. Plan with that which is in my pocket.' In Reinhard Bonnke's pocket were a few copper coins; God would have to provide the rest. With a boldness that surprised even himself, Reinhard Bonnke ordered the tent.

His many engagements took Reinhard away from his family; it was not easy for Anni and the children to share him with the many people who demanded his time and attention. Often when Reinhard travelled away on long journeys Anni would make a calender with cut out windows. A window was opened each day he was away. The last one opened on the day he would be home again. Fulfilling his high calling was a sacrifice the whole family had to make.

The frustration of being separated from home was compensated by the joy of seeing many won for the kingdom of God. The words 'We are going to plunder hell and populate heaven' were never far from Reinhard's heart.

The team ventured into remote areas. One such place was Giyani, a village on the border of Vendaland and Mozambique. The school hall was packed to capacity and many sat outside listening to the gospel message. Soon the team had to move to the agricultural showgrounds several miles away where a crowd of over eight thousand people gathered.

One day Reinhard went into the local Post Office and the

young counter attendant gaped at him with wide eyes 'Pastor Bonnke?'

'Yes', said Reinhard.

Tears filled the teller's eyes as he spoke again: 'Umfundis (a local term for pastor or teacher) I must tell you something. I was a heathen, a real heathen. I never set foot inside a church. I had nothing to do with Christianity. I was a drunkard. I tormented my wife. Then one night I had a dream. Two men appeared to me dressed in snow white garments and said: 'Go to the school. There you will be shown the way of life.' So I went to the school and heard you preach. I am now born again. I am a child of God'.[7]

A further encouraging testimony from that crusade came when Pastor Bonnke bade farewell to the school teacher, who told him, 'Normally in such mass meetings people make heroes of the evangelists. But the people are not talking about you or Pastor Kolisang. All they talk about is Jesus.'[8]

Despite the warm testimonies and the reports of church growth, particularly in rural areas, criticism began. 'Reinhard Bonnke shouts when he preaches, and he won't stand still behind the pulpit.' Many refuted the miracles. One German newspaper, commenting upon a photograph of a pile of crutches collected at the end of the Giyani crusade, stated that it was 'typical of the African people . . . they were absent-minded.'[9]

Other critics stated that Bonnke stirred the crowds using emotionalism to achieve his objective. The African is generally an expressive person who prefers lively, enthusiastic messages and responds accordingly. Singing lively choruses and clapping is not irreverent. 'In the stifling of the emotions beware of the suffocation of the soul,' said Thomas Shaw. Shakeskpeare put

---

[7] Steele page 101.
[8] Ibid page 101/2
[9] Ibid page 102

it better: 'Why should a man whose blood is warm within, sit like his grandsire cut in alabaster?'

When Livingstone preached, his messages, according to Robert Moffat, were always simple and confined to the atonement for sins by Jesus Christ and the destiny of the believer and sinner. Reinhard Bonnke also preaches a very simple message, often speaking in parables so as to make a message more clearly understood. Examples such as 'You can work in a soap factory and never be clean—you have to apply the soap to yourself; likewise you can go to a church and never receive forgiveness from the blood of Jesus which can wash away all sins—you have to apply the blood by faith and ask Jesus to forgive you'.

Preaching the gospel in Africa is not without its problems. Remote areas do not have electricity; generators must be bought, serviced and maintained. During 1977 and 1978 gospel meetings were often held in darkness as the generators failed. Rough dusty roads made journeys hard for the trucks, and heavy rains lashed the crusade tent.

David Livingstone showed perseverance, and this is also evident in the life of Reinhard Bonnke, who relentlessly pushes himself and his team to new efforts. Not long after the massive ten thousand-seater tent arrived he was already considering an even larger one, though he was reluctant to tell the team— they were having enough trouble carting the present one throughout the countryside!

Since his attack of fever—and the knowledge of Mrs Kohler's intercessory prayers being answered—Reinhard realised the importance of committed prayer support. Miss Suzette Hattingh joined the team, and her responsibility was to pray for the team and the crusade meetings, as well as teach and encourage people to pray.

In addition to full time team personnel praying, pastors and members of their congregations united to intercede for lost souls to be won to Christ. Prayer meetings would often start several hours before the crusade service and continue throughout, only concluding at the end of the meeting.

As the work continued even the new tent proved too small to hold the crowds, so early in 1979 Pastor Bonnke called the team together and announced the next major challenge. A tent large enough to seat thirty thousand people would be ordered. Engineers were contracted and calculations made. A tent of that size would cover eleven thousand square metres. From the back one would need binoculars to see the pulpit. It would be nearly the size of two football fields. The fabric would have to be waterproof, windproof, fireproof and very flexible. Furthermore, Reinhard Bonnke's directive was that it must be 'a structure that goes up and comes down with no fuss, is forgiving to uneven ground and folds up and transports easily. It must have good acoustics and little or no internal obstructions.'[10]

As much as the members of the team admired their leader they seriously doubted his judgement. Where would so many people come from? At the time crowds attending the crusades numbered between ten and fifteen thousand, but the big tent was being made to house double that number. And where would the money come from? The project would run into millions.

The CfaN board again questioned Reinhard Bonnke—had he really heard from God? The evangelist was adamant, God wanted to 'harvest many souls, the days of the sickle were over, these were the days of the combine harvester.' The tent was necessary and although it would test the faith of every member of CfaN it was ordered. The fabric was to come from America; an Italian firm was approached regarding the construction of the canopy, and South African firms were to be involved in the making of the masts and rigging. This would be the largest movable structure in the world, and Reinhard

---

[10] 18 February 1984 CfaN Souvenir Brochure, centre page

Bonnke wanted it designed and built within two years. Like Livingstone, Bonnke was ever an optimist.

Soon churches throughout the world heard of the project. Invitations followed as people were interested in meeting the man who had ordered a tent, costing millions, in the belief that God would supply the money.

Having accepted an invitation to conduct several crusades in England, Reinhard Bonnke there met a couple formerly from Zimbabwe, Peter and Evangeline Vandenberg, who were fulfilling a music ministry of praise and worship.

They felt a call to join the Christ for all Nations team, especially as Peter's training as a motor mechanic and engineer would assist in the handling of the Big Tent's transport fleet. Within a short while the Vandenbergs had moved to South Africa. Bonnke noticed Peter Vandenberg's skills in diplomacy and management, and within months he was given the responsibility of general manager, thus freeing the two evangelists, Bonnke and Kolisang, to carry out their ministry.

Reinhard Bonnke is a visionary; he sees projects and, like Livingstone, storms ahead, often to the frustration of the rest of the team who struggle to keep up with him. Peter Vandenberg is able to stabilise the vision with practical backing. While one maintains high public profile, due to the calling of the ministry, the other is content to see that all is functioning correctly. The result of this partnership is the enabling of the team to 'reap the harvest of souls'.

Future crusades were planned. Harare, in Zimbabwe, was one venue under consideration, as was Lusaka, the capital of Zambia, and Soweto, the sprawling suburb of Johannesburg.

But criticism was again aimed at Reinhard Bonnke. The tent project was too expensive. To ask God to help was a crime. Others did not agree with the way people were healed— it was all well and good to pray for the sick but actually to expect a miracle—wasn't that taking God to his limits? Bonnke had to learn quickly how to handle criticism, and he decided to abide by John Wesley's advice, a man used greatly by God, who stated 'I am too afraid of God to be afraid of men.'

Reinhard Bonnke decided not to read any press articles on himself. If the articles praised him he could be dangerously close to falling into the sin of pride, or if they criticised he might be so discouraged that faith would not be able to operate in his life. He would allow God to be his defender.

The Christ for all Nations policy would not permit the taking out of loans from banks or private individuals, instead they chose to 'trust God, to whom silver and gold belongs.'[11] The target date for the opening of the new tent was revised and set for March 1982.

Crusade meetings in South Africa were now intermingled with trips to Germany, Africa and even India. In Calcutta Bonnke was coldly warned that this city of starving millions was also the graveyard of great evangelists. Reinhard Bonnke's reaction was simple: 'Well, I don't have to worry . . . I'm not a great evangelist.'[12]

A five-month intensive preaching campaign was planned for Zambia. Venues included Lusaka, the capital, as well as towns like Kabwe, Ndola, Kitwe and, of course, Livingstone.

People came in their thousands to hear the gospel and often sinners came forward to return stolen articles to rightful owners.

Hymns such as 'Jesus is my Saviour, day by day, mine, mine, mine, Jesus is mine' were not far from the lips of countless folk. The newspapers and television service gave coverage to the crusades and interest in the gospel of Jesus Christ was aroused. The Lusaka newspaper, the *National Mirror* on 17th July 1981 said:

CfaN is fulfilling the message of nearly 2000 years ago when Jesus said: 'Go ye into all the world and preach the gospel to every

[11] Steele page 154
[12] Ibid page 158

creature . . . and these signs shall follow them that believe. In my name they shall cast out devils . . . they shall lay hands on the sick and they shall recover.'

Indeed miracle healing is being witnessed. On the second day of the two-week crusade four blind people received their sight. The following day two people left their crutches behind . . . and scores of others had demons cast out of them. The power of God was certainly at work.

Bonnke then formally met President Kaunda.

Gradually throughout 1982 the Big Tent began to take shape, but it was not until 31st July 1983 that the first pitching took place. The massive canopy stood seven stories high, dwarfing all the surrounding structures.

A date—18th February 1984—was set for the dedication of the enormous structure, to be followed by a two week preaching crusade. Significantly this was to be in Soweto. This date was also set aside as a special day of prayer for the salvation of Africa.

The team was now poised to move north, but in order to fulfil the divine commission, the gospel needed to be first preached in Cape Town. However, on 6th May a high wind whipped across the Cape Peninsular and, directly in its path at Valhalla Park sports field, was the tent. As the freak wind increased, small tears began to appear in the fabric and within several hours the canopy had been ripped to shreds. Those who had worked on the tent for several years wept openly on seeing their dream for the salvation of many literally torn apart.

Pastor Bonnke was preaching in Calcutta, India, when he received the news. Amazingly, after a moment of prayer in his hotel room, he felt a tremendous peace sweep over him. He turned to his wife, Anni, and remarked, 'I'm worried that I'm not worried!'

Christians throughout the world on hearing the news telephoned in and pledged their support and prayers. The publicity brought thousands of people from Cape Town and the surrounding region to the crusade which was still being held. The size of the crowd grew from twenty thousand to fifty thousand on the final days. By then a decision had been made to order another canopy, whether or not the insurance company would pay.

Ironically the tent would not in fact have been able to hold fifty thousand people. Later Reinhard Bonnke was to say, 'The Big Tent awed me. God allowed the tent to be destroyed. I thought the devil had done it, yet now I believe the Lord wanted to tell me "Just listen! This roof is too little for you, I have a bigger one—the sky.'"

Remarkably, without an appeal for support, folk from all denominations, from Protestant to Catholic, rallied round.

By then Reinhard Bonnke and the CfaN team realised that they could not cope with the demand for crusades and evangelism on their own, so they planned to motivate Africa's top evangelists to pursue their God-given vision that Africa would be saved.

Since 1972 Reinhard Bonnke has had a vision for a 'blood-washed Africa'—an Africa and her peoples cleansed from sin by the precious blood of Jesus—and he seized every opportunity to bring that to pass holding Christian conferences in Nairobi and crusades in Kampala, Uganda, and Zaire.

The 'Fire Conferences' were a success and evangelists soon returned enthusiastic reports to the CfaN offices. A date was fixed for a 'Fire Conference' to host four thousand evangelists from Africa, and world-famous Christian leaders were invited to preach. The venue chosen was the then new Harare Sheraton Conference Centre in Zimbabwe; one of the few centres in Africa having multi-language translation facilities.

It became apparent that the former 'dark continent' was showing a hitherto unforeseen enthusiasm for truth and divine revelation as vast numbers of people willingly bowed the knee to their Lord and Saviour, Jesus Christ.

Crusades throughout Southern Africa including Zambia and Zaire were held and the post-crusade teams, inundated with the demand to organise follow up counselling, worked overtime.

However a tragedy occurred during the return journey from a Zaire crusade when CfaN lost two of their valuable team. Milton Kasselman and Horst Kosanke lost their lives when their truck had a head-on collision with a fuel tanker. The tanker, due to the thick dust, had edged over to the wrong side of the road and had rammed into the CfaN truck. The huge blaze was seen for miles around. The CfaN convoy team looked on helplessly, stunned. This was a great loss, for the members had grown close to one another through many trials and tribulations. The reality that one could be called upon at any time to pay the supreme price in the service of Christ hit home to all on the team.

Despite the blow the team rallied and the members busied themselves with the preparations for the conference in Harare, Zimbabwe. The new canopy arrived and the big tent was erected in time for the Harare 'Fire Conference' in April 1986. There were, however, objections to the forthcoming crusade. Muslims took CfaN to court in order to ban the meetings and the case was referred to the High Court of Zimbabwe. Many Christians united in prayer, and at the last moment a ruling was given in favour of freedom of religion. The crusade went ahead.

As literally thousands responded to the call to make Jesus Lord of their lives further miracles were witnessed. A young African girl, totally blind, received prayer, and when the Pastor took his hands away from her head a look of sheer bewilderment came on the child's face. She swung her head to look into the bright lights, then on to the faces of those about her. Tears welled up and collected in the corners of her eyes, blurring her vision and causing frustration—she wanted to see! She rubbed her eyes hard. Then her mouth hung open as she gazed around, scarcely able to believe what had happened. It was real, no child could have feigned the incident. God had performed a miracle.

The success of this conference in spreading Christian joy and enthusiasm to villages and cities throughout Africa was later to prompt similar conferences in Europe, from Frankfurt in Germany to Birmingham in England and then to Lisbon in Portugal.

Following the Zimbabwe crusades, gospel meetings were planned for Blantyre, Malawi, to be held from 9th to 24th August 1986. One hundred and sixty churches gathered together to help reap the harvest. Attendance grew from approximately twenty thousand people on the first few nights to over one hundred thousand at the end of the crusade.

The area where David Livingstone had laboured and seen so much devastation was now being won for Jesus Christ.

Christ for all Nations was invited to have another crusade in Lilongwe, Malawi, and it was opened personally by the President, Dr Kamuzu Banda.

It was during this week-long crusade that Reinhard Bonnke read, before a silent crowd, the words written by David Livingstone one hundred and thirty three years earlier not far from where the present gospel meetings were being held:

> Another century must present a totally different aspect from the present . . . Future missionaries will be rewarded by conversions for every sermon. We are their pioneers and helpers. Let them not forget the watchmen of the night, we who worked when all was gloom and no evidence of success in the way of conversion cheered our path. They will doubtless have more light than we, but we served our Master earnestly and proclaimed the same Gospel as they will do.[13]

These prophetic words of Livingstone had come to pass. It is also quite amazing to note that at the same time a Christian

---

[13] Sunday 19 June 1853 P J page 168

Zambian union official, searching for an even deeper relationship with God, drove to the Crusade site before the meeting, looking for Reinhard Bonnke. The evangelist was away, but members of his team prayed for the union official, that he would receive the annointing of the Holy Spirit upon his life as spoken of in the book of Acts. This zealous young man was 'carried away in some kind of tongue' which he couldn't understand . . . 'He was overjoyed at having received the gift of the Holy Spirit in speaking in other tongues. This experience had a radical effect upon his life' approaching the Bible changed, understanding it changed. The words of the Bible became alive, real. 'Now I was able to read and sit, meditate and understand.'[14] This was Frederick Chiluba the man who later went on to become President of Zambia.

In between 'the Malawi Miracle Meetings', as they came to be known, gospel crusades were held in several cities in Nigeria as well as in Tamale, Ghana, where many Muslims were converted to Christianity.

By the end of 1987 the meetings were reaching an average of seventy thousand people or more per crusade. The Big Tent, despite its capacity for thirty thousand was now inadequate while the logistics of hauling it across Africa were staggering. In addition a new base was needed, preferably in Europe, to cater firstly for the 'Euro Fire Conferences' and secondly to be a permanent headquarters for the work in Africa.

While in prayer, Reinhard Bonnke visualised the map of Africa. Two arrows moved slowly northward, one on the east and the other on the west. Connecting the arrows was a fine net. Reinhard Bonnke came to the conclusion that the best strategy was to create two crusade teams with ancillary equipment, on either side of the continent. Twelve crusades would be held each year and dividing the load between two teams would help ease the pressure of pre-crusade planning

---

[14] Interview with President Chiluba, 20 May 1993.

and follow-up. Regional bases would be established to handle the work load: Lagos, Nigeria, to the west and Nairobi, Kenya, in the east. A headquarters based in Frankfurt, Germany, would oversee Africa, the 'Euro Fire Conferences', and any other international crusades that might be planned from time to time. The Big Tent, together with its ancillary equipment of trucks, fuel and water bowsers, generators, lights etc., all in all costing nearly two million US dollars, would be *donated* to a mission organisation in Mozambique.

The teams in Africa would be trimmed to a mere five people on the east and five on the west, two technical staff, and three involved in prayer, pre-crusade planning and ministry. The offices in Kenya would have a small contingent of staff, as would the headquarters in Germany, the latter having a total staff of twenty.

Hearts throughout Africa were opening up to the message of the gospel. In two years nine gospel crusades had been held in Ghana. Kenya had opened its doors, with the State President, Daniel Arap T Moy, his Vice President and eight government ministers attending the gospel crusades. Cities such as Kampala in Uganda, Bujumbura in Burundi, Warri in Nigeria, Abidjan on the Ivory Coast, Kigali in Rwanda, Machakos and Meru, Bamenda in the Cameroons were challenged and uplifted by the preaching of the gospel.

A source of worry for many preachers in recent years is the lack of integrity shown by many carriers of the gospel, who have allowed themselves to become enslaved with the trappings of this world. Reinhard Bonnke, in a report to ministers and Christians wrote: 'My dear fellow ministers, hear the Word of the Lord. We MUST MIND IN THE BEGINNING WHAT MATTERS IN THE END. Carry your very souls in your hands and walk circumspectly.' In their CfaN conferences the theme 'Evangelism and Integrity' is given much coverage, for in today's world it is so easy to be distracted from the God-given goals and fall into the many snares of the devil. Regarding his acclaim Bonnke recently told a crusade gathering: 'I am a normal human being, I put my trousers on the same way as you men do . . . I like fish and chips the same way as you do. God uses the willing and he will use you if you will let him.'

As the gospel 'Combine Harvester' moves forward, so the hunger to hear the word of God preached appears to increase. Crusades in Nigeria have recorded crowds of over half a million people in a single meeting!

But it has not been without many trials and frustrations. In September 1990 in the Ugandan town of Jinja, on the banks of the Nile the gospel crusade was stormed by armed soldiers and closed down. Many were beaten with sticks as the soldiers dispersed the dissapointed crowd.

Despite exciting crusades in Lome (Togo), Bouake (Ivory coast), Kinshasa, Kananga, Mbuji-Mayi and Kisangani (Zaire); where C130 Hercules transporter aircraft were hired to carry the crusade equipment over impenetrable terrain, there was a major setback in the town of Kano, northern Nigeria. A crusade was due to be held in October 1991 but Reinhard Bonnke left without even preaching a word. Muslim fanatics, incited by one of their imams, ran out of control, killing hundreds of people not dressed in muslim clothing. They burned down and looted banks, churches and stores. Crazed with murderous intentions religious extremists went searching through the Central Hotel where it was presumed the CfaN team would be. They were elsewhere in an ordinary guesthouse.

The Nigerian army was called in to restore order and evacuate Reinhard Bonnke and the team. A curfew was imposed and all religious meetings cancelled.

The Muslims were angry because the Nigerian Government had refused permission for them to invite one of their religious leaders from South Africa to speak, but had granted Reinhard Bonnke, who had been invited by the Christians, permission. Thus CfaN were caught in the crossfire resulting from this dispute.

Other nations more tolerant of Christianity opened their doors and invited the evangelist in. The first ever open-air crusade was held in the Central African Republic in February 1992. Over ten thousand Christians crowded the airport to welcome them. The President supplied Reinhard Bonnke with the Presidential escort and limousine. He also invited him to address the nation's parliament.

In July 1992 Christ for all Nations reported in their 'Revival Report' magazine that in the God-given task of preaching the gospel from Cape Town to Cairo they were 'about half way'.

There are critics of mass evangelism who say that conversion of souls should be carried out on a one-to-one basis. That is an ideal and noble suggestion. Sadly, however, too many Christians are not fulfilling their responsibility to share their faith and win the lost for Christ. Mass evangelism is therefore seen by many as a vital part of God's plan to reach people. As Reinhard Bonnke stated:

> In Matthew chapter 13 we are told that the Kingdom of Heaven is like a dragnet cast into the sea, and gathering fish of every kind . . . and Jesus said when it was filled they drew it up on the beach; and they sat down, and gathered the good fish into containers, but the bad they threw away . . . The duty of the casting out of the net and pulling it in is ours . . . This is our justification, we need to go into all the world and preach the Gospel to every creature, not the selected creatures, then leave the sorting out to God the Father, God the Son and God the Holy Spirit.

These crusades do bring church growth. A minister, Willie Crew, visited a tea plantation in Malawi in August 1988. He told how he came across a congregation of between three and four hundred people. The leader of the church said he had been to one of Pastor Bonnke's meetings and had become a Christian. On his return to the plantation, although not a pastor, he simply started to gather people together for church meetings.

Speaking at the 1990 Keswick convention in England Rev Kennith Ononeze, in addressing the 'issue of witnessing to Christianity among the Muslims' in the Jos, Nigerian crusade, centred on the astounding miracles and movement of the Holy Spirit:

> The greatest miracles were to the Muslims as a sign and a wonder to that community . . . and the Christians were blessed primarily with more numerical strength . . . not only in the strengthening and multiplication of the two hundred and fifty participating Churches, but twenty brand new Churches have sprung up since the crusade.[15]

That tells a story of God and just one of his obedient servants working together. The African situation is even bigger than Livingstone could ever have imagined!

Operation World, a Christian research organisation, reports that in Africa 'The dramatic ingathering into the churches is unique in history. Africa is the first continent to become majority Christian within a single century.'[16] They go on to point out that

> tremendous prayer and effort will have to be made to conserve the fruit of growth and prevent spiritual tragedy on a massive scale.
> (a) Much church growth has been without a deep repentance from sin and the works of darkness. In many churches there are still people bound by the fear of witchcraft. The decisive confrontation with Satan's forces has yet to be made in many areas.
> (b) Many have come to faith, but lack teaching. Syncretism is widespread because the Word of God is not adequately taught and understood.
> (c) The critical lack of trained leadership is crippling growth. The

---

[15] CfaN Revival Report F/90 E page 10.
[16] Operation World by Patrick Johnstone fourth edition page 45

poverty of most churches makes it hard to support those in training or in the ministry.

(d) There have been few Christians prepared to speak out for moral uprightness and ethical standards in societies riddled with corruption, greed and favouritism. Often church leaders have become, themselves, part of the problem.

(e) Denominational confusion and barriers are more often caused by personalities and tribalism than doctrine. Spiritual unity across denominational barriers is too rare.[17]

Christians are urged to recognise the need and fulfil the Great Commission—'Making disciples of all men'. The need is very great for good teaching to support the mighty work of evangelism. The author has known pastors in rural areas to cycle more than fifty kilometres to attend a Christian leadership Bible seminar, such is their hunger. With good Bible teaching the many who are still bound by the fear of witchcraft and who have not fully repented will by the grace of God see the need to do so.

As Operation World has pointed out, the problems are great, yet not insurmountable. God is looking for men and women who are prepared to surrender their personal ambitions and submit their desires to his will.

In the words of the Christian President of Zambia, Fredrick Chiluba:

I want to appeal to the Christian Community. This is their hour ... The hour in which we must promote Calvary, the Christian faith. We must promote in every heart the belief in The Lord God that He is The King, He is The Lord and with Him nothing is impossible. We can only pray that those who have not known Him yet and those that believe in other gods will know that there is The God, the Father of our Lord Jesus Christ. The God of Abraham, the God of Isaac and the God of Jacob. We can't explain God to people sufficiently for them to understand Him. The Lord

[17] Ibid page 46

will reveal Himself to them, we can only pray that The Lord will use us as His instruments to try and get the Gospel out. The Lord will do the convicting. He will bring them forth.

Organisations such as All Africa School of Theology, Christian Vision, and others too numerous to mention, are moving throughout Africa encouraging Bible training courses and helping equip the saints. If God can raise up men to evangelise Africa—answering the prayers of the saints—so too can he mobilise men and women to preach and teach the Good News.

God is looking for men and women who, like David Livingstone, will consider it a joy to lay down their lives in the fulfilment of a higher calling. Our motive should be the same as his; that of giving glory and honour to God.

Jesus Christ in the Garden of Gethsemene and at Calvary sowed in tears as he gave of his life so that the Father, our Father, may reap with joy and bring about the union and fellowship he so longs to have with mankind.

Reinhard Bonnke . . .

. . . preaching to 90,000 people in the sports stadium in Bukavo, Zaire in July 1989.

Biographical Notes
David Livingstone (1813–1873)

Obtained from the National Archives of Zimbabwe

For details of Livingstone's life, reference must be made to his own works and to the standard biographies, notably W G Blaikie, *The Personal Life of David Livingstone*, (Murray: London, 1880), and J I Macnair, *Livingstone the Liberator* (Collins: London, 1940).

The following is an outline

1813	Mar 19	Born at Blantyre, Co. Lanark
1823		Commenced work in a cotton factory
1836		First attended classes in Glasgow, intended to qualify him as a medical missionary
1838	Sep 5	Examination for appointment as a missionary of the London Missionary Society
1840		Meeting with Robert Moffat, choice of Africa as his sphere of work
	Nov	Qualified as licentiate of the Faculty of Physicians and Surgeons, Glasgow, and ordained as a missionary
	Dec 8	Embarked for Africa
1841	Jul 31	Arrived at Kuruman
1843	Sep	Established a station at Mabotsa

1845	Jan 2	Marriage to Mary Moffat
1846		Move to a new station at Chonuane
1847	Aug	Move of the station from Chonuane to Kolobeng
1849		Journey to Ngamiland with Oswell and Murray
	Aug 1	Reached Lake Ngami
1850		Second journey to Lake Ngami, accompanied by Mrs Livingstone and children
1851		Journey with Mrs Livingstone, the children and Oswell to the Makololo
	Aug 4	First sight of the Zambesi
1852	Mar 16	Arrival in Cape Town
	Apr 23	Departure of Mrs Livingstone and children for England
	Aug	Destruction of Kolobeng by Boers
	Dec 14	Departure from Kuruman for the north
1853	May 23	Arrival at Linyanti
	Nov 11	Departure from Linyanti
1854	May 31	Arrival at Loanda
	Sep 20	Departure from Loanda
1855	Sep 10	Arrival at Linyanti
	Nov 3	Departure for Quellimane
	Nov 16	Discovery of the Victoria Falls
1856	May 20	Arrival at Quellimane
	Dec 9	Arrived back in England
1857	Nov 10	Publication of *Missionary Travels and Researches in South Africa*
	Dec 4	Address in the Senate House at Cambridge Resignation from the London Missionary Society
1858	Feb	Appointment as H M Consul at Quellimane for the East Coast of Africa, south of Zanzibar
	Mar 12	Departure of the Zambesi expedition from Liverpool
	May 14	Arrival at the mouth of the Zambesi

The spelling of 'Livingstone'

Blaikie relates that the original form of the name was 'Livingstone' but that the missionary's father had shortened it to 'Livingston'. David for many years spelled it the same way his father had, but in about 1857, at his father's request, he restored the original form of 'Livingstone'.

Post Mortem Report

Examination and Verification of the Body of the Late David Livingstone

(From the British Medical Journal, 18th April 1874)

The arrival of the body of Dr Livingstone in London on Wednesday last was followed by an examination of his body by Sir William Fergusson, with the view of settling all doubt as to the identity of the body with that of the great missionary and explorer. The following account is from the pen of Sir William Fergusson.

Happily, it was borne in mind by many old friends that he had one condition of body which would mark the identification of his remains, even if years and years had elapsed. The skeleton of the human frame being the last part which decays and falls into impalpable dust, it was thought by those who knew some part of his physical condition that if it should be proved, on anatomical examination, the remains of an old ununited fracture in his left humerus (arm-bone) could be recognised, all doubt on this subject would be settled at once and for ever.

It has fallen to my lot to have the honour of being selected to make the crucial examination to this end, and I have accordingly performed that duty. From what I have seen, I am much impressed with the ingenious manner in which those who have contrived to secure that the body should be carried through the long distance from where Livingstone died until it could reach a place where transit was comparatively easy, accomplished their task. The lower limbs were so severed from the trunk that the length of the bulk of package was reduced to a little over four feet. The soft tissues seem to have been removed to a great extent from the bones, and these latter were so disposed that by doubling and otherwise the shortening was accomplished. The abdominal viscera were absent, and so were those of the chest, including, of course, the heart and lungs. There had been made a large opening in front of the abdomen, and through that the native operators had ingeniously contrived to remove the contents of the chest as well as of the abdomen. The skin over the chest, sternum, and ribs had been untouched.

Before these points were clearly ascertained, some coarse tapes had to be loosened, which set free some rough linen material—a striped coloured bit of cotton cloth, such as might have been an attractive material for the natives, among whom Livingstone travelled—a coarse cotton shirt, which doubtless belonged to the traveller's scanty wardrobe, and in particular a large portion of the bark of a tree, which had formed the principal part of the package—the case thereof no doubt. The skin of the trunk, from the pelvis to the crown of the head, had been untouched. Everywhere was that shrivelling which might have been expected after salting, baking in the sun, and eleven months of time. The features of the face could not be recognized. The hair on the scalp was plentiful, and much longer than he wore it when last in England. A moustache could not be distinguished, but whiskers were in abundance. The forehead was in shape such as we are familiar with from memory, and from the pictures and busts now extant. The circumference of the cranium, from the occiput to the brow, was $23\frac{7}{8}$ inches, which was recognized by some present to be in accordance with such measurements when alive.

In particular, the arms attracted attention. They lay as if placed in ordinary fashion, each down by the side. The skin and tissues under were on each side shrunken almost to skeleton bulk, and at a glance to practised eyes—there were five, I may say six, professional men present—the state of the left arm was such as to convince every one present who had examined it during life, that the limb was Livingstone's. Exactly in the region of the attachment of the deltoid to the humerus, there were the indications of an oblique fracture. On moving the arm, there were the indications of the ununited fracture. A closer investigation and dissection displayed the false joint which had long ago been well recognized by those who had examined the arm in former days. The Rev Dr Moffat, and in particular, Dr Kirk, late of Zanzibar, and Dr Louden, of Hamilton in Scotland, at once recognized the condition. Having myself been consulted regarding the state of the limb when Livingstone was last in London, I was convinced that the remains of the great traveller lay before us. Thousands of heads, with a like large circumference might have been under similar scrutiny; the skeletons of hundreds of thousands might have been so; the humerus in each might have been perfect; if one or both had been broken during life it would have united again in such a manner that a tyro could easily have detected the peculiarity. The condition of ununited fracture in this locality is exceedingly rare. I say this from my personal professional experience, and that such a specimen should have turned up in London from the centre of Africa, excepting in the body of Dr Livingstone, where it was known by competent authorities to have existed, is beyond human credibility. It must not be supposed by those who are not professionally acquainted with this kind of lesion—which often causes so much interest to the practical surgeon—that a fracture and new joint of the kind now referred to, could have been of recent date or made for a purpose. There were in reality all the indications which the experienced pathologist recognizes as infallible, such as the attenuated condition of the two great fragments (common under such circumstances), and the semblance of a new joint, but actually there was a small fragment detached from the others which bore out Livingstone's own view, that the bones had been 'crunched into splinters'. Having had ample opportunity of examining the arm during life, and conversing with Livingstone on the subject, and being one of those who entertained hopes that the last reports of Livingstone's death might, like others, prove false, I approached the examination with an anxious feeling regarding this great and most peculiar crucial test. The first glance at the left arm set my mind at rest, and that, with the further examination, made me as positive as to the identity of these remains as that there has been among us in modern times one of the greatest men of the human race—David Livingstone.

The accompanying extract from Dr Livingstone's *Missionary Travels and Researches in South Africa*, published in 1857, will be read with peculiar interest at the present date. It bears specially upon the matter now in question. In giving an account of an attack on a troop of lions in the village of Mabotsa, Dr Livingstone says: 'In going round the end of the hill, however, I saw one of the beasts sitting on a piece of rock as before, but this time he had a little bush in front. Being about thirty yards off, I took a good aim at his body through the bush, and fired both barrels into it. The men then called out, "He is shot! he is shot!" Others cried, "He has been shot by another man too; let us go to him!" I did not see any one else shoot at him, but I saw the lion's tail erected in anger behind the bush, and, turning to the people, said, "Stop a little till I load again". When in the act of ramming down the bullets, I heard a shout. Starting, and looking half round, I saw the lion just in the act of springing upon me. I was upon a little height; he caught my shoulder as he sprang, and we both came to the ground below together. Growling horribly close to my ear, he shook me as a terrier dog does a rat. The shock produced a stupor similar to that which seems to be felt by a mouse after the first shake of the cat. It caused a sort of dreaminess in which there was no sense of pain nor feeling of terror, though quite conscious of all that was happening. It was like what patients partially under the influence of chloroform describe, who see all the operation, but feel not the knife. This singular condition was not the result of any mental process. The shake annihilated fear, and allowed no sense of horror in looking round at the beast. This peculiar state is probably produced in all animals killed by the carnivora, and, if so, is a merciful provision by our benevolent Creator for lessening the pain of death. . . . Besides crunching the bone into splinters, he left eleven tooth wounds on the upper part of my arm. A wound from this animal's tooth resembles a gunshot wound; it is generally followed by a great deal of sloughing and discharge, and pains are felt in the part periodically ever afterwards. I had on a tartan jacket on the occasion, and I believe that it wiped off all the virus from the teeth that pierced the flesh, for my two companions in this affray' (who were both bitten, one in the thigh and the other on the shoulder) 'have both suffered from the peculiar pains, while I have escaped with only the inconvenience of a false joint in my limb. The man whose shoulder was wounded showed me his wound actually burst forth afresh in the same month of the following year.'

As quoted in Michael Gelfand, *Livingstone the Doctor* pp 294–296.

Abbreviations Used in Footnotes

Chamberlin	*Some Letters from Livingstone 1840–1872*. Edited by David Chamberlin, London 1940.
Mssny. Corr.	*Livingstone's Missionary Correspondence 1841–1856*. Edited by I Schapera, Chatto & Windus: London 1961.
Fam. Lett. I Fam. Lett. II	*David Livingstone Family Letters 1841–1856 Vol I 1841–48, Vol II 1849–56*. Edited by I Schapera, Chatto & Windus: London 1959.
P J	*Livingstone's Private Journals 1851–1853*. Edited by I Schapera, Chatto & Windus: London 1960.
A J	*Livingstone's African Journal 1853–1856 Vol I*. Edited by I Schapera, Chatto & Windus: London 1963.
M T	*Missionary Travels and Researches in South Africa*. David Livingstone, John Murray: London 1857 and 1873.
Zam. & Tribs.	*The Zambesi and Its Tributaries 1858–1864*. David & Charles Livingstone, John Murray: London 1865.
LJ I LJ II	*The Last Journals of David Livingstone in Central Africa 1865–1873*. Horace Waller, John Murray: London 1880.

Birkinshaw   *The Livingstone Touch.* Phillip
                 Birkinshaw, Purnell: Cape Town 1973.
Blaikie   *The Personal Life of David Livingstone.*
                 William G Blaikie, London 1880 and
                 1910.
Campbell   *Livingstone.* R J Campbell, Ernest Benn
                 Ltd: London 1929.
Coupland   *Livingstone's Last Journey.* Sir Reginald
                 Coupland, Collins: London 1945.
Zam. Doc.   *The Zambesi Doctors—David
                 Livingstone's Letters to John Kirk 1858–
                 1872.* Edited by R Foskett, Edinburgh
                 University Press: Edinburgh 1964.
Gelfand   *Livingstone the Doctor—His Life and
                 Travels—A Study in Medical History.*
                 Michael Gelfand, Blackwell: Oxford 1957.
Jeal   *Livingstone.* Tim Jeal, Heinemann:
                 London 1973.
Johnston   *Livingstone and the Exploration of
                 Central Africa.* H H Johnston, George
                 Philip & Son: London 1891.
LMS   London Missionary Society.
Macnair   *Livingstone the Liberator—A Study of a
                 Dynamic Personality.* James I Macnair,
                 Collins: London & Glasgow 1940.
Ransford   *David Livingstone—The Dark Interior.*
                 Oliver Ransford, John Murray: London
                 1978.
Ritchie   *The Pictorial Edition of the Life and
                 Discoveries of David Livingstone.* J Ewing
                 Ritchie, James Sangster & Co: London
                 c 1880.
Robertson   *The Life of David Livingstone—The
                 Great Missionary Explorer.* J S
                 Robertson, Walter Scott Ltd: London
                 c 1902.

Stanley   *How I Found Livingstone; Travel,
                      Adventures, and Discoveries in Central
                      Africa.* Henry M Stanley, Sampson Low:
                      London 1872.

NAZ   National Archives of Zimbabwe

MacDonald   *Zambesi River.* J F MacDonald,
                      Macmillan: London 1955.

Moorehead   *The White Nile.* Alan Moorehead,
                      Hamish Hamilton: Middlesex 1973.

Montefiore-Brice   *David Livingstone: His Labours and His
                     Legacy.* A Montefiore-Brice, Partridge:
                     London.

Martelli   *Livingstone's River: The Story of the
                     Zambezi Expedition 1858–1864.* George
                     Martelli, Victorian & Modern History
                     Book Club: Newton Abbot, 1972.

Mary Moffatt   *Beloved Partner: Mary Moffatt of
                     Kuruman, A Biography based on her
                     letters.* Mora Dickson, Botswana Book
                     Centre & Kuruman Moffatt Mission
                     Trust.

Lloyd   *Livingstone 1873–1973.* B W Lloyd,
                     Struik: Cape Town, 1973.

MacLachlan   *David Livingstone.* T Banks MacLachlan,
                     John Ritchie: Kilmarnock, 1931.

Adams   *David Livingstone: The Weaver Boy
                     Who Became a Missionary.* H G Adams,
                     Hodder & Stoughton: London 1874.

Hughes   *David Livingstone,* Thomas Hughes,
                     Macmillan: London, 1928.

Worcester   *The Life of David Livingstone.* Mrs J H
                     Worcester, Jr, Moody Press: Chicago.

Boreham   *A Bunch of Everlastings or Texts That
                     Made History.* F W Boreham, The
                     Epworth Press: London, 1922.

Wallis	*The Matabele Journals of Robert Moffat 1829–1860* Vol I. J P R Wallis, National Archives of Rhodesia: Salisbury, 1976.
Rhod. Soc.	*Rhodesiana*, Pub. No. 20—July 1969. Edited by W V Brelsford, Rhodesiana Society: Salisbury, 1969.
LMS Pioneers	*Blazing the Trail—London Missionary Society Pioneers* by A H Cullen, London Missionary Society, 1916.
Trail	*In Livingstone's Trail—Universities' Mission to Central Africa*. Revised by P Benham, Universities Mission to Central Africa, 1939.
Steele	*Plundering Hell: The Reinhard Bonnke Story*. Ron Steele, Sceptre: Johannesburg, 1984.
Bonnke	*Evangelism by Fire*. Reinhard Bonnke, Kingsway Publications: Eastbourne, 1989.
CfaN	Various Publications from CHRIST FOR ALL NATIONS.